MW00647333

The Lost Submarine

A True Story of Love and War

Nancy Kenney

By Nancy Kenney

The Lost Submarine

A True Story of Love and War

Published by

splatteredinkpress.com

ISBN 978-9848542-8-8

Note to the Reader

This book is a work of non-fiction. It includes personal letters, entries from diaries, war journals and logs, newspaper reports, official letters from the Navy, and excerpts from e-mails. Only minor editing, in the interest of shortening a lengthy book was done, but nothing changed the factual content. The editing is apparent when the reader sees ... between words or sentences.

The author attempted to include a photo or mention of each member of *Lagarto's* crew. There were a few for whom no picture or information was obtained. After so many years, some sailors' families still haven't been found; hence, the author regrets she has no information to share with the reader. If anyone has any information on any of the *Lagarto* crew, please feel free to contact Nancy Kenney at nancykenney11@yahoo.com.

The *Lagarto* families have been generous. They shared letters, photos, and stories. I am grateful to every one of you. However, limited space prevented inclusion of them all. I hope you understand.

Finally, eighty-six young men perished on *Lagarto*. This book attempts to tell their story. Although we can't know everything about their lives in the silent service, or what they endured in their last few minutes (perhaps blessedly for those of us left behind), we know where *Lagarto* was lost and that she went down fighting.

The Foreshadowing

No one in my family is a practitioner of the paranormal, and I sort of and sort of don't believe in that kind of thing. But in May 2005, something happened that affected us deeply. Its first sign was a dream.

On Memorial Day week end 2005, my 33-year-old son Bill visited my husband and me on our farm in Lake Leelanau, Michigan. Soon after he arrived, we sat together in the kitchen, and he told me of a powerful dream he'd had earlier that month. His wife Linsey woke him when she saw tears streaming down his face. Billy told her of a dream he'd had about his grandfather and namesake. This is what he said:

One day, while driving down Lake Shore Drive in Chicago, Bill approached McCormick Place on Lake Michigan and decided to stop. He walked into a tent, brimming with light and full of sailors – namely the crew of U.S.S. Lagarto, the submarine on which his grandfather had served. Lagarto had been lost late in World War II and was, in fact, still missing.

As Bill walked through the tent looking for his grandfather, he saw sailors playing cards and engaged in conversations. After inquiring about his granddad Bill Mabin, who had been a signalman on the boat, he was directed to a man sitting quietly in a corner, whittling small objects from a piece of wood. As Bill approached him, there was instant recognition in the sailor's eyes.

The sailor stood to greet the young man, and Bill said, "You're my grandfather." "Yes, I know," said Bill Mabin. They embraced warmly – a big grandfatherly bear hug.

"Are you healthy?" inquired Bill Mabin.

"Yes, I am," his grandson said.

"That's good. That's all that really matters," said sailor Mabin.

Those were the only words exchanged between them, and Bill awoke from his dream. My son told me he had never had such a beautiful dream and his only regret was that he, not I, had experienced it. I thought it was wonderful and was happy he'd had a visit from his grandfather.

A small detail of the dream I found intriguing was that of Bill Mabin whittling. His father – my grandfather – had taken up whittling as a hobby in his later years, long after the death of his son in World War II. Neither of the Bills knew of Gordon Mabin's penchant for wood carving. What an odd and eerie and wonderful coincidence, I thought.

A week later, the significance of the dream became odder and eerier and more wonderful. I learned that the submarine, in which my father and 85 other men had perished on 3 May 1945, had been found on 18 May 2005 – almost 60 years to the day after the boat's loss. This extraordinary and unexpected discovery of *Lagarto* came the same week as my son's dream visit from his grandfather.

There was another connection from the past. The wood carving that Gordon Mabin was doing when he died 50 years ago was a statue of a sailor dancing with a woman. The lovely unfinished statue adorns the hall table in my home.

Dedication

FOR THE CREW OF *U.S.S. LAGARTO* (SS -371)

Crew of *Lagarto*, taken at commissioning party, Manitowoc, WI. 1944.

CTM Harold D. Andrews
Malden, Missouri

CMoMM Charles Anker
St. Petersburg, FL

LTJG Frederick L. Auchard
Woodston, Kansas

F1 Charles H. Bjornson
Newton, Massachusetts

Y2 Charles W. Breithaupt
Vicksburg, Mississippi

CRM Wardour L. Britain
Longton, Missouri

S2 Aaron Brock
Busy, Kentucky

F1 Clark R. Byrer
Canton, Ohio

RM1 William E. Carleton
Los Angeles, California

MoMM3 Lloyd F. Cathey
Nicoma Park, Oklahoma

QM3 Sylvester G. Catozzi
Bedford, Indiana

TM3 George E. Clouse
New Hampton, Missouri

MoMM1 Caldwell T. Cook
Columbia, South Carolina

TM2 John E. Davis, Jr.
Little Rock, Arkansas

RM2 Leslie M. Doud
Alva, Oklahoma

TM3 Alvin H. Enns
Gray, Oklahoma

MoMM1 Richard L. Fisher
Pekin, Illinois

S1 John J. Franze
Ellwood City, Pennsylvania

MoMM1 Oakley R. Frasch
Manitowoc, Wisconsin

F1 James N. Gerlach
Toledo, Ohio

F2 Richard F. Grace
Wilmington, Delaware

QM1 William Graves
Portland, Oregon

EM2 Dennis J. Gray
Trinity, Texas

StM2 Robert Green
Titusville, Pennsylvania

EM1 Richard L. Gregorick
New York, New York

S2 James P. Gregory
Union, South Carolina

RM3 Glen E. Halstead
Lynn, Indiana

MoMM1 Thomas Hardegree
Two Rivers, Wisconsin

MoMM3 George C. Harrington
Hamilton City, New York

MoMM2 Thomas J. Harrington
Fall River, Massachusetts

S1 James B. Harris
Baltimore, Maryland

MoMM3 James C. Harrison
Royal Oak, Michigan

TM3 Walter Hinken
Grand Rapids, Michigan

EM3 William F. Honaker
Sandstone, West Virginia

LT Lloyd G. Irving
Cleveland, Ohio

S1 Hezekiah Jefferson
Bronx, New York

CEM Jesse Jobe
Tunnel Hill, Illinois

S1 Fred Johnson
Pontiac, Michigan

CEM John R. Johnson
Vallejo, California

S1 William H. Jordon, Jr.
Charleston, West Virginia

LT A.H. Keeney, Jr.
West Hartford, Connecticut

RT1 Philip M. Kimball
San Gabriel, California

StM1 Albert Kirtley
Springfield, Ohio

MoMM2 John W. Kneidl
Dayton, Ohio

CDR – CO Frank D. Latta
St. Helena, California

S1 Noah B. Lee, Jr.
Smithfield, North Carolina

F1 Russell W. Lee
Amite, Louisiana

MoMM2 Robert J. Lewis
Louisville, Kentucky

F1 Louis J. Lynch
Cleveland Heights, Ohio

SM1 William T. Mabin
La Grange, Illinois

S1 Joy M. Marriott, Jr.
Columbus, Ohio

SC2 James H. McDonald
Mattoon, Illinois

TM3 Justin M. McGee
Rockford, Illinois

LT – XO William H. Mendenhall
Edmond, Oklahoma

F1 Willis L. Moore
Lansing, Michigan

S1 William G. Moss
Richmond, Indiana

RT2 Lloyd R. O'Hara
Cleveland, Ohio

F1 Howard E. Ortega
Pastura, New Mexico

S1 Dick M. Paper
Davenport, Iowa

LTJG Joseph S. Pash
Niagara Falls, New York

RM3 Robert R. Patterson
Roanoke, Virginia

EM3 Robert C. Perry
Alderson, West Virginia

TM3 John W. Peterson
Philadelphia, Pennsylvania

QM3 Robert F. Peterson
Chicago, Illinois

LTJG Walter B. Phelps
West Hartford, Connecticut

F1 Harry R. Plushnik
Ceresco, Michigan

CMoMM Gerald A. Price
Elida, Ohio

EM2 Morris D. Reeves
Atlanta, Georgia

F1 Raymond E. Reichert
Toledo, Ohio

BM1 Eugene T. Robison
Boggstown, Indiana

MoMM1 John H. Root
Maribel, Wisconsin

LT Robert T. Ruble
Denver, Colorado

S1 Walter J. Rutledge
Tupelo, Mississippi

SM2 Wesley C. Shackelford
Great Bend, Kansas

TM2 Ralph E. Simmerman
Rogersville, Missouri

CPhM Robert B. Spalding
Eugene, Missouri

GM2 John E. Stehn
Philadelphia, Pennsylvania

EM2 Donald G. Stiegler
Rochester, New York

EM3 Ulysses M. St. John, Jr.
Lincoln, Alabama

MoMM2 Floyd Tait
Costa Mesa, California

LTJG Harold A. Todd, Jr.
Wauwatosa, Wisconsin

CGM Frank D. Turner
Spartanburg, South Carolina

S1 Arthur M. Wade
Mason City, Iowa

S1 William M. Warnick
Raymondville, Texas

MoMM2 Max M. Wicklander
Seattle, Washington

S1 John L. Williams
Sayre, Pennsylvania

And my friend and hero, Jamie Macleod

Table of Contents

Preface

When I was a little girl, my grandmother showed me my father's favorite jacket.

She kept it in a storage closet in her basement. A conservative tweed, the sport coat was cut in a casual style. I loved it.

When I stayed with my grandparents, I would often steal down to the basement to visit my father's jacket. I held its sleeve to my face and felt its rough fabric next to my cheek. There was a faint whiff of cigarette smoke lingering in the sleeves, and my senses took everything in. As a child, this was the closest I could get to my father. No one knew this jacket was important to me. Because I thought they would worry I was sad, I didn't tell my grandparents or my mother about my visits. The basement jaunts were a secret between my father and me.

Growing up in the same town in which both my parents were reared, I knew more about my father than many war orphans. Bill Mabin was a hometown hero – a handsome young man, an exceptional athlete, and the nicest guy in the world. Everyone said so. I was surrounded by those who loved my father and would talk about him if I asked. But I rarely asked. I didn't want to upset anyone.

That's the way I lived my life – a very happy one – but with a piece of me missing. Until I was sixty-two years old.

On June 5, 2005, my son John called with the astounding news that *U.S.S. Lagarto* (SS-371), my father's submarine which had been missing for sixty years, had been found. Finding that important piece of my life began a healing process for me and others who had lost someone in that submarine. We call it peace.

Bill Mabin at 22 years old.

Overdue and Presumed Lost 1945

Three months before the end of World War II, the American submarine *U.S.S. Lagarto* (SS-371) was on her way to Fremantle, Australia. One of the 28 subs built in Manitowoc, Wisconsin; she had just finished her first patrol in the South China Sea and was scheduled for refit and R & R for her crew.

On May 2nd, the submarine's commander, Commander (CDR) Frank D. Latta, received an urgent call for help from Lieutenant Commander (LCDR) Ben Jarvis, the captain of her sister ship, *U.S.S. Baya. Baya* had barely survived a harrowing attack on a Japanese convoy – an oil tanker, a cargo ship loaded with supplies and two heavily armed escorts, including the escort-minelayer *Hatsutaka.*

The captains of the two American warships stood on the bridges of their submarines, their streamlined battle-weary boats bobbing in the Pacific Ocean only twenty feet apart, and made plans to attack the Imperial Japanese convoy the next day. Commander Latta had much experience in dangerous missions and never shied away from taking the sharp end of the stick. According to Theodore Roscoe's *United States Submarine Operations in World War II*, "It was agreed that *Lagarto* would dive on the convoy's track when a certain point was reached, and *Baya* would strike from a point some 12 miles ahead. The submarines parted company, and the convoy chase went on."

The two boats exchanged contact reports during the day, and LCDR Ben Jarvis directed a midnight attack on the enemy. *Baya* was again driven off by the convoy's escorts. After many attempts to contact her, *Lagarto* was never heard from again. She was reported missing-in-action when she failed to return to port at her scheduled time.

What happened to *Lagarto*? Japanese records released after the war revealed a possible explanation for the submarine's disappearance. They reported depth-charging an American submarine at that location and bragged about their heroic circumstances. One of the enemy escorts, the minelayer *Hatsutaka*, a ship that had been bedeviling American submarines in that area for some time, was herself sunk by the *U.S.S. Hawkbill*, another Manitowoc submarine commanded by CDR Worth Scanland, a friend of CDR Frank Latta. Thus, there was no direct eye-witness account of *Lagarto's* sinking at war's end.

In the intervening six decades, little was known by the loved ones of *Lagarto's* crew in regard to the fate of her eighty-six submariners.

Margy and Bill

Bill Mabin and Margy Miles were sweethearts. In their early twenties, they were both residents of the comfortable Chicago suburb of La Grange. They were my parents.

After two years at the University of Illinois and jobs at Wrigley's (chewing gum) and *Downbeat Magazine*, Bill decided to join the Navy – planning to get in his service and then return to college. Margy had a job she loved at *This Week Magazine* in Chicago. After dating for several years, both were looking forward to getting married in the near future.

The fair-haired, blue-eyed Margaret Miles and the dark-haired, brown-eyed William Mabin made an attractive couple by any standard. They were deeply in love.

On November 25, 1940, Bill Mabin enlisted in the United States Navy. He had just turned twenty-two and made the commitment to serve his country for the next four years. At the time of Bill's enlistment, the U.S. was not engaged in war, but his enlistment contract included the phrase, "IN THE EVENT OF WAR OR NATIONAL EMERGENCY DURING MY TERM OF SERVICE, I FURTHER OBLIGATE MYSELF TO SERVE THROUGHOUT THE WAR OR NATIONAL EMERGENCY, IF SO REQUIRED." This caveat was, indeed, enacted by Commander Frank D. Latta, as the *U.S.S. Lagarto* made her way to Pearl Harbor to play her part in World War II.

After basic training, Seaman 2nd Class Bill Mabin was sent to San Diego, California to serve on the destroyer *U.S.S. Crosby*, under the command of LCDR R.J. Penny, where his rating was changed to Seaman 1st Class. For the next year, he and Margy muddled through, missing each other, while looking forward to the future.

21 January 1941 – La Grange, Illinois

Dearest Bill –

Remember me? I'm the gal to whom you used to write. I'm also the gal you are engaged to. (Doesn't that look startling?) And the gal who loves you very much and worries when she doesn't hear from you --- You know, the tall blond with the good legs.

--- Honey, I sure hope you have written me a letter that I will get when I get home tonight. Last night I went over to see your mother and took my two new records over. She just about went nuts about "My Man" and "Somebody Loves Me." I sure wish you were here so we could enjoy them together. Darling, it's absolutely not right for us to be so far away from each other, but what the hell can we do about it? I get so lonesome for you, especially when I hear some record I know you would be crazy about.

I'm so glad you'll be able to wear civilian clothes after February. I know it will be a great treat. By the by, speaking of clothes, is your suit blue or white? Your mother and I are going to make a questionnaire out in duplicate with blanks for you to fill in, so we'll finally find out a lot of things we've both been wondering about.

Darling, every time I can't think of what to say I start feeling like telling you how much I keep loving you and how I want to be with you. Honey, I just can't help worrying about our getting into the war, though I keep saying that I know we won't. Sweetest, will you please comfort and soothe me a little the next time I write. I know you get awful lonesome, and even though I have my family and friends, I weaken occasionally.

I sure do love you.

Yours,

Marg

Less than a year later, hell arrived for everyone.

War!
Letters 1942

For the United States, World War II was in its infancy. On December 7, 1941 – a date that truly has lived in infamy – the Japanese Empire attacked American military forces in Pearl Harbor, Hawaii.

In January 1942, Signalman Third Class (SM3) William Tucker Mabin was assigned to duty at Headquarters Communication Office, Signal Tower, Eleventh Naval district. Everyone knew that service men were now in the war for the long haul.

Three weeks after the Pearl Harbor attack, Bill's mother Nancy went to San Diego to spend the New Year's holiday with her son. She wrote Margy Miles, Bill's fiancée, the following letter. It was written on Hotel San Diego letterhead.

1 January 1942 – San Diego, California

Dear Margy:-

My first letter this year! I am a little shaky today – not from too much to drink but from being up all night and I haven't been able to sleep all day as I thought I would – just not sleepy.

Well, Bill came in about 5:30 and we went downstairs and had a nice steak dinner first and then stopped in the cocktail room and had a drink. It was raining and we were glad we had planned our evening inside. I had gotten some sliced turkey and ham at Hamilton's in the afternoon for sandwiches and Bill got a bottle of Seagrams & some cokes. He invited a young chap, Carl Franzen, from the ship who has also been to school but has graduated and is waiting around for the Crosby. Bill and I played rummy 'till he came about 9 o'clock. He is an awfully nice chap from Chicago, about 27 years old, and he was pretty homesick and seemed glad to be here. We drank and talked and listened to the radio (I had gotten one in my room for the night) and listened to the Empire Room and Trianon in Chicago. When ten o'clock came, we celebrated New Year's Eve with you all back there. By the time 12 o'clock came we were talking (Bill doing most of it, believe it or not) and didn't much care about the New Year's Eve here. There was a lot of noise in the hotel – lots of parties going on. About one o'clock we decided to go out and see what was going on and Carl took us out to the Alpine Gardens on Pacific. We were there in time to see some of a very good floor show. Things really close up out here at 2 AM, as far as serving drinks were concerned. We stayed around 'till about 3 AM and came back to the hotel. The boys were too tired to send them out, so I made them lie down and sleep until 6 o'clock. I worked a crossword puzzle and cleaned up the room and woke them and sent them on their way about 6:15 and went to bed.

This hotel was really a mess today – parties still going on until 7 AM. I went down and had coffee about 11:30 – came back and got in my robe, trying to sleep but not successful. Bill will be in about 5:30 and we will stay pretty low tonight. I will send him home early because to tell you the truth, Bill was a little the worse for wear this morning. Don't mention it to him because I mean he was just tired out and all in. Anyway, we had a very nice New Year's Eve and if you could see how homesick these poor devils get on holidays, it makes you determined to get into some kind of work to help them along.

The Crosby has not been in – no one seems to know where it is. The other ships have all been in. Some wives got letters telling them to go home; their chances of seeing their husbands were too poor for them to stay here. Bill told me to tell you this because he can't write anything anymore and DON'T mention it when you write him, as all letters are being censored. Even x x x for kisses are forbidden. From now on we will hear very little from Bill. I can explain better when I come home just how hard it is for Bill to write and will be worse when he gets back to the ship. I do hope the Crosby comes in before I leave. Don't tell anyone but Gordon (Bill's father) *about this, as they really impress upon you out here to mention NOTHING about a ship...*

The following month, Margy wrote to her aunt and uncle, Marie and Charles Fox, about her impending marriage:

19 February 1942 – La Grange, Illinois

Dearest Aunt Marie & Uncle Charlie,

This is to tell you of some very good news! At least from my point of view it couldn't be better! Bill and I plan to get married sometime in April.

Of course as you know we have wanted to get married for some time but it looked like a pretty impractical desire but now things have certainly happened to give us a break. I don't know whether or not you heard of Bill's good fortune, but here's the story.

After he finished school and got his Signalman third Class rating he was put back on his ship but this only lasted for about a week and a half due to the fact that there were too many rated Signalmen on the Crosby. But – to his surprise and delight he was given shore duty in Broadway Tower with double his pay for subsistence which totals $140.50! Which was so much more than either of us ever expected to have happen.

This of course puts a very different light on our getting married. I will not be alone for great lengths of time, in fact his hours are eight on and twenty-four off (Uncle Charlie thought his hours were pretty good last year – I guess he's a lucky guy.) Of course both of us realize that even though he has been told this is permanent duty there is nothing really permanent in the navy, and he might be transferred again sometime to another ship, but we feel that about all a guy and a gal can do these days is take their happiness while they can, that there's no "security" to wait for, so long as we know we can lead a fairly normal life for awhile. We're sure not going to let the chance slip away from us. Mother feels this way too and is very happy for me even though I don't suppose she is anxious to get rid of me.

So - - - I'll be seeing you again soon. And one of the luckiest things about the whole set-up is that Bill is in San Diego, for as long as I can't be near my immediate family there is no place where I could possibly find people I love more dearly than in San Diego. You've been so marvelous to me always.

I'll undoubtedly want to look for a job after we've sort of settled, but least we won't exactly have to worry about the "wolf at the door" in the meantime. However, I think it would be very wise of me to work and save everything I make – and besides I really like working and it would keep me from sitting around with nothing much to do.

I don't expect I'll find a job as nice as this one. I'm now working for the Western Manager of THIS WEEK MAGAZINE. It's wonderful work and the best experience I could possibly get – I'm the Office Manager. My boss, whom I adore, has a daughter and four sons and is very understanding about my wanting to get married and is anxious to help me any way he can. He's really one in a million.

The head of the Gray Ladies here in Chicago has advised that I try to finish my course here so that I can do that sort of work when I get to San Diego. I think I'll want to do something in the way of "helping out," and I can't think of any more interesting kind of work.

With all my heart I hope I have your hearty approval and that you too think we were "pretty lucky fellows." I hope Uncle Charlie is not working too hard, though I can't imagine him any other way.

Even though Bill and Margy had gone together for four years, Bill sent a formal note to Marg's mother on March 7, 1942.

Dear Mrs. Miles,

As you know, Marg and I have gone together for a long time, close to four years. We've also wanted to get married for some time but there always seemed to be, oddly enough, a financial situation that was a little tough to cope with. At long last that situation no longer confronts us.

I love Marg very much and am sure she must feel the same way about me. Naturally, being in the Navy, my position is none too secure, but whose is nowadays? Luckily, we have a better break than most to start out with. If we can only be together a week it's more than worth it.

Our biggest problem now is that if both families will approve. It means a lot to us, and I pray to God they will.

Both the Miles and Mabin families did approve, and in April 1942, Margy and her grandmother Margaret Cossitt boarded a train in Chicago and headed to San Diego for the wedding.

Maggie Cossitt, then in her mid-seventies, was a wealthy woman. Knowing that Margy couldn't afford sleeping accommodations on the long trip (and would be too proud to accept her grandmother's offer to pay for both of them), Mrs. Cossitt – known to her grandchildren and great-grandchildren as "Yammy" – sat up in the regular passenger cars with her 24-year-old granddaughter all the way to California.

Yammy's brother, Charles Fox, was a prominent La Jolla surgeon, whose patients included the famous

Hollywood cowboy star Tom Mix, as well as those of more modest means. One of Dr. Fox's patients, unable to pay his bill, reimbursed the surgeon with a beautiful pearl, which he gave to Margy's mother, Jean Miles.

Charlie and Marie Fox lived in a gorgeous hillside estate in the Grossmont area of La Jolla. Their home stood in the midst of a large orange grove and had a spectacular view of the Pacific Ocean. It was there that Marie's mother, the famous German opera star, Madame Ernestine Schumann-Heink, visited her daughter and son-in-law. It was also at the Fox estate where an intimate wedding reception was held for the Mabin newly-weds, whose guests were Margy's handful of relatives and a few close Navy friends of Bill's – including his best man, Ed Stuart. Prior to the reception, Margy and Bill were married in a Roman Catholic ceremony, held in the chapel of St. Joseph's Cathedral in San Diego. It was presided over by the Reverend James R. Keane, a noted Catholic scholar, who authored *Novena: in Honor of Our Sorrowful Mother* in 1938.

After the wedding, Margy received this note from her new mother-in-law:

23 May 1942 – La Grange, Illinois

Dearest Margy:-

I was so glad to get your letter and to know that everything came up to your expectations (including Bill).

I know it is going to be hard on you both when you leave, but just think how lucky you are to have seen each other after five months. Rather cold consolation when the parting comes I know...

The happy couple settled down in California, and the new bride wrote her mother:

6 June 1942 – San Diego, California

Dearest Mom,

I so enjoyed your last letter, with the enclosures. I honestly was thrilled to death with the letter written by Jeannie (Margy's 3-year-old niece); *I could just see her grasping a great big pencil with such ease and writing 'Mowgy' a letter. I also like very much the little card with the prayer, and I shall make use of the penny postcard.*

You needn't worry about my working too hard. Bill is a big help and as you ought to know, I'm just born lazy, so couldn't work too hard if I wanted to. It isn't nearly as hard to get work as I thought it would be, I can get back and forth in a half hour (each way). I manage to get the bed made and dishes done before I leave in the morning, and Bill does the shopping for supper plus miscellaneous errands.

He had his back opened up Saturday and is home today as he isn't good for much signaling. He feels 'not too hot' and was in quite a bit of pain Saturday night, but is getting along alright I am sure.

Last week I got a check from Midgie for a wedding present which wasn't hard to take. Then Saturday I got a beautiful quilted stocking box from Bud and Belle (brother and sister-in-law) *for my birthday – so the mailman has been pretty good to me. (It's easy for him to be with all the swell people I know.)*

For the next four months, the Mabins lived happily together in San Diego. Bill applied for submarine duty, and his request was approved. In August, Bill was transferred to New London, Connecticut for submarine training, and Margy returned to La Grange to live with her mother. She was four months pregnant.

Bill wrote his wife the following letter:

<u>14 September 1942 – New London, Connecticut</u>

My Darling Margaret,

Unfortunately this will be short 'cause it's my last till my tonsils are out, and it's written on borrowed paper. I checked into "sick bay" (not hospital) this afternoon. My tonsils will be jerked in the morning, and I will be glad to be rid of them.

Your check arrived this afternoon, and it's more than enough. I don't spend much but I like to feel as though I have it in case of emergencies. Sorry about getting a little 'panicky' when my cash was dwindling.

I love you more than the world itself, and when I finally get settled shall send for you and small flags. ('Small flags' or 'Flags' was the Mabins' nickname for their unborn baby.)

I've gotten in pretty well with the 'chief in charge' (not the hospital), and he offered me a pretty good job, which it turned out I was not eligible for because I hadn't gone thru the tank, due to my tonsils. It'll probably be too late after they're out, but it at least shows I can get along, from the start, with some 'chiefs in charge.'

Your Air Mail stamp is not available, so I'm afraid I'll have to send this 'free.' Without going ashore it's hard to get hold of stamps; that's why I've sent my letters free.

Sometime within the next month, you should get a check of about $200 from the Navy. It's that new dependents allotment allowance.

Honey, I miss you so much it terrifically affects my daily routine. Keep your fingers crossed and I'll have some definite plans after I get out of sick bay.

The following month, Margy traveled to New London to spend some time with her husband before he shipped out. While there, she wrote her mother:

<u>23 November 1942 – New London, Connecticut</u>

Dear Mom,

I hoped to write a gay letter this morning but due to a phone call from Bill, I'm definitely out of the mood now.

Things look very unpromising for his leave; in fact, he was turned down. The need for signalmen now happens to be great – so that's that.

Bill will need some bucking up & if I'm a mess it certainly won't help him. He usually doesn't count on anything, but strangely he was counting on this, was almost certain of it – so I know how disappointed he is. But that's life. He'll leave with a draft (group of men) *to go somewhere on Monday. He doesn't know where of course.*

I owe a few other letters this morning but don't feel like a choice correspondent so I won't write any more today. Please warn Nancy. I'll write her as soon as we know anything definite. Got a nice letter from her this morning.

Will probably be home very soon –

Margy wrote lovely poetry. On 26 November, she wrote this poem for Bill:

A Thanksgiving Song to My Bluejacket Husband

Darling, these things I'm thankful for -
That every day I love you more,
That I am sure you love me, too,
And I am close and near to you.

And even when you go away
I'll still be thankful every day
Knowing we're really not apart
Because we have each other's heart...

So take good care of mine my dear,
I'll guard yours carefully back here,
I'll know that though you've gone to sea
You'll sometime bring it back to me.

Dumps (Margaret Mabin)

Bill Mabin in San Diego. 1942.

Found!
2005

It was Jamie's turn to take the first dive. After picking up their new boat in Singapore, British divers Jamie Macleod and Stewart Oehl arrived at the possible location of a lost American, World War II, diesel-powered attack submarine. Moored in the Gulf of Thailand, over what could be *U.S.S. Lagarto,* the divers stood sweaty-palmed with their eyes glued to the sonar screen.

Their first GPS mark had been passed with nothing remarkable showing on the screen. Then a bit of scatter began to show – at first a build-up of yellow, changing to red. Stewart Oehl recalls, "We couldn't even blink." An image of solid red appeared on the screen. The signal was given to lower a shot line. "Whatever was down in the depths was now marked to be explored," said Oehl. Macleod went down the line first, while everyone else on the dive boat held their breaths, waiting for his signal.

The conditions were good for diving, and it took only a few minutes to reach 65 meters. Macleod was greeted by the sight of the bow of a submarine, beckoning to him through the blue waters. The boat sat solidly on the bottom of the ocean and was covered with crustaceans clinging to everything, including the silent guns on the deck. To prevent the divers from drifting away from the boat, Macleod attached a shot line (a weighted guideline) to the periscope shears and sent a marker to the surface to tell Trident's crew that he had found a wreck.

Macleod swam aft and saw a 5" gun and a conning tower. But his time was up, so he started his ascent. As he made his way up through the clear blue waters of the Pacific Ocean, the implications of the discovery hit him, and he reflected on the sailors he had just left behind.

A third of the way up, he encountered Oehl going down; Macleod waved his arms and gave him the V for victory sign. Adrenalin rushed through Stewart Oehl' s veins. He knew this could mean only one thing – *LAGARTO!!!* He gave Macleod an underwater cheer in response. Two other descending divers were not far behind him.

Oehl's first vision of the submarine wreck enthralled him. "Standing on the bottom of the ocean, I looked up in awe; it was an unmistakable sight." He followed the contours of the bow upwards onto the deck and started moving aft. First he saw the forward gun, then the conning tower, and then the rear gun. There was no doubt in Oehl's mind they'd found *Lagarto.*

It had started in Wisconsin. Retired submariner Roy Leonhardt and his fellow SubVets, an active group of men who had served their country on submarines did more than the usual activities expected of retired veterans. The Wisconsin and Manitowoc SubVets held meetings, sent out newsletters and did the many things that go along with membership in such an organization. These SubVets went beyond that.

In 2005, the SubVets petitioned Wisconsin's Governor Jim Doyle and the state legislature to officially proclaim May 3rd annually as "*Lagarto* Remembrance Day" in honor of their state submarine (which each state had). Leonhardt e-mailed divers in Thailand inquiring if there was any new information on *U.S.S. Lagarto,* presumably lost in those waters in May 1945. He knew learning anything new was a long shot, but his attitude was – why not give it a try?

Leonhardt contacted Steve Burton, a British technical diver/engineer in Thailand who was well acquainted with other technical divers in the area. Burton contacted Macleod and Oehl, who had purchased a dive boat in Ranong and would be bringing it back to Koh Tao, their base of operations in Thailand. He informed them of Leonhardt's inquiry and asked if they were interested in diving in the area of *Lagarto's* last known location to see what they could see.

On 28 April 2005, Leonhardt received this e-mail response from Steve Burton:

> "I have, by coincidence, a friend with a book of fisherman's net snag marks. He has 4 reported abnormalities on the seabed at the USS *Lagarto's* sinking position. He'll run a scan over the reported wreck site next week for you, weather permitting, as

he brings his new boat around from Phuket to Koh Samui Thailand. I'll keep you informed if the vessel is found. This is the first time this sort of equipment has been used at this location to try and locate the vessel."

Commander Antonio San Jose 2005

United States Navy Commander (CDR) Antonio San Jose was on a salvage operation at sea when news of *Lagarto's* discovery reached him. He was onboard *U.S.S. Safeguard* (ARS 50), the U.S. Navy's diving and salvage vessel, floating just off the coast of Indonesia. After the 2004 tsunami disaster, a Marine Corps aircraft, involved in the relief effort, crashed and sank in 5,000 feet of water. *Safeguard* was searching for the plane, using their side scan sonar and a deep ocean remote-operated vehicle (ROV). The search operation for the aircraft had gone cold and after two weeks of searching the ocean bottom, the plane eluded them, so the crew needed something to lift their spirits.

When CDR San Jose was contacted by the American Embassy in Thailand in May 2005, his first thought was to shift from their current search and sail directly to Thailand to go down for a look at *Lagarto* since they had a deep ocean ROV onboard. He was ready to go and requested some information from Jamie Macleod to assist the Navy in their identification.

On 2 June 2005, CDR San Jose e-mailed Jamie,

> Tony San Jose here...I am a USN Diving and Salvage Officer stationed in Singapore...I need some assistance regarding the submarine you have found.

Tony asked Macleod about the sub's position, the topography of the ocean bottom and the depth. However, two days later, he was given another assignment and advised Macleod to address any further inquiries to the American Embassy in Thailand. He was hopeful that the *Lagarto* issue would be revisited after certain questions had been answered.

For one thing, the Naval Historical Center (NHC) wanted to make sure the Navy was not chasing a false lead. Also, prior to conducting U.S. Navy dive and salvage operations off the coast of a foreign country, adequate notification and detailed information would be needed by the U.S. country team in Thailand prior to commencement.

So, the verification of *Lagarto's* discovery was put on hold, but not forgotten.

The News
2005

Sunday, June 5th was a beautiful day, and I spent much of it lounging in a comfy chair on our screened-in porch, reading the newspaper. In the background, I could hear the pounding of horses' hooves as they galloped in the pasture adjacent to our farm in Lake Leelanau, Michigan. They were Belgian Draft horses, and I loved to watch these huge, fascinating animals romp and play.

It was a quiet day, and I was getting a little drowsy, so I decided to take a nap. I curled up on my bed with a good book and fell asleep. A short time later, the bedroom phone rang and woke me. The excited voice on the phone was my son John's. "Mom, are you sitting down?"

I was still shaking off my nap, but his news jarred me awake. He told me that information on the internet stated that my father's long-lost submarine, *U.S.S. Lagarto* had just been found.

Stunned and confused, I couldn't comprehend what my son was telling me. "Honey, I want you to talk to John," I said to my husband, who had just entered the room. Since he had served as a lieutenant in the Navy, I thought he might be able to make some sense of this. As he listened to our son's news, his facial expression became serious. John Jr. told him that *Lagarto's* discovery appeared in several places on the internet, and it sounded pretty authentic. We headed to my laptop as soon as we hung up.

The internet articles sounded pretty definite, but we needed to know more. Maybe, I thought, there would be something on the evening news. We were disappointed. There was nothing on the news that night about *Lagarto's* discovery.

My mind in turmoil, I called my other children, Bill and Beth. Although I seemed calm, I was in shock the remainder of the day. I kept thinking I had to do something, but I didn't know what. My family and I agreed I must find some way to confirm this information as soon as possible. I also knew I had to tell my 88-year-old mother very soon.

The next morning, I was up at dawn. Before he left for the day, I assured my concerned husband I would be fine; I had lots to do and would be very busy. He gave me a gentle hug and left for work.

The first call I had to make was to the Wisconsin Maritime Museum in Manitowoc. For several years, they had held an annual *Lagarto Remembrance Day* to honor the lost submarine, one of the four built in Manitowoc lost in World War II.

USS Lagarto (SS-371) was the designated state submarine of Wisconsin. As a result of a project initiated by the World War II Submarine Veterans Association (SubVets), every state had a state submarine – representing the 52 lost in WWII. New York and California each had two.

The morning dragged, and I saw nothing about *Lagarto* on any of the news channels. Our Michigan home was in the Eastern time zone, and the museum was in the Central time zone, so I knew it would be a few hours before I could reach anyone there. I spent a few agitated hours drinking coffee, nibbling toast, and watching CNN to see if there was any news about *Lagarto*.

It was time to call. When I reached the museum, I asked the receptionist if she had heard anything about *Lagarto's* discovery.

"Is it true?" I asked.

"Yes, isn't it wonderful," she said.

With that, I burst into tears.

My life changed with the words, "Yes, isn't it wonderful!" How could I describe the jumble of emotions I felt when I heard those words? It was the impossible news I never dreamed I would hear.

All my life, *Lagarto's* fate was murky to me. Since I was only two years old when my father died, I had grown up knowing little about what had happened to him and his shipmates. This fact of life became more difficult to accept as I grew older. I knew only that my father died on a submarine in World War II, somewhere in the Pacific Ocean, close to the end of the war. At least, I thought this was certain, but when someone is missing, there is always doubt.

Lagarto's last known location was in the Gulf of Siam (Gulf of Thailand), and it was last heard from on 3 May 1945. This was all we knew for sixty years.

After the war, Japanese sources reported that the minelayer *Hatsutaka* had attacked an American submarine in the area of *Lagarto's* operations, but the sinking was never confirmed by either side in the war.

Furthermore, *Hatsutaka* herself was gone. The Japanese minelayer was sunk by CDR Worth Scanland, the skipper of the American submarine *U.S.S. Hawkbill,* who was a friend of *Lagarto's* CDR Frank Latta. *Hatsutaka* survivors refused rescue, so there were no living witnesses to confirm her possible attack on *Lagarto.*

After my brief conversation with the museum's receptionist, I took a few minutes to regain my composure and thought – now what do I do? At that important moment in my life, I was standing alone in my kitchen, my husband at work, my children in Chicago, and my closest friends hundreds of miles away.

My mother lived in the vicinity, but that presented another problem. How would she take the news? She adored my father, but had put her life back together 57 years earlier when she wed my stepfather – the man she always said "saved her life." My mother's second marriage lasted 45 years before my stepfather died in 1993, and it gave me three siblings. Hank Chambers was the only father I knew. He came into my life when I was five, and he was a good father.

I had no idea how my mother, eighty-eight years old and frail, would react to this stunning news. My brother Dan was visiting Mom, and I knew he would be helpful to both of us. Since he was leaving the next day, and Mom might need some company after receiving this extraordinary news, I had to tell her that afternoon.

In the meantime, I had things to do. The news reaching us through means of the internet left me a little unsettled. I knew there had to be some kind of official announcement, but at the time, I had no idea how hard it would be to get.

I put my past political experience to work. Since I was a fairly new resident of Michigan, my political contacts in Illinois seemed a better bet for getting information.

My first call was to the office of Illinois Senator Richard Durbin. When I ran for the Illinois State Senate in 1996, Durbin was making his first run for the United States Senate. We had become acquainted through attending many of the same Democratic campaign events in the Chicago area.

After explaining the reason for my call to a member of Senator Durbin's staff, I was told that in order to get a response to my question (Did they have any information on the discovery of *Lagarto?*), I had to fax my request to his office. This, I found, was standard procedure.

My next call was to Illinois Senator Barack Obama. His office required the same contact procedure. By this time, I was beginning to get very emotional.

Hysterical was more like it. Senator Obama's aide reacted with compassion to my sobbing plea for help in confirming the discovery of my father's lost submarine and promised to get back to me as soon as he could.

I had one more call to make before I went to see my mother. Before I moved to Michigan, my congressman was the powerful William O. Lipinski of Chicago. Congressman Lipinski and I had become friends during my state senate race, and we respected each other. When I reached his office, then held by his son, Dan Lipinski, I asked for Lipinski aide Christopher Ganschow, an old and trusted friend. Ganschow wasn't there, so I spoke to another staff member, Lenore Goodfriend. She was sympathetic to my situation, and I was relieved to find someone I knew who was responsive. All I had to do was send a fax.

Those calls were all I could manage that morning, so I took off for my mother's house.

My mother had always been pretty. As she aged, she became patrician looking. Margaret Mabin Chambers was one of those lucky women with high cheek bones and a perfect nose. Her hair, always soft and lovely, was now streaked with platinum-blonde gray.

When I arrived, she was sitting in her usual spot on her blue couch, working on a piece of needlepoint. All of Mom's children and grandchildren have an abundance of Grammy's colorful needlepoint pillows. Sitting across from her, on the other blue couch, was my brother Dan, who must have been as apprehensive about Mom's feelings as I.

"Mom, I have something strange, but really wonderful to tell you. The *Lagarto* has been found." I could see confusion in Mom's eyes. I tried to explain the inexplicable to her, but I wasn't certain she grasped the news. This wasn't surprising, as I had difficulty grasping the news myself.

Dan got on the internet to see if there was anything new about *Lagarto*. We were certain that the discovery of a World War II submarine, lost for sixty years, would merit some news coverage. After all, the U.S. had been at war in the Middle East for two years, and the country was awash in patriotism. By the time I left my mother's house, there was nothing new on the internet or cable news stations.

The Mess Cook and Jack Benny 1942

In December 1942, Signalman Third Class Bill Mabin was transferred from New London to Portsmouth, New Hampshire for duty on *U.S.S. Balao* (SS-285). The day before the assignment was made, he wrote to his wife:

14 December 1942 – New London

My Dearest Marg,

First off, I wasn't transferred today. I went to the office this morning to find out what time and where I was to go. They told me I wasn't on today's list to go, but that tomorrow myself and three or four others will be sent out. They would not say where we were to go, which may mean a lot or may mean nothing at all. All those leaving today have known for several days where they were going. Those to remain here on old boats have already been transferred, and the Key West draft left this noon, so it doesn't look like I'll get either of those.

This will be my only letter for several days because I have no idea of how long it will take me to reach my destination. It may be Pearl Harbor or it may be Electric Boat Company, but in any case they haven't even told us. So don't worry if you don't hear from me for awhile.

I've felt terribly lost ever since that train pulled out of Chicago. I couldn't miss you more if I'd spent 20 years with you.

All the love in the world,

Bill

22 December 1942 – Portsmouth

My Darling,

At last the mail is beginning to come through, although not in the order written. Your letters have never meant more than they do now, and as time progresses they will mean even more, if possible.

Yesterday I was caught in a position that I thought I was past being vulnerable to, that of being selected as a mess cook. Actually it's a break, although surprising 'cause it rids me of numerous watches and shore patrol. It seems each ship has to supply a certain number of mess cooks to the sub barracks, and I, being the only one not yet going to school, was more or less drafted into the job, only for a week though. Last night Jack Benny and his show, including Mary Livingstone, Rochester, Don Wilson, Abe Lyman & band, etc. gave a two hour performance at the yard. First they ate at the sub barracks and the mess cooks got an introduction and autographs of most, because they were given a special dinner, served by us mess cooks. The one that impressed me most was Rose Blane, singer with Abe Lyman. I was standing about five feet from her, staring into space, and I happened to look at her, and she gave me quite a smile and called me over. We talked of generalities for two or three minutes. She was actually the biggest hit of the show. She sang "A Haven," which is a record out at Doc's that I played quite a bit while home. She has quite a personality.

Will soon send you our Christmas menu with three autographs.

All the Love in the World to the Most Wonderful Expectant Mother and Wife in the World,

Bill

24 December 1942 – Portsmouth

My Darling,

This will be short, it's primary purpose to send you enclosed Menu.

You must have been in bed close to a week now, haven't you? Has it done you some good, and do you feel any better? I hope to God you follow the doctor's orders to the letter, and don't find excuses, as before, to stray a bit. I know it must be damn tiresome to stay in bed all the time, but he must have some reason for putting you there.

Well, darling, take awfully good care of yourself and let me know your progress.

At this point in her pregnancy, Marg's health was of concern to everyone. Not wanting to worry Bill, she was not candid with him about her precarious pregnancy. Her physician, Dr. James Clarke, diagnosed her condition as toxemia of pregnancy, and she was ordered to have complete bed rest. Margy's mother left her brother Dwight to run their real estate business and stayed home to care for her daughter. In addition to bed rest, Margy's diet was limited. Unknown to Bill, Dr. Clarke was so concerned about his patient, that he advised her to have a C-Section and deliver the baby two months early. Marg refused, believing the health risks to a seven-month infant were severe. Bill knew nothing of this. In late December, he wrote:

28 December 1942 – Portsmouth

My Darling Wife,

Yes, honey, I think I shall be in the States when Flags is born, but that's not for sure. My guess is that my ship will be commissioned in about a month, then will probably lay around the States for awhile (that is not for publication).

I'm glad you've lost weight and know it will help when Flags comes. I'm not worried about money, and hope you don't. In about another month I shall get a good increase, and then things should go quite smoothly. Found I definitely can't make second class 'till we start operation, which will be some time yet.

I have been without a cent for two days now and don't even care. I have two cigarettes left and shall give up smoking when I finish those. I don't even care about that. I look to being broke 'till after New Years and am puzzled by my new outlook of not caring.

Good night, darling; take care of yourself and Flags.

Frustration
2005

The weeks that followed the news of *Lagarto's* discovery were a frenzy of phone calls, e-mails, and emotion. My initial shock turned into obsession, and I became disinterested in anything but *Lagarto*. My father! I knew where my father was! The first week after the news was rough. I paced around the house, I took long walks, I insisted that my children drop everything and visit. As word spread, I burst into tears at the mere mention of the subject. I was stressed, I was exhilarated. My husband thought I should seek professional help.

Everyone wanted to help, but didn't know what to do. When I told one friend the news, she could tell I was shaken and called a few days later. "I wanted to send you a card, but couldn't find any that were quite right. I don't think Hallmark makes any which address this situation," she said. Being so far from most of my friends, I sent them e-mails with the news. It became quite the amazing story, and most of them responded with awe and sympathy, but no one knew what to say. I didn't know what I wanted them to say; I just had to talk about it.

Indeed, it was confusing for everyone to know how to comfort me, especially when my emotions were so mixed. I was dealing with the knowledge of where my father was which made his loss real. The discovery of his submarine was stark proof he was gone. I knew this, of course. But because his death was always a mystery, it became almost mythical in my mind. Long suppressed feelings of loss came to the forefront of my emotions. I became acutely aware of all the years I hadn't had my father. I had missed him, but until his ship was found, I hadn't known how much. I wanted so much to talk to my mother about this, but most of the time, she was unreachable. Her mental confusion impaired her ability to discuss many things and sadly, a conversation on this subject was impossible to have.

Thank goodness for my husband and children. John was my rock and listened hours on end to my musings on *Lagarto*. My children called often and made the long trip from the Chicago area to Michigan's Leelanau County soon after the news broke.

A turning point came when John asked me what I wanted most to come from this discovery. He knew me well and realized that I needed to focus on the future.

"I want to meet the other families," I said. "I want a memorial service for *Lagarto's* crew."

Those became my unwavering goals. From that point on, every waking moment was spent on the phone or internet seeking information on the submarine or her families. I was driven to know more about the discovery and to hear from the Navy. They must know something, I thought. For the most part, I ran into brick walls. Through e-mail, I contacted the American Embassy in Bangkok. Jamie Macleod had informed them of the discovery of *Lagarto* two weeks earlier, and I assumed they must know something. They didn't.

On Thursday, June 9th, I received a polite, if not helpful, response from the American Embassy in Bangkok. I was told a "number of internet searches had been done on the *U.S.S. Lagarto,*" and I was referred to the Naval Historical Center's website. I was assured there was nothing more that could be done; my request (for information) fell beyond the scope of their capabilities.

On Friday, June 10th, I received a phone call from an official with the Joint POW-MIA Accounting Command (JPAC), the military agency charged with searching for, recovering, and identifying the remains of MIAs from all past wars involving the U.S. The military official was professional and warm, and she referred me to the Navy Personnel Casualty Assistance Department at the Department of Defense (DOD). The contact at the DOD directed me to a website: oceanexplorer@NOAA. No help. Then I called the Department of POW/MIA Office (DPMO) and left a message. No response.

In the meantime, I had begun corresponding with Jamie Macleod – both to thank him and to learn, first-hand, what the divers had found. Macleod and I became partners. In fact, important partnerships were forming between the key participants in the *Lagarto* quest. The folks at the Wisconsin Maritime Museum, at that time chiefly Karen Duvalle and volunteer Roy Leonhardt, gave me every support they could. Ray Krause, a computer expert, asked for my input for a *Lagarto* website he was designing. Duvalle and Leonhardt sent me every piece of information they had. Chris Ganschow, my friend who was an aide to Congressman Lipinski, became an advocate for *Lagarto* issues.

Karen Duvalle and I decided that it was important to find as many *Lagarto* families as possible. At that time, only four family members (including me) were known to the museum. Where does one begin? We began with the roster of the crew. Duvalle and I developed a routine that worked well; she did most of the original research, then sent me the names and phone numbers of the possibilities. I made the calls.

There were others who helped. Through internet research, my brother Dan found two families and forwarded me the information. He was also the first person to make an inquiry to the Naval Historical Center (NHC).

While all this was going on, I kept a close eye on my mother. It was difficult to get a read on her reactions when I raised the subject of *Lagarto.* She was always subdued, never excited. One minute, she said she wanted to know more, and the next she'd say, "Things like this are better left in the past." When I broached the subject of *Lagarto's* discovery, I never knew what reaction I would get. Mom had saved most of her correspondence that dated back to 1946, a dark period in her life. In addition to the letters from my father, there were more letters exchanged between her and other *Lagarto* family members. These missives were honest and heartbreaking.

Over the years, Mom had suggested I read my father's letters to "see what he was like." For some reason, I resisted. Now, I knew I had to read them; more importantly, I wanted to read them. I took my mother's box full of letters from the 1940s home. These letters opened the door to a time that brought my father and his *Lagarto* shipmates to life for me.

In the meantime, two of my children began to consider visiting the location of *Lagarto* themselves. This meant traveling half-way round the world, from Chicago to Thailand. I considered going with them, but decided against it. I rationalized that a *Lagarto* trip was a gift that Bill Mabin's grandchildren, not his sixty-two-year-old daughter, could give him. The truth was that I was not up to it. My children were.

My daughter, Beth Kenney Augustine, broached the possibility with Jamie Macleod. In an e-mail dated 14 June 2005, she wrote:

> Dear Jamie,
>
> Thank You! Thank You! Thank You!
>
> I hope you truly understand the chain reaction of joy that your discovery of *Lagarto* has set off. For our family and all the others to know that the *Lagarto* has been found brings some much needed closure to an otherwise sad chapter in their lives. Who would have thought that after all these years – she would be found?

Macleod responded with a gracious welcome to the Mabin grandchildren to join the MV Trident crew on the next excursion to *Lagarto's* site.

Beth and John had little more than a month to plan their trip and arrange their work schedules for this emotional journey. Their brother Bill, starting a new job, was unable to join them on this visit to their grandfather's gravesite.

The Baby and the Balao
1943

In 1943, two huge events in the lives of Bill and Margy Mabin were about to converge – Bill's first submarine patrol in enemy waters and the birth of their baby, a risky event for both mother and child.

2 January 1943 – Portsmouth
My Dearest Marg,

This is the first chance I've had to write for a few days, and even now I don't have too much time. Going to school from ten 'till midnight every time you get the duty, and you get the duty every three days. Besides that, you get watches many of the days you don't even have the duty. For example, I have the duty tonight, and tomorrow I have to go out to Sea on a trip 'cause they need a signalman on it. The other night I had to go to some town about twenty miles from here and help test running and searchlights. Otherwise they are very short of men, especially signalmen here.

Well darling, I'm back after spending all day out on a tug and I'm a little tired. So I must say good-night, honey.

From Margy to Bill:

5 January 1943 – La Grange, Illinois
Dear Bill –

I'm expecting the Doctor today, he said the first of the week and he wasn't here yesterday. I imagine when he comes he'll decide definitely what he's going to do & when.

This may sound silly dear but if I get a little scared (and I probably will), I'm going to think of how courageous you have been & will especially have to be – in this war. So much more courageous than I'll be even if I'm a very brave gal – for you'll be having many risks while mine is just one.

I dreamt last night that you and I were casually lying in bed & the Dr. (who was a priest in my dream) gave you the shot instead of me, which was to start me in labor. We thought it was very funny – but were wondering just what affect it <u>would</u> have on you – since you certainly couldn't have a baby. It still strikes me funny and I'm still wondering. I love to dream about you – even a crazy dream like that – we're together for awhile anyway and it sure is nice.

I have no news – not even a book review, so will close now. I'll add anything exciting that might happen later.

Later – same letter.

The Doctor came. My blood pressure is down a little but he thinks now that the baby is 8 months along. Perhaps I should go to the hospital where I will be under observation for a few days I imagine, and he possibly will induce labor maybe during the week end.

My state of mind at the present is very good. Right now I'm not scared or don't dread it at all. I hope, and imagine, I'll keep feeling this way. Doctor Clarke wondered if I counted wrong because he thinks I'm very small. (Of this I am rather proud – especially after being told so often how fat I was.)

I don't know just how much I'll be able to write at the hospital. I will be able to receive letters however. My address will be c/o MacNeal Hospital, Berwyn, Ill. – for heaven's sake USE IT, please darling.

Now I can get back to my favorite subject – how much I love you. Every night I go to sleep wishing & sometimes pretending you have your arms around me – but that day will come again soon – and in the meantime aren't we lucky to be married and have each other. And pretty soon we'll have another one, a symbol of our love.

Your father is going to be the chauffeur tomorrow – at least he won't have to worry this time about beating the stork.

<u>6 January 1943 – Portsmouth</u>

My Dearest Marg,

Received a couple of letters from you this morning, one complaining about my lack of writing and the other about the possibility of an eight-month Flags.

The first subject is one I realize and am afraid I can't help too much. I write when I get the chance, and consequently haven't written my folks for a long time. I realize, especially now, how much you like to get mail, but please try to realize I don't have all the time to write I want. Right now I'm trying to sink this dope about new Subs in my thick head, trying to study for second class, and standing at least my share of watches.

I don't like the sound of your having your baby early, but suppose the doctor knows what he's doing. Please keep me well posted on the developments, and if anything important happens, instruct my folks to send a wire immediately. I feel kinda helpless this far away, not being able to do anything for you, much less not even knowing what's happening to you.

Please darling, take perfect care of yourself, and I'll try to be a little better with my writing.

<u>8 January 1943 – Portsmouth</u>

My Darling,

Things are certainly moving fast. This afternoon's mail tells me you've been in the hospital since Wednesday.

I went in town last night and tried three times to phone you at home. While waiting for the operator to call me back, people kept using the phone so I never did get the call through. As long as you weren't home it's probably just as well anyway. I suppose by the time you receive this you will have already had Flags.

Originally the Balao was supposed to go in commission the fifteenth of this month. Now they have put it off 'till the fifteenth of February, and I doubt even that. They used to commission these boats long before they are ready to put to Sea, but starting with Balao, they will not commission them until they are ready to put to Sea. Fine thing.

Give the little guy the first kiss for me, and I'm afraid you're going to have to wait a little while for yours. All My Love to You Both.

As anticipated by Dr. Clarke, Flags was a difficult and dangerous delivery for both mother and child. There had been a real possibility that one or both of us might die. Never the less, Flags arrived – via Cesarean section – on January 11, 1943. The Red Cross contacted Mabin to apprise him of the situation, and he got leave for 9 days to be with his wife and baby girl. All turned out well, as I am that baby girl!

3 February 1943 – Portsmouth

Dearest Marg,

Tomorrow at eleven A.M. we go into commission, and I am detailed to hoist the Union Jack at the proper moment. There will be an Admiral, the Captain of the Yard and some other big-wigs at the ceremonies, plus reading of a personal letter from our dear Secretary of the Navy to the Balao crew.

To answer a couple of your questions when I think of them; naturally mother may wear my white muffler with her new coat, and I haven't seen Rose since getting back. I have found a new and much better saloon, no waitress thrown in this time.

I am sure glad to hear Nancy is gaining weight so fast. Hope Mr. Anderson soon develops those pictures of her. I could never forget that cute face of hers, but I am anxious to see those pictures.

Well darling, another short letter, but I hope it's better than nothing.

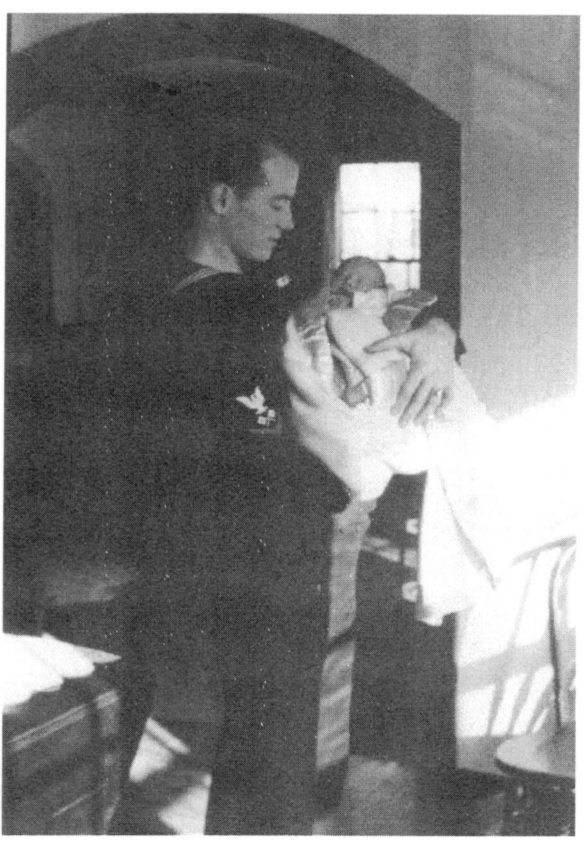

Bill Mabin, home in La Grange, on emergency leave. He is holding his daughter, who was a few days old. 1943.

On 4 February 1943, *U.S.S. Balao* (SS-285) was commissioned.

<u>7 February 1943 – Portsmouth</u>

My Dearest Marg,

Since last Thursday I've been drawing submarine pay, so next payday should be a pretty good one. I think I'm going to run into a little difficulty in making out an allotment to you. You are only allowed to make out a certain percent, ninety percent I think, of your base pay. That seventy percent extra I now make is not considered as base pay. Actually my base pay is only seventy-eight dollars, and twenty-two of that is taken for your present Govt. allotment, plus about three dollars and a half for insurance. Don't worry darling 'cause I'll make some arrangements to send you money. Incidentally, did you receive fifty or sixty-two this time?

I found out yesterday that one of our officers, Lt. Kimmel, is the son of Admiral Kimmel, the admiral who was at Pearl Harbor. The son is a darn nice guy. In fact all of our officers seem to be 4.0 guys.

A week from next Saturday, February 20th, the Balao holds her commissioning party. It will cost each man $10.00, and he gets three tickets for wife or friends. We get quite a fancy and costly dinner, all the whiskey and beer you care to drink and an orchestra. The American Legion is handling the whole affair for us and is trying to make a big thing of it. They expect close to three hundred. Of course it's a strictly invitation affair. Sure wish you were well enough to come here on the train. I think you'd really enjoy it. Incidentally, I think we'll be around the States for close to three months.

I'm sure glad you enjoyed the last phone call I made. I was a little blue and just wanted to talk to you for a minute. I was pretty sure you'd be awake 'cause I knew it was close to feeding time.

I saw a darn good show last Sunday night. It was "Stand By For Action," with Charles Laughton, Robert Taylor, etc. It was all about the old four stacker (a destroyer) like the Crosby. Think I may go over and see "Casablanca" tonight.

You seemed surprised that I am doing Quartermaster work. A Signalman on a submarine does almost entirely Q.M. work. After I make SM2 (Signalman 2nd Class) I think I shall change my rate. A S.M. and a Q.M. do exactly the same work on subs. Our chief Q.M. is a swell guy and gives me a lot of help.

Every bit of my love to you and Nancy.

10 February 1943 – Portsmouth
My Dearest Marg,

Tomorrow will be our darling's first month of real life. It should be an occasion for some sort of celebration, but due to a few miles separation I guess I'll have to be content to just celebrate in my mind. Say "Happy First Month" to Nancy for me. I just hope it won't be many more months before I can tell her myself.

Boy, do I ever wish you and Nancy were here. I could rent a place through the Navy pretty cheap and we'd really be on top of the world. I guess I can't complain though, 'cause we've been pretty damn lucky.

I shall probably write the Folks tomorrow night. I have really neglected them.

Every Bit of My Love to You Both.

14 February 1943 – Portsmouth
My Darling Marg,

Today being Sunday, I'm going to try to accomplish a few things, such as write a few letters, wash clothes, get some rest, etc.

You mentioned some while back about using that "Down Beat" stationery. Certainly, use it, that's what it's for. Anything I have is yours to use as you please. There's only one exception. If you ever run across some "Indian Head" pennies I have stowed some damn place, don't cash them in.

A rather amusing incident happened yesterday. It seems someone stole a pistol from some place and it was suspected it may have been hidden in a locker in the sub barracks. So it was announced there would be locker inspection. You've never seen such a mad rush to get rid of the bottles in the lockers. If they couldn't find a place to hide their bottles, they would drink them up and throw them away. The ground outside the barracks was covered with whiskey bottles. I don't think they found the gun.

I think it will be another month or six weeks before we start making our trial runs. It will probably be another month after that before we leave Portsmouth. I don't know what my chances are for getting five days before we leave the States. With the baby and your condition, I suppose it's not even remotely possible that you could visit me for a few days in case I can get five days? Your condition may be O.K. by that time, but I guess you couldn't very well leave the baby.

I'd do most anything to see you, I miss you so much. I guess that will make our lives even much happier after the wars over. The three of us will really be starting life together when we're finally reunited. I pray I won't be too much of a stranger to Nancy when that time comes. I don't think I could ever feel like a stranger around you again.

Take care of yourself honey, and don't try to do too much work. Mention me to Nancy now and then so she won't forget she has a pop.

18 February 1943 – Portsmouth

Darling,

Those pictures you sent are all actually perfect. You have no idea the thrill I get looking at them. They are going to get worn out with me taking them out of my pocket so much. The one I love is the one of you and Nancy. You both look so darn perfect in that picture it seems impossible that you both belong to me. I keep thinking of how perfect it will be when the three of us can go for a walk together on a beautiful, Midwestern fall afternoon. That probably sounds like a funny thought, but I can actually picture it in my mind, in fact have been thinking about it since I got the pictures.

After this, be kind of careful what you say in your letters, and don't refer to anything I may write when we may be leaving, etc. Not that you have been writing anything you shouldn't, but censorship has started for the Balao crew because we're in commission. I think you're familiar with what you should and should not write, if you're not, just use common sense.

Although I'm very poor at expressing it, honey, I love you very much.

21 February 1943 – Portsmouth

My Dearest Marg,

Well, this is the day after the big party, and there are a lot of hang-overs walking around. It was one of those affairs that everyone gets drunk at. Yes, even me. That's about all there is to it. From now on I'm going to stay aboard and only go ashore for a definite purpose.

I made out an allotment to you the other day for $50.00. I could have made it out for $52.00 but figured if my submarine pay ever stopped, for some reason or another, it would be better to get $2.00 a month than nothing, although I don't know what good $2.00 a month would do me. It starts March 1st, and you will be sent your first check the first of April.

Those pictures of our baby still look just as good to me now as they did the first day they arrived. I look at them just as much.

My hand seems to be shaking quite a bit, due to last night, and I want to do a little work on my second class course before the lights go out. My thoughts are always with my small family.

25 February 1943 – Portsmouth

My Dearest Marg,

I think it's about time you see the doctor and find out if you will be able to make the trip out here. The way they are rushing things to completion on the ship, it's hard to judge just how long we'll be here. I would say if you could make it around the first of April, it would be about right.

After I receive word that you can come, that is, if you can, I will have to start that old search of a place for you to stay. If you were to be here for some time, the task would be fairly easy. But this finding a room for a few days or a week will be hard. The three hotels here are actually dives, and from what I hear, quite crummy inside. Anyway, the thing to find out first is whether you can come or not, and for how long will you be able to leave the baby! There's always the question of money, but we seemed to have been able to work that out before, so I guess we can again.

I feel quite funny when I think of the possibility of seeing you again. It really hasn't been so long, but it seems longer than ever before. Just to be able to jump into my blues after work, have a couple of beers in town, then come home to "my old lady." Such a simple pleasure, but what a wonderful one. To my "well traveled wife" to be with me again before I go off to the wars?

I seem to be in quite a rut, that of writing on only one subject, whether you will be able to come to Portsmouth or not. It's the only thing I've been able to think about for some time.

You know, it's a shame that lights are out when I get home from drinking a few beers. If they were on I could sit down and write you a letter that would probably make you blush. I can think of the most romantic things to write to you when I've had those few beers. If I see you before I leave I shall try to make you fall in love with me all over again. The kind of love you feel when you first discover that you're in love with someone.........Listen to the line "old baldy" is giving out with.

Today is an anniversary that we seldom mention anymore. It was four years, eight months ago that we started going together. Tomorrow will be ten months of perfect, and I do mean perfect, wedded life. Take things easy, darling, and let me know if you will be able to visit me.

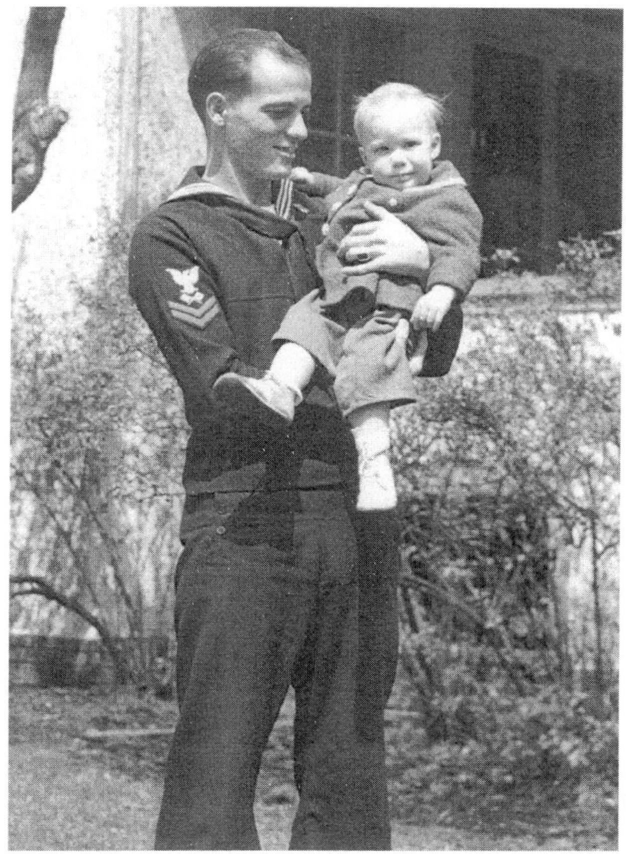

Bill Mabin in La Grange holding his daughter.

Finding the Families 2005

The few *Lagarto* families known by the museum gradually multiplied. Karen Duvalle, Roy Leonhardt, Ray Krause and I made progress. It was exciting to realize that we were writing the book on how to address this kind of unusual situation.

Two more *Lagarto* relatives learned of her discovery through the internet. I received a call from a man who became a friend and confidant. What would I have done without Dick Armstrong? Armstrong's uncle was Fireman 2nd Class Richard Fox Grace, a twenty-year-old resident of Wilmington, Delaware at the time of his death on *Lagarto.*

The Armstrong/Grace family still lived in Wilmington and was a steadfast and colorful component of the city's social fabric. Virginia Grace Armstrong, Dick's mother, had many vivid memories of her younger brother. Armstrong and I spoke several times a week, and I often chatted with Ginny. After sixty years, a long marriage and two sons, Fred and Dick, Ginny Armstrong still missed her handsome younger brother. The Armstrongs pledged to do everything they could to honor *Lagarto's* crew. Armstrong offered to contact Senator Joe Biden's office to solicit his support.

Illinois resident Brad Stahl whose great uncle, Chief Electrician's Mate Jesse Jobe on *Lagarto's* crew, got involved. One of six Illinois residents serving on the submarine's crew, Jobe had lived in Tunnel Hill. His naval portrait showed a handsome, dark-eyed sailor – an attractive man, who undoubtedly had a bright future ahead of him. Stahl told me that his grandfather, WWII submariner Chester Jobe, had always carried a heavy burden over his brother's death. Often family and friends of those who die in war wonder why they were spared when someone close to them was not. It was Jesse Jobe's choice to serve on *Lagarto*. He was a chief electrician and was offered the chance to go back to the States to train others in this work. He chose to fight.

Stahl was anxious to help. He contacted his representative in Congress, then Republican Speaker of the House Dennis Hastert, to see what he could do.

We found the families of Lieutenant (LT) Arthur Keeney and Lieutenant Junior Grade (LTjg) Joseph Pash. LT Keeney and LTjg Pash were both married and fathers of baby sons when *Lagarto* disappeared. Old photographs of these dashing Naval officers showed two attractive and intelligent young men. I learned that LT Keeney's granddaughter, Laura Keeney Zavala, had been seeking information on her grandfather. As we found *Lagarto* families, we learned that many adult grandchildren felt the loss of their grandfathers. That was true of my children.

In the meantime, George Weeks, a friend and syndicated political columnist, suggested I contact

Harold Chase, an aide to Michigan senator Carl Levin in his Traverse City office. Mr. Chase promised to see what he could do.

Squeezing In A Little Time 1943

<u>1 March 1943 – Portsmouth</u>

My Dearest Marg,

It seems there are several questions I would like to answer if I can think of what they are.

In the first place, I did receive Nancy's footprint from you, quite awhile before getting the one from Clarice (brother Jim's wife). *The reason I didn't mention it, if I didn't, was because the pictures came shortly afterward, and I was too interested in telling you how much I enjoyed them. Clarice's letter came via Charleston, South Carolina, so I suppose that was the reason for its delay.*

Tomorrow morning I report to <u>the dentist</u>, so you may stop worrying about that. Although I don't look forward to it, it will be a relief 'cause my mouth has been bothering me of late. Normally I don't mind going to <u>the dentist</u>, but I have a lot of work to be done on my teeth. I guess I'm just as much a baby as all men are when they have to go to <u>the dentist</u>. (Did I mention "The Dentist?")

About your coming for a visit. I want you here an awful lot, darling, but it looks like you're the one who will have to decide whether we can afford it or not. I certainly hope you decide we can, and that the doctor will let you go.

<u>7 March 1943 – Portsmouth</u>

My Dearest Marg,

I was so glad the Dr. gave his permission for you to come; I was afraid he wouldn't. At least the problem is solved. Now the remaining obstacle *seems to be that of money. Right now I have about $70.00 that will have to last me for some time. I have been fortunate in winning about $11.00 in the last three days, playing poker. I'm going to quit while I'm ahead.*

The first thing I want you to do is find out what your round-trip fare will be, and let me know as soon as possible. I have the duty the first week end in April, the third and fourth. I won't have the week-end duty for the next two weekends. I would suggest you arrive April 5th or 6th. I think we'll both have enough money to swing the deal by then. In the meantime, I shall try to live the next month on as little as possible. It will take sacrifices on both our parts, but they will be small ones in comparison to the happiness we will receive as a result of them.

Now for a little statement you made that makes me mad. I can't tell you how sorry I am that you "let yourself in for so much trouble by marrying me." If I've ever heard a stupid statement, that's it. All you've given me is more happiness and contentment than I've ever before known, plus a beautiful perfect baby daughter. All that, in less than a year. If that's trouble, let me have more of it. All the trouble we've had, you've had to bear.

Give the little guy a big fat one for me, and hundreds for yourself.

P.S. Just finished writing my folks, and it dawned on me I hadn't mentioned in my letter to you that I love you. So, I love you.

I love you very much, darling. Below are listed the four things I love most in life.

1. *My wife and daughter*
2. *My folks*
3. *Good beer*
4. *My wife's mashed potatoes*

Please don't feel hurt that I place "Good Beer" ahead of your mashed potatoes. I love you darling.

<u>9 March 1943 – Portsmouth</u>

My Dearest Marg,

This will be a fairly short letter, more or less to try to get a couple of points straightened out, or maybe more muddled.

Your train fare rather staggered me also. I don't like the idea of your traveling in day coach, just because it's cheaper. A year ago it was a different story, but today your condition is not the same. Will have to work it out so you can come Pullman.

The second thing that has me a little perplexed right now is the time for you to come. As I mentioned in my last letter, we should plan on about the 5th of April, due mainly to our being in a better financial state, plus the fact that I have the duty April 3rd and 4th. Unless I can figure things differently, we'll plan on that time. Now the only reason against the above mentioned time, and it is a good reason, is that we will <u>probably</u> be aboard ship about the first of April. That means it won't be long before we start making trial runs, thus, less liberty. Unfortunately, they're rushing the Balao through and she has all priorities. For that reason it's hard to figure on just how much longer we'll be here. This will probably make you all the more confused, as it does me, but I know things will work out for us as they always have.

I guess the only thing for us to do is plan on April 5th and trust to our usual good luck. In a couple of days things may be a little clearer. Now don't go getting low, 'cause that will only hinder, instead of help, the situation.

Was amused, in reading last night's paper, to find out that the "Dennis O'Keefes" have something in common with the "William Mabins." (Dennis O'Keefe was a movie star and had a baby the same day Nancy Mabin was born.)

I love you very much, darling.

Marg found a way to spend some time with her husband in Portsmouth. While there, she sent the following letter to her mother:

24 March 1943 – Portsmouth
Dearest Mom –

You probably wonder why I'm not answering the letter you wrote me last week, and the reason is because I have not yet received it!

Bill got a letter to me from you Monday at the Base but he didn't get home Monday night, & last night he very shamefacedly told me he left it in his locker so I still have it to look forward.

I just moved over here this morning. This place has a good many advantages (one being a good heavy table on which to write letters). It has a private bath which is very nice and is sort of like an apartment. That is our room is huge (old house – first floor) and divided into two sections; one a sort of sitting room and the other is a bed room. These can be separated by pulling across a heavy velvet curtain on a rod – so we have a regular sitting room. The furniture is old, heavy and grotesque, but the other advantages make up for that. The main advantage is the complete privacy and also having a sane landlady; the other was nuts I'm sure.

Bill may make second class before I leave. He'd probably kill me for mentioning it in case he doesn't but keep your fingers crossed and say a few "Hail Marys." It would make my allotment all screwed up again for awhile – would of course cut out that government check I get for myself & Nancy, but would mean a better base pay for Bill and of course the main thing to me – it will help his morale. He's worked so hard. He sews on the sewing machine – and does all sorts of cute little jobs. I'm going to have him sew for us after the war.

Met a few shipmates last night. Tough mugs, but interesting. If I could only write I think I could write an interesting tale of my life in "the Navy." It has certainly been a busy one – and quite different from anything I had known previously – but very broadening to say the least. Of course that goes for Bill too. It certainly isn't the life he was brought up in but the difference is more apparent to me because I'm in and out of it so much. I'm still thrilled to death to be with Bill, but so lucky to have a nice momma & baby to come home to when he goes.

<u>3 April 1943 – Portsmouth</u>

Dear Mom –

"It never rains but it pours" as you know. Thursday Bill was sad about not getting his rate – yesterday he was sadder – someone stole his submarine coat with all but $100.00 of his pay in it! It leaves us kinda short, so I wonder if you'd forward one of my checks from the Govt. – I'll need money for the train ride plus what we'll use here. Hate to use the check – any of it right now, but hate not eating worse.

Will write a more acceptable letter soon. I'm not at all sad about the money. Those things don't bother me sometimes. Well, I am, but I'm not letting it spoil our happiness together.

On April 12th, Margy left for La Grange, and Bill continued getting things ready to leave for war on his new submarine, *U.S.S. Balao.*

<u>12 April 1943 – Portsmouth</u>

My Darling Marg,

Can you imagine me writing the same day you leave? It must be love. Darling, it's going to be tough not to be able to come home to you from now on, even though I did go to sleep on you a few nights.

Sure hope you made your train connections with no trouble. I was a little worried about it this morning.

One of the main purposes of this letter is to tell you to listen to the "March of Time" program next Thursday night. <u>I think</u> it comes on about 9:30 P.M. Chicago time. Be sure to listen 'cause our Executive Officer told us this morning it would probably be of much interest to our family and friends. I don't know myself just what it is to be about.

If I don't cut this letter off right now it may be sometime before you hear from me.

It was at this point that Bill began to make notations in his small Navy journal regarding the operations of *U.S.S. Balao,* the first submarine of its class and the first submarine on which Bill served.

13 April 1943 – *U.S.S. Balao* started shake down.

17 April 1943 – Portsmouth

My Dearest Marg,

It gave me a funny sensation to read your last letter, and the remarks about your coming to the door and calling to me, our last morning together. I'm glad I didn't hear you 'cause it would have been just that much harder in leaving you. Those were perfect days, and I sure felt swell inside, showing you off around town. You surpassed my expectations of you, and they were plenty high. My gal can fit into any type of company, one of the traits I hope our daughter will inherit from you.

I sure do love you.

18 April 1943 – same letter

A little bit more tonight, darling. Maybe if I continue to do this you'll someday have a full length letter from me.

I still can't get over our perfect timing of your visit. You came at just the right time, and it wouldn't have done any good to stay on any later than you did.

Give that marvelous daughter a big fat one for the old man and try to pretend you're getting one yourself.

<u>6 May 1943 – Portsmouth</u>

My Dearest Marg,

It's been some time since you've heard from me, and it's been equally long since I've heard from you. The last letter I wrote was the last day I received one from you. I guess from now on, our mail will be chasing us around.

I burned my right hand the other day, and this is the first I've been able to write. It wasn't serious and it's all right now, but it was uncomfortable for awhile and prevented me from writing a couple of days I had the chance to.

I'll have to make this rather short 'cause if I don't I won't be able to mail it for a couple of days, and it's been pretty long already.

Darling, I love and miss you so much, I wish I had more chance to tell you. I think of you constantly. My next letter I shall try to make a little more romantic, but just wanted to get a bit of news off to you while I had the chance. Give my love to the folks and more to you and Nancy.

<u>9 May 1943 – Portsmouth</u>

My Darling Marg,

Today I received quite a batch of back mail, and it was a shot in the arm. You complain about your letters, and say they're putrid and dull, but none of them ever affect me that way. I admire the ease with which you write. It sounds just as though you were talking to me.

A Quartermaster was transferred off the ship and disqualified for further submarine duty. He wasn't very well liked aboard the ship and was a very lazy bastard. The Chief spent about ninety five percent of his time checking up to see if he had done the work he told him to do, and about nine out of ten times he hadn't. So now I am trying to straighten out some of the mess he made. Needless to say I <u>didn't</u> get rated May first, even though Mr. Seymour told me I would. The boat seems to be very stingy on rating. We're expecting a striker, or third class, in our gang to report today. If it is either, I shall still be second in charge.

Our days are numbered here, and if we're in Tuesday night, I plan on going to Howard Johnsons for dinner, then stopping by Irlandis (good friends). *Both will be very pleasant memories and remind me of some very happy days. It's hard to figure where we were the happiest, probably San Diego. Every bit of time spent with you has not been short of perfect though.*

It's hard for me to write about Nancy 'cause I've been with her so little. (It had been 3 months and 18 days since he had seen his infant daughter.) *So keep on writing just as much about her as you can.*

19 May 1943 – Portsmouth

My Darling,

I guess my letters have been few and far between, but this time with good reason. I rate liberty tonight but am standing-by for Eddie Miller. I don't feel much like going ashore any more, especially in this town.

I was quite surprised about Bo Hutchinson and Ruth Smith getting married. If I recall right, Bo used to date her occasionally but could never make much headway.

I miss you and the baby so much darling. I wish I could see you both for a little while. I won't say how lucky we've been in the past 'cause that doesn't help a bit. I might just as well be in China as where I am.

We got a Q. M. 3/c on board the other day. He's just out of school and has never been to sea before, so consequently has much to learn. He seems willing, and that's more important than knowing his stuff and being lazy.

It's been a long time since I've been to sea, but I got back in the swing of the routine surprisingly fast. Now it seems like I've been to sea all my life. In a short time I shall really know what it is to be at sea for a long time.

Well, for three years now I have failed to give you a birthday present. This last time could not be avoided though. I was afraid I wasn't even going to be able to call you. It was a tremendous thrill to hear your voice, and I think I heard a small squeak out of Nancy. I wish I could make those calls more often.

Were you expecting me to call? You answered right away and didn't seem surprised, although pleased. My time is so mixed up that I can't recall what night it was I talked to you, although your voice is still ringing in my ears – actual music, and you sounded so well and happy.

I'll try to make one more phone call before I leave for good, but don't know just when that will be. It will probably be around the same hour.

<u>27 May 1943 – Portsmouth</u>

My Most Darling Marg,

Well darling this will be the last for quite some time. My letters have been so few and far between you probably won't notice the difference.

It looks like I'm going to get second class the first of June. It seems to be the real thing this time. Dennehy told me to go ahead and buy second class rating badges, due to the fact I'll be at sea when my rate goes in effect. I can almost say it for sure this time but there have been so many false alarms before. I won't believe it 'till I start to draw the money.

On this last night there are so many things I'd like to say to you. I will never be able to express to you, by letter, just how much I love you and how strongly I want you. I guess you'll just have to be satisfied with my crude attempts of writing until we're together again.

It hardly seems possible that I am about to leave the States for God knows how long. From now on, all the places I go will be new to me.

My darling, I know it will be hard for you not to be able to receive letters from me for long periods of time – It will be damn tough for me, too. Anyway, I won't even have this secondary method, very often, to tell you how much I love you. You must never doubt for a second that I love you terrifically. It's a feeling that will last for a lifetime and never wear out. You must never doubt this, and keep praying for the day you, Nancy and I will be together for good.

I know I don't need to tell you to take good care of Nancy. I hope the little doll won't think her old man too much of a stranger when she finally gets to know him. I would like so much to watch her go through her early stages of life. (It had been 4 months and 1 week since he'd seen his daughter.) *When I get new construction again next year, the three of us shall get acquainted. I won't waste time sending for you.*

I must write the folks tonight, so I'll close and repeat I love you more than the world itself.

The Press, The Navy and Numa 2005

After ten days of making inquiries to the Navy and waiting for a response which didn't materialize, I took matters into my own hands. I called our local newspaper, the *Leelanau Enterprise,* and told them I had a great story.

On Friday June 17th, the *Enterprise*'s Eric Carlson came to my home for an interview. Carlson is a journalist who also served in the Marines, assigned to their public information office. After the interview, he gave me some advice on how to work with the military. Keep it positive, he said. He told me that the military usually makes special arrangements to honor the discovery of those who have died in war. Carlson promised to do some research on his own and let me know what he found.

He was true to his word, although I considered the news far from good. Carlson had placed a call to the public affairs office of the Commander Submarines Pacific (COMSUBPAC) in Pearl Harbor. He was told that the location of *Lagarto* had been known for a long time, although the Navy had never gone down to look for it. The public affairs officer added the United States Navy (USN) most likely would not go down now. As far as honoring those lost sailors, he said, the Navy holds a ceremony in Pearl Harbor twice a year for all the submarines lost in WWII, so they probably would not be doing anything special for *Lagarto.* He added that it was possible the Navy may throw out a wreath the next time they pass near *Lagarto's* location. I was stunned by this casual response from the Navy, especially since this was the first and only submarine discovered since the war that had been identified by independent divers.

Jamie Macleod's interaction with the USN was positive. In an e-mail, he wrote:

> It's a shame you haven't had a good response from the U.S. Navy. I rang the U.S. Naval Attaché soon after the find, and he made all the relevant departments aware. Soon after, I had messages from JPAC, the dept. responsible for accounting for MIA/POWs. After that I received a message from Diving and Salvage asking for more information. I'll forward you their e-mails; they seem very interested and very grateful for our work...
>
> I'm sure the Navy did have a rough idea where she lay, but the ocean's a big place and searches are difficult. There are two more *Balao* class subs missing in this area, *Wahoo* and *Tang.* NUMA has been trying for years to locate them.

> Let me know how you feel after you've read their responses. Hopefully you'll feel better.

Macleod also informed us that National Underwater and Marine Agency, better known as NUMA, had taken an active interest in *Lagarto's* discovery. NUMA was founded in 1979 by Clive Cussler, an author of popular fiction and non-fiction adventure books. According to its website, NUMA was a "non-profit, volunteer foundation dedicated to preserving our maritime heritage through the discovery, archaeological survey and conservation of shipwreck artifacts." My daughter, Beth Kenney-Augustine received the following message from Macleod in regard to MV Trident's next trip to *Lagarto* and NUMA:

> <u>*17* June 2005</u>
> Hello Beth,
>
> I think NUMA are the right people to do the job but apparently we have to be very careful what we say as they are still under negotiations with the Pentagon and production companies.
>
> I think they have a new presenter so you won't be able to meet Clive – but I'm told the new one is great. I have no idea of their timeframe.
>
> We are trying to organize a trip very soon. I'd like to take a few photos for ID

purposes and it'd be a perfect time for you to make your memorial.

As usual we are trying to raise the money for the next expedition, so you and your brothers would be more than welcome. When could you come?

Costs would be about $700 per person (ouch!). Duration of the trip would be 5 nights/days, we could pick you up from Samui airport, and then we have a 15 hour voyage to the site. The boat is comfortable (A/C, hot water, etc., but not luxury).

The same day, Beth informed her brother John of Jamie's note and said:

"Here's the invitation...what do you think?"

John replied:

".....It sounds great. I think we need to talk tomorrow with Billy and see what could work. Let's seize the moment.

Mom doesn't have to worry about my diving. I am certified, but not to the extent I would need to be to go to 200 ft. The deepest dive I ever took was 80 feet, and that was with an amazing need to carefully monitor my ascent/descent."

Two of Bill Mabin's three grandchildren (with best wishes from his namesake) began to make plans for the most poignant adventure of their lives.

Off to War
U.S.S. Balao (SS - 285)
1943

Bill's Mabin's first submarine, *U.S.S. Balao,* sailed for the Pacific theater of operations and joined the 7th Fleet at Brisbane, Australia on 10 July 1943. The following excerpts are from the Mabin letters and notations he made in his naval diary.

31 May 1943 – U.S.S. Balao left States*
10 June 1943 – U.S.S. Balao arrived Panama*

11 June 1943 – Panama Canal Zone
My Dearest Marg,

It's been sometime since I've written, darling, and will be quite awhile before I write again.

Honey, since I last saw you I've realized more than even before just how much it means to have a wife that can mean so much to life as you have. All the tough times and troubles we had before we were married, and there were plenty of them, served as a pretty good foundation for our long married life. We sure saw the ugliest part of each other in that four years, and yet still got married. Consequently, the rest of our lives will be smooth sailing or damn close to it. Have I made any sense in this letter so far?

(Most of the couple's problems had been centered on religion. Margy was a Roman Catholic, and Bill was a Presbyterian. Bill's parents, although they liked Marg, opposed the marriage on religious grounds.)

This weather is damn warm and bananas are very cheap. I guess you probably know I made second class. There must have been some mistake. If so, they may overlook it.

Love to you and Nancy; she's the best thing we've ever done.

P.S. In rereading this mess I realize what I said about seeing the ugliest of each other in that four years. It goes without saying what perfect times we had in those four years. Those are times that will never be forgotten.

14 June 1943 – *Balao* left Panama*

6 July 1943 – At Sea

My Dearest Marg,

It's been a long time since I've written a letter, and much longer since I've received one. The last communication I had was the phone call to you, and that seems years ago.

I've missed you so darling, it's hard to realize the time we'll be separated. Fortunately, I received pictures of Nancy from both you and the folks the day after I made the phone calls. They make me feel just a little closer to you both, although not much. Gosh! Nancy must be a big girl now. It just dawned on me that she will be six months old in a few days, and it's been about five and a half months since I've seen her. I used to feel quite a martyr at not being able to see Marcia and Mike grow up (his brother Jim's children). *Now I can't even see my own daughter.*

Most of my thoughts are taken up with you and Nancy. Time seems to go much faster that way, and it makes me feel warm to think of the perfect times we've had together, those in San Diego being the most prominent in my mind. We were sure on top of the world then, weren't we darling?

9 July 1943 – *Balao* arrived in Brisbane, Australia*

12 July 1943 – Brisbane

My Dearest,

I finally got quite a bunch of mail from home, and the feeling it gave me to read your letters can't be expressed. You may think it quite foolish to write so often, when you know I can't receive them for a spell, but it isn't. It gives me a day-to-day idea of happenings, and you don't seem so far away that way. Don't sacrifice sleep or anything in order to write me, but do write every time you're in the mood. When you've been out at sea for a spell, it's a disappointment to get only a few letters. Just remember that I will eventually get them.

It's been quite a stretch since I've had anything to drink. No liquor sold on Saturday or Sunday, the two days I made my liberties, and week days, the saloons are only open for about two or three hours during the day. It looks like I'll have to get healthy in spite of myself. And I thought it was tough because the saloon closed early in Portsmouth. The further away I get from home the better home looks. That sounds as though I only miss home because I can't get a drink, but I guess after five years you pretty well know how my mind works.

*Subs' locations were secret. They are added here in hindsight and as reference points to the ships movements.

Father's Day 2005

__*19 June 2005 – Father's Day – Nancy Kenney's Diary*__

Worked this morning, then went to Mom's. Had a nice visit; she seems a little more comfortable talking about Lagarto. Spent hours this afternoon, reading my father's letters. Mom has urged me for years to do this, but for some reason I just couldn't. I decided that today was my day to get acquainted with my father. There were just over a hundred letters – starting in the early 1940s. I got through most of them (about 70) and decided to leave the rest for tomorrow.

One thing I did learn was how much my parents were in love. Beautiful letters. Quite moved by them. Mom also save scores of letters from others during that period. I intend to get through them all.

The week has been busy with odds and ends. My husband is still concerned about the emotional trauma of dealing with the discovery of Lagarto and talked me into seeking professional counseling to help me deal with my feelings. I met with a clinical psychologist in Traverse City who is a therapist and a Catholic nun. She listened as I talked, and her presence calmed me. She came up with a wonderful idea. Get a map of the United States and have it mounted, she suggested. As you find Lagarto families, pinpoint them and see how many lives are changed with this news. Great idea!

Things are happening. Karen Duvalle heard from Wisconsin senator Herb Kohl's office. Senator Kohl is interested in the Lagarto situation and is going to look into it. Our congressional effort is gaining momentum.

Jamie Macleod is trying to raise enough money to make use of a remote operated vehicle (ROV) offered by Mermaids Maritime of Bangkok, to do a video survey of the Lagarto wreck. The funds are needed to pay a pilot to run it.

Karen told me she came across a clipping on Torpedoman 2nd Class George E. Clouse, a former resident of Missouri. The newspaper article noted that Clouse's widow lived in New Hampton, MO, and he had two children – a daughter Judy and a son Terry. She gave me some phone numbers to call, and I reached Beulah Clarke, Clouse's widow. She was shocked, of course. Beulah Clarke was the sweetest lady in the world. At the end of our conversation, she took my phone number and said her son would call.

Roy Leonhardt told me he received a response to his inquiry to the Naval Historical Center (NHC) for information on Lagarto. In a nutshell, the folks there don't know anything we don't know. Apparently e-mails were exchanged between members of the NHC staff, as well as someone at the State Department, and aside from doing a quick google search, no one knows anything. It doesn't sound like any more is going to be done.

I'm getting pretty frustrated. Enough time has passed, with no response from the Navy, that it seems obvious we Lagartos are going to have to do something ourselves. We will probably need to get some press coverage. My background in PR work should help me figure this out.

The decision to not wait for the Navy to take the lead in confirming *Lagarto's* discovery was somewhat liberating. It gave me the freedom to pursue my own goals.

I sent an e-mail to Karen Duvalle and Roy Leonhardt:

> 21 June 2005 – Lake Leelanau, MI
>
> Dear Karen and Roy,
>
> This week, I have slowly nudged the news of the *Lagarto* to the local press, qualifying that there has not yet been Navy or U.S. government confirmation. I've thought long and hard about how to do this and realized that we have to get some press coverage for two reasons:
>
> 1. Help find relatives.
> 2. Get the powers that be to take us seriously.
>
> The first story will appear in the *Leelanau Enterprise* this Thursday. The slant will be a Father's Day story. I think they

said it will be on the front page, and you can get it online.

The second will be either this week end or next week end in the *Suburban Life,* a newspaper distributed in the western suburbs of Chicago (where I lived for 60 years). I am very familiar with both papers and believe they will do a good job.

Don't know what you are intending to do about press coverage, but thought I'd let you know how I handled it. Thought about it being premature, but then decided, if the news is handled well (from the standpoint of confirmation), it would be good to do. Let me know how you're handling this on the other side of Lake Michigan.

23 June 2005 – Kenney Diary

Received a call from Norma Bishop, the new Executive Director of the Wisconsin Maritime Museum. Loved her. Fabulous credentials.

Continued to try to find Michael or Patrick Latta, the sons of Lagarto's captain. No luck.

Spent the afternoon with Mom. Got home and found Naval History magazine had come in the mail. It had an article about a submarine lost during a test in 1941. E-mailed the magazine's editors to try to interest them in writing something about Lagarto.

The next few days were busy, gratifying and odd. I received a call from a stranger who had heard about *Lagarto's* discovery from a woman I had chatted with in a yarn shop. He had served with the Merchant Marine in WWII and asserted that *Lagarto* should not have been operating in the shallow waters of the Gulf of Siam (Thailand) at that point in the war. He suggested that the sub must have been involved in espionage. With my emotions so raw, this suggestion scared me, and my husband decided he would handle this man if he called again. However, after giving it some thought, I decided the man may have been right: many submarines were engaged in spying on the enemy and other clandestine operations.

A few days later, I received a call from Joe Meredith, a representative of the Grand Traverse/Leelanau Counties Department of Veterans' Affairs. Meredith had seen the article about *Lagarto's* discovery in the local paper and got in touch with me. He told me that my mother was entitled to receive a monthly benefit as a war widow, since her second husband was deceased. As Mom's health was declining and the cost of her care increasing, this was a godsend.

In the meantime, Karen Duvalle and I continued to look for the Latta family. It was our first priority. On June 29th, Duvalle had good news. She had received an e-mail from a friend of Michael Latta. We were happy to know we had found Mike Latta, but saddened to also learn his brother Patrick was deceased.

We still had a problem. How would we connect with Latta? He was retired and lived on a sailboat without a phone. We had no address for him; we only knew he spent a lot of time in Mexico. That worry was soon dispelled because Mike Latta found me.

June 2005 – Kenney Diary

Rollercoaster Day! In the AM, I received a call from a gentleman, Hank Henderson, who served with Lagarto's executive officer (XO), on the submarine Pompon. He thought Mendenhall's widow was still alive and living in Oklahoma. I couldn't follow up immediately because I had to get to Mom's, but by the time I got home, he had already tracked everything down. LT Mendenhall's widow, prominent Oklahoma attorney Jane Looney-Montgomery, had passed away the previous year. However, Mendenhall's daughter Nancy was still living in OK. Henderson gave me the information I needed to reach her.

Henderson also told me of his experiences with LT Mendenhall. Bill Mendenhall was a Communications officer aboard Pompon. Another submarine built in Manitowoc, they prepared Pompon for commissioning. At the time, Henderson was a Radioman 3rd Class, and Mendenhall was an LTjg. They made three war patrols together, then Mendenhall was transferred off to go to new construction back in the States – which turned out to be Lagarto. Henderson stated that Bill Mendenhall was one of the finest Naval officers with whom he had served – and a heck of a guy, too! Henderson went on to make all nine Pompon patrols, and became the senior radioman as a Radioman 1st Class on the last three patrols. Henderson told me that he had thought of Lagarto many times over the years because of his great respect for Bill Mendenhall.

Later that day, I called Nancy Mendenhall Ford and left the message: "We have something very important in common. Please call as soon as you get this message."

A little later, I received the return call from Nancy Ford. I could tell she was driving when we first began to talk, but she soon pulled out of traffic. We two Nancys, both in our 60s with fathers we never knew who died together, had a lot to talk about. We were perfect strangers with a strong and terrible bond.

Ford was two months old when her father died. They never saw each other (they bear a strong physical resemblance), but she still has the precious baby blanket her father sent her after she was born.

We spoke of many things and cried, acknowledging that only we two could know what a penetrating, lifelong loss we shared. Ford told me something I didn't know – our fathers spent their last Christmas, 1944, in Pearl Harbor. She knew this because her uncle, Mendenhall's brother, ran into him there. Bill Mendenhall expressed concern to his brother about the waters to which Lagarto was being sent. He thought they were too shallow for submarine operations.

After this conversation, we two Nancys, both women with handsome dads named Bill, parted as

Lagarto sisters, hoping for a chance to sit down one day to have a good long talk.

Today has been full of emotional moments. The aide from Senator Obama's staff called. I could tell by the sound of his voice he was frustrated. He said the Lagarto situation was one of the most difficult with which he had ever had to deal. His inquiry started with the Naval Public Affairs office on and on to "you name it." He was ultimately referred to the NHC. I was a little mystified as to why confirmation of Lagarto's discovery ended up there, but it did.

As time passed, I began to believe that the discovery of *Lagarto* was seen as a historical issue, while the *Lagarto* families saw it as personal. This created much angst among everyone for some time.

Senator Obama's aide also said he understood the Navy would not take any steps to confirm *Lagarto's* discovery. He was told the NHC was aware, however, of the discovery made by Macleod and Oehl.

This made me sick to my stomach. It confirmed my impression the Navy was not going to do anything. We were on our own.

UNTITLED

"To you I now belong, each part of me
Is yours – my body, heart, and so much more
You have me with you, rolling across the sea
And shall have still, on every shore.
Thus, when the sordid work of war is done
The good of me, my love, and yet the bad
I fear is yours, and will be till I die.
Oh God, I ask all grace that can be had
To be the wife for him, my love, for I
Must be the warmth that thaws the chill of war -
The solace to a heart grown sick with fear.
Part of this thing – so great – he's fighting for.
Have I the strength? God grant it – for my dear."

Margaret Mabin

On Patrol In the South Pacific 1943

<u>26 July 1943 V-MAIL – Somewhere in the Pacific Ocean</u>

Dearest Marg,

Today I received a couple more letters from you. I sure enjoy news about the baby, but can you give me a little more dope about her color, such as eyes, hair, and complexion. She should be getting to the age by now that those things are becoming more prominent. Every day I become a little more conscious to the fact that I have a little daughter, although I don't know why. God knows I've seen little of her.

Tonight I had one of my biggest liberties in the last month and a half. I had six beers this time and lucky to get that many. For once in my life I can't find a place to spend my money.

This has been a very unromantic letter, but it's written under difficult circumstances. My darling, my feeling for you is far from unromantic!

<u>First patrol, July – September 1943 – 50 Days</u>

The following entries are from a small diary that Bill Mabin kept while on patrol:

<u>25 July 1943</u>

Left Brisbane for Patrol

<u>29 July 1943 – 5th Day</u>

Two depth charges dropped on us by one of our own ships.

2 August 1943 – 9th Day

Also my 25th birthday.

6 August 1943 – 13th Day

Sighted Jap hospital ship and closed within a thousand yards of it, but didn't fire. It was zigzagging.

7 August 1943 – 14th Day

Spent all morning chasing and getting in position to fire on 3 Jap cargo ships and 2 Destroyer escorts. Just when in position, enemy changed course and were out of range.

10 August 1943 – 17th Day

Sighted 2 Jap Merchant Mar. and one escort. Gave chase, and were sighted by escort. Jap escort dropped first depth charge at 0845 and last depth charge at 1120. Dropped about 20 ash cans in all. Naturally lost contact with rest of convoy.

12 August 1943 – 19th Day

Sighted one Jap Mer. Mar. and one destroyer escort. Attempted to get in position to fire on them, with no success. Returned to Battle line.

14 September 1943 – Last Day

Second patrol, October – November 1943 – 43 Days

17 October 1943

Sighted two Jap destroyers and four merchant mar. Fired six fish at one merchant and missed. Possibly first fish hit. Received very heavy depth charging. Official count was nine but it seemed like many more. If they had been any closer, or there had been any more we probably wouldn't be here now. The most scared I can ever remember being. Terrifically hot for several hours. No fun.

18 October 1943

Met up with Silversides. Found she had sunk one of above-mentioned convoy and had watched us take our depth charging. We both made contact with convoy again tonight, and we lost it after trailing it all night and fumbling some good chances. I counted 8 ships in convoy that night.

22-23 October 1943

Silversides and we made contact with another large convoy. We fired 10 fish a little after midnight. Many explosives and much smoke from Japs. Japs fired on us with deck guns. Came back in to finish off convoy and escort, and freighter started firing at us. Finally shells got too close & we had to dive. They dropped 3 depth charges on us. We did all our firing on surface. Great panic among Japs. We are following them now in order to take another (we sunk one and damaged two) crack at them when it gets dark tonight. We have eight fish left.

Last above convoy. *Silversides* sunk three of them.

26 October 1943

I qualified. (author's note: for dolphins)

28 October 1943

Refueled and took on four more fish at Tulagi.

<u>3 November 1943</u>

Fired 6 fish at large merchant mar. in 3 ship Jap convoy. Escort kept us down several hours with depth charging. Conservative estimate – 10 charges dropped. Six fish left. Have fired 22 so far this run.

<u>5 November 1943 – Somewhere in the South Pacific</u>

My Dearest Margaret,

It's been a long time since I've called you that. It's a name I like but almost forget you possess. I guess about the only time I use it has been when I'm very serious with you.

Nancy's almost ten months old now and it's been almost that long since I've seen her. I still picture her as that eleven-day-old baby, even though I have pictures of her at six months old. Seeing her that one time is almost worse than not having seen her at all. The picture I got of her then is still quite vivid in my mind, and it's hard to think of her any different. When I do see her again she'll be walking, and maybe even saying a few words. I'll undoubtedly be just another stranger to her, but I hope I'll see enough of her this time to become a permanent fixture, at least in her mind.

I've been wondering lately if you allow anyone to talk "baby talk" to her. If anyone starts that just pick up the nearest object and hit them over the head with it. That's one of my pet peeves. A kid has a hard enough time learning to talk without a lot of older people talking "assey" to it. I suppose you'll tell me it's impossible not to do, but just remind the offender of what an ass he sounds like, and give him my regards.

It's been over six months since we've been separated. That's the longest separation we've had since we've known each other, and it seems at least six years. I wonder if we'll seem strangers to one another the next time. God knows we love each other enough to never become strangers, even for a second, regardless the length of our separation.

I wish it were possible to record all my thoughts of you on paper. I've written you enough mental letters to keep you busy reading the rest of your life. When it comes time to put those thoughts down on paper I'm a total loss.

Incidentally, while I was on leave, I read the condensed story of "The Human Comedy" in liberty and meant to write you on how much I liked it. On returning from leave, the first letter of yours I read mentioned the same story. My opinion of William (can't remember how he spells his name) went sky-high as a result of his fondness for the 220 yd. low hurdles, although I have always thought highly of his writing.

I must clear off this table so it can be set-up for supper, but will write again soon, and I promise there will be more letters this time than last.

16 November 1943

Pulled into Milne Bay, New Guinea for end of second run. Forty-three days. Two sunk, one damaged. Started two weeks leave aboard *Fulton* (*Fulton* was a submarine tender).

Loss

A fascinating aspect of the *Lagarto* project was finding other families. After years of suppressing the quiet pain of my father's loss, I knew there would be others who felt the same. We lived in distant corners of the country, and didn't know each other. Our grandparents and many of our mothers were gone. Widows who had never forgotten their first love and others who had lost a beloved brother, would want to know this news. Nieces and nephews, who had lived with their parents' grief and heard of their uncle's bravery for years, would also want to know.

I related to the children, many of whom knew little about their fathers. I felt compelled to do something. Nothing interested me more than getting to know the other *Lagartos*.

To understand this obsession, one must be a war orphan – especially if your father's status is missing. Many orphans of WWII, all in their sixties or early seventies, described this feeling of loss in almost identical terms. The phrase "a hole in my heart" was repeated over and over again. Many adults believed that a child couldn't miss his/her father because they never knew them. Some children were left out of funerals or memorial services and never said good-bye to their fathers. Questions went unanswered; the past was the past and better left alone. Many widows remarried and felt disloyal to their new spouses if they talked about their former husband. Some parents couldn't bear to talk about their precious son. Some siblings were left behind in the grieving process and didn't deal with their own sorrow.

In discussing these life-long feelings of bereavement, sons and daughters told me they were reluctant to ask their mothers and grandparents about their father because they didn't want to hurt them. They grew up sacrificing their own need to know their father for the sake of protecting their mothers and often grandparents.

I was lucky. My mother and grandparents were always willing to talk about my father when I asked. My grandfather assumed the role of surrogate father. I don't remember anyone else ever holding my hand, as a child, when we took walks together.

Still, I didn't ask too often or too much for fear of making my grandparents sad. My questions about my dad were held within my heart.

When I asked my mother about my father, she talked about his warm nature, his athletic ability, and his many friends. Mom said his best quality was that he was nice to everyone. Others said the same thing; Bill Mabin was the nicest guy in the world. "He was a marvelous man," she said one day when I was driving her home from a doctor's appointment. Mom was in her late eighties then, but she remembered that. She told me he was the only person who always put her first. "How could you miss him," she said. "You never knew him." This response always ended the conversation.

This was common; other war orphans told me that their mothers reacted the same way.

The discovery of the WWII submarine presented an opportunity for *Lagarto*'s children to get to know their fathers. Their reactions often differed from other family members' feelings. We wanted to know our fathers, to take action and do something for them. Some families attained closure. *Lagarto* children agreed that we opened, rather than closed a door. Behind that door stood our fathers.

To Numa Or Not To Numa And Other Mishaps 2005

On its website, NUMA described itself this way:

> "The National Underwater and Marine Agency (NUMA) is a 501C3 non-profit, volunteer foundation dedicated to preserving our maritime heritage through the discovery, archaeological survey and conservation of shipwreck artifacts."

This organization, founded by adventure writer Clive Cussler, was both fact and fiction.

In Cussler's novels featuring his action hero Dirk Pitt, NUMA is well known to readers. His website notes that in his first non-fiction book, *The Sea Hunters,* "Cussler explores the special world of undersea adventure that inspired and has its fictional parallel in the Dirk Pitt novels. He describes his lifelong love for the sea and ship, and how his involvement with the search for John Paul Jones' famous Revolutionary War ships, the Bonhomme Richard, led to his establishing the NUMA.....Foundation, a non-profit organization dedicated to the discovery and preservation of historic shipwrecks."

Known only to a few, Jamie Macleod had entered a discussion phase with NUMA Australia. It sounded very promising.

On June 5th, 2005, Macleod sent a simple straight-forward message to NUMA, relating that they had found a wreck "believed to be the *U.S.S. Lagarto,* a Balao class sub that went MIA in May 1945." He asked if they were interested in the story.

Macleod received an almost immediate response from NUMA, indicating that they were. Thus began a cryptic flirtation between the divers and NUMA, which took many months to end.

At first it seemed exciting. Macleod was informed that the organization was developing a series of programs which would be the basis of a major Hollywood project. There were meetings in L.A., and there were press releases and negotiations with the Pentagon. There were PR teams all over the world. And there was the prospect of a residual economic boom for the dive industry in Thailand. Contracts had to be signed.

Macleod was advised to keep things quiet. The caveat was clear.

However, the press did get involved. After a positive article written by Reuter's reporter Ed Cropley, CYBER DIVER News Network (CDNN) News Editor Lamar Bennington published a scathing article with the provocative headline "Thailand dive shop owners deny they want to rob US war grave." In addition to stating unequivocally that U.S. officials had denied permission to local dive shop owners (i.e. Macleod and Oehl) to dive the wreck of *Lagarto,* they added that U.S. officials "may have to anchor a U.S. Navy ship over the wreck to protect the war grave from Thailand's dive shop owners."

The blast went further. Continuing to defame Macleod, the article went on to say, "While Thai dive industry kingpin MacLeod, 43, claims that he and other dive shop owners in the area who promote and sell wreck diving tours just want to 'study' the wreck, and do not want to disrespect a war grave, many are skeptical given the failure of Thailand's diving industry to protect local reefs and their callow business-as-usual response to the horror of tsunami damage and deaths."

Needless to say, this article and others that jumped on the anti-diver bandwagon were very upsetting to Jamie Macleod, Stewart Oehl, Karen Duvalle and me.

After reading these articles, Karen Duvalle and I e-mailed each other dozens of times that morning, and I was beside myself with anxiety, thinking that the negative publicity would end any further dives on *Lagarto.*

Macleod and his crew were abashed and worried the publicity would end any hope of receiving Pentagon approval for more dives. We tried to reassure each other that all would turn out well, and it did. But the articles horrified us all. Macleod was burned by the press, and it took him almost a year to trust most reporters again.

Michael Latta and Other Noble Beings 2005

The First week of July 2005 – Kenney Diary

The best part of the week was connecting with Mike Latta, the son of Lagarto's skipper, Frank Latta. He lives on his sailboat in Mexico, and although communication is difficult, I feel like I've found my big brother.

Mike told me that years ago he spoke to CDR Ben Jarvis, captain of U.S.S. Baya, the last person to speak to CDR Latta before Lagarto went down. We thought that there was much confusion over Lagarto's demise and wanted to know more about it.

A wonderful story about Lagarto in Springfield, Missouri's News-Leader newspaper reported that there are three Lagarto families who live in that area. Amazingly, none of them knew each other!

People send me lovely things. One was a poem about Lagarto written by Al Alessandra. He wrote the poem after watching a History Channel program "The Color of War." A segment of the series, "Silent and Deep," featured Lagarto and two other subs. I'll send his poem with John and Beth when they go to Thailand.

The only seriously down note of the week – and it is very upsetting – was a call I received from Senator Obama's aide, who read me the response they had received from the Navy in regard to Lagarto's discovery. Basically, the USN is not going to do anything. I can't believe it!

The response from Mike Latta was a shot in the arm. As the son of *Lagarto's* skipper, he had a unique perspective on the submarine. He remembered going along on training exercises in Lake Michigan and had fond memories of that experience, including his mingling with the crew. Latta had earned his stripes in life, and lived it then his own way. From the first time I spoke with him, I knew I'd found someone supportive – but someone who would also appraise things with honesty. He had no fear of speaking his mind. That made two of us.

A man of a certain age, Latta had reached that age with much grace. He was handsome with white hair, chiseled features and intense blue eyes. No stranger to fitness, he was wiry and strong. Latta's resourcefulness enabled him to live independently on his sailboat with no phone or television or many of the superfluous luxuries we earthlings think important. But like all *Lagarto* children, he carried the emotional baggage of a lost father. In his first written message to me (e-mail), he said in part:

> Dear Nancy,
>
> I am astounded. I had no idea anyone was interested, let alone discovered, the resting place of our fathers' sub, the

> *Lagarto*. I knew that she had gone down in very shallow waters off the eastern shores of Malaysia. In fact I managed to fly over the general area and say a few thoughts while on a trip from Singapore to Bangkok some few years ago. Before sailing off to Mexico 4 years ago I even attempted, via one of his diving exploration associates, to get the famous Mr. Ballard interested in finding the *Lagarto* for one of his *National Geographic* special features... but to no avail. And now here you are, out of the blue, with this wonderful news.
>
> And I want to hear it all...

The next day, Latta wrote more:

> Dear Nancy,
>
> Thanks again for bringing me into the new LAGARTO information fold. It has my head spinning as I drag up old memories. Sorry that I couldn't reach you at home earlier by phone. As a cruising sailor the past few years, it is difficult for me to simply pick up the office phone and communicate whenever I please. And vice-versa. I now must walk to a road nearest the harbor, catch a bus into town, find an open cyber café and check my e-mail. Phone calls are another matter!........

> ...Our family lived in Manitowoc during the building and subsequent trials of *Lagarto*. My dad even managed to sneak me, aged 8, aboard while testing out on the lake! I am sure that your dad was one of the many crew members that had to put up with my curiosity and stumbling efforts to stay out of the way. Often a huge pair of arms would swoop me up and safely over a coaming or up the last rungs of the conning tower ladder. It was such a happy experience. I had no idea at the time, that being the son of 'the old man' was probably a somewhat sacrosanct position. It is forever etched in my memories.

Communicating with Mike Latta became a balm to my anxiety. At that point, I had the pressure of dealing with many issues at once, not the least of which was continuing to push the Navy to recognize *Lagarto's* discovery. My touchstone was this: *Lagarto's* crew, who so long ago gave their lives for this country, will be honored. The thought that galvanized me was that those dear young men, whose lives were cut short in such a violent way, could not speak for themselves. If we *Lagartos* didn't pursue getting them the recognition they deserved, who would? Who loves them more than their own families and friends? If we didn't act, no one else would.

Mike Latta was in this with me now – in a quiet but strong way.

A Third Christmas At War And Other Lonely Times 1943

19 November 1943 – New Guinea

My Dearest Marg,

Got quite a bunch of letters yesterday so I'll keep busy answering for a while now. It took me practically all day yesterday to finish reading my mail, with various interruptions every time I'd be in the middle of one.

Nancy seems to be growing so fast I can scarcely believe the things you say. She'll undoubtedly have all her first teeth, be walking and talking when I next see her. Would that I had the chance to be there while these things were being developed. Her development in her first nine months must have been tremendous.

I am now on two weeks leave; and what a leave (We later learned he was in New Guinea at this time.) *I've often heard jokes of guys spending their leave aboard ship, now I'm one of those guys. Yes, we're in a spot now where it would do no good to go ashore 'cause there's nothing there, and I do mean nothing. So for two weeks I will sit aboard the tender and do nothing. There is supposed to be a few cases of beer aboard for us, but as yet that hasn't been broken out. When they do break it out there will probably be only enough to just tease one with. Yes, I guess I've spent more pleasant leaves, and in much more interesting places.*

20 November 1943 – New Guinea

Dearest Marg,

Yesterday we took a few cases of beer over on the beach and had a ball game. There were only about four bottles of beer per man, but even a little tastes pretty good when it's the first in a long time. Besides that, it was "states side" beer, the first I've had since last May. The worst they brew back in the states is many times better than the best they brew in this part of the world. Yesterday was the first beer I've had that has been reasonably cold. When you get it, all the beer over here is green and warm. I shall never again complain about my beer not being cold enough when I get back.

I've often thought what a great comfort it is to have a wife and baby waiting for me back home. Also when you're blue and scared, and I've been both, it's a comfort to think there's someone besides yourself that gives a damn. Those are a few practical advantages of being married. Besides these advantages I've got as perfect a wife as any man ever had, and one that makes me look good in spite of all my faults. So far all the advantages of married life have been mine, but some day, when I'm home for good, maybe you too shall be rewarded by a few advantages.

Today we shall again have our few bottles of beer and a ball game. That's been the real highlight of this so-called leave of ours.

Take care of yourselves, my darlings, and someday I'll be able to take care of you both myself.

22 November 1943 – New Guinea

My Darliug,

This afternoon I received two letters from you that would normally get no more than a routine answer,........but I just happen to be in the mood to tell you how much I really appreciate your letters. I'm always in the mood that I appreciate receiving them but I'm seldom able to put in words how much I really enjoy every one of them.

You often mention, my darling, how much I must tire of your saying, "I love you." Yes, but if that was that was all you said it still wouldn't be half enough. Knowing that you really love me and want me home as soon as possible is enough to keep me going for time eternity.

Incidentally (one of my favorite words for starting a paragraph, as if you didn't know) don't worry about being too romantic in your letter writing. The censors seldom, if ever, read your letters to me. Anyway, I bet I can tell you more military secrets than you can tell me.

The most important thing about your letters to me is your saying, "I love you," and the news, any news no matter how small, of Nancy. Those are the two things I'm coming home for, so please keep me posted on both.

While I think of it, darling (I won't use the word incidentally this time) if you ever find a good investment, even if it's a gamble, for what little money you've saved for us, don't hesitate about it. I shall plan on coming home when the war's over, with no money in the bank. If we have more than $10.00 to our name, after the war, it's all to your credit. I mean it honey. I never saved a cent when I was single, so there's no reason why I should claim any money since I've been married.

5 December 1943 – New Guinea

Darling,

Just about fifteen minutes ago I got a letter from mom with some pictures of you and Nancy, taken in front of dad's office. There is one really perfect one with you, Nancy and Bev (Simcoke) *and her baby* (Jimmy). *I've been waiting for a long time for a really good picture of you and the baby, one where you look at the camera instead of the baby. That's the best picture so far. I can't keep my eyes off you and Nancy; it's such a good picture of you both.* (Jim Simcoke's father, Sam, was a navy pilot and was also killed in the war.)

You may be interested in knowing that your allotment has been increased. You will now get $145.00 a month, in two separate checks. The government has increased the family allotment, and the $37.00 affair is no more. I don't know just what this new set up is but I think I receive about $20.00 a month more now, due mainly to having a child. If my submarine pay stops for any reason, such as transfer back to new construction, I will receive about five dollars a month for myself. So when that does happen, be prepared *to send me money upon request. Things will be a little fouled up when that happens, but I'll worry about it then. I start drawing longevity (5%) now too. I just figured out that all in all, I make $236.90 a month. Not bad, but at times I've also thought not half enough either, and I don't mean because I'm such a valuable man to the Navy either. We should be able to save a bit to help out on that wonderful day we're finally back together for good again. Good night, my darling, I love you, and give that perfect baby of ours a kiss from her old man.*

Margy and Nancy Jean, Christmas time. 1943.

Third patrol, December 1943 - January 1944 - 38 Days

7 December 1943 – Mabin Diary

Awarded Submarine combat pin. We now have a new captain, C.C. Cole.

25 December 1943

Christmas Day, about sixty miles from Truk. Held one minute's silence for boys in states who couldn't get home for leave.

27 December 1943

Spotted two Jap. Heavy cruisers and two destroyers making about 25 knots, headed for Truk. Fired four stern fish. Dove and heard three explosions about 4 ½ minutes after firing. Possibly a hit, but not likely due to their high speed. We received no depth charges.

Another year of war was almost behind the sailors aboard *Balao,* but they were destined to bring in the new year with plenty of fireworks!

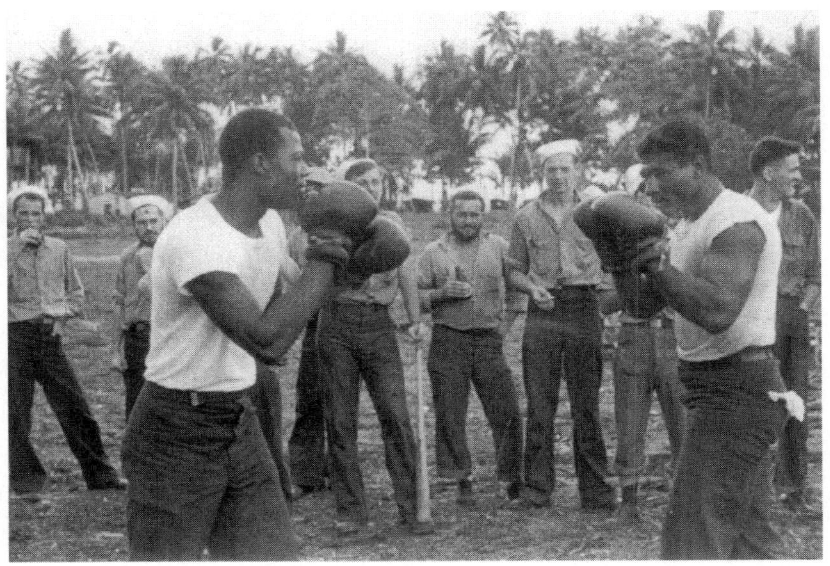

Rest and relaxation (R&R) while in New Guinea, serving on U.S.S. Balao (SS-285). Bill Mabin, far left, drinking beer. 1943.

Response From the Navy 2005

Early in July, I received a copy of the response to Senator Obama's office on the question of confirming the discovery of *U.S.S. Lagarto.* One thing I learned about making inquiries to the Pentagon is that they are generally made through "officials." That official, in this case then Senator Obama, notifies the interested party. The author of the response was a Navy captain, then acting Director of Naval History:

Dear Mr. Obama:

I am writing in response to your letter of June 9, 2005, regarding the recently reported discovery of the wreck of USS Lagarto (SS 371) in the Gulf of Thailand. I understand that your constituent, Ms. Nancy Kenny's (sic) father, Signalman First Class Bill Mabin, was a crewmember on board Lagarto when the submarine was lost on May 3, 1945.

The Naval Historical Center (NHC) was notified on June 1, 2005 that divers had located what is believed to be the wreck of USS Lagarto in the Gulf of Thailand in approximately 70 meters of water. It was reported that the submarine appeared to be intact with no visible damage and the hull number was clearly visible (author's note: the hull number was not visible, and to my knowledge was never reported as such). *We later learned that a dive company in Thailand, under the direction of Mr. Jamie Macleod, was the group that had located the submarine. We contacted Mr. Macleod to thank him for locating what appears to be Lagarto and informed him of the U.S. government's position that the wreck not be disturbed in anyway (sic), that as a war grave, it should be treated with dignity, honor, and respect. Mr. Macleod assured us that he had no intention of disturbing the wreck. He stated that he plans to do a video survey of the submarine and has agreed to provide us with copies of the video as well as any other images of the wreck. We understand that Ms. Kenny had also been in touch with Mr. Macleod and that he has promised to keep her apprised of their upcoming survey.*

At present, the Navy has no plans to visit the wreck site. The Naval Attache in Bangkok and the U.S. State Department are aware of this situation and has informed the government of Thailand of its position of non-disturbance. For your information, a new law titled the Sunken Military Craft Act was passed last year that affords sunken U.S. military ships and submerged aircraft wrecks further protection from unauthorized disturbance.

I hope that this information provides your constituent and her family some comfort. The Navy and the nation honor William Mabin's memory and all those who have given their lives in the service of the United States.

While I appreciated the captain's response, I found his letter disturbing, not comforting. It seemed the Navy had decided to shed itself of any responsibility in confirming the submarine's discovery or subsequent honoring of *Lagarto's* crew. Again, my stomach was tied in knots, and I began to feel disappointment in the Navy I had loved so much all my life.

Smoke on the Horizon 1944

Bill Mabin's journal entries and letters to his wife show the opposite poles of love and war.

1 January 1944 – Mabin Journal

Spotted smoke on horizon. At 2348 fired 6 fish into ten thousand ton merchant mar. sunk it with three hits. There were two escorts. Dropped nine depth charges on us.

Fired on surface & almost rammed one escort that came out of a squall. Dove and abandoned conning tower. Had trouble closing C.T. latch. After about five hours down came to the surface at full on the batteries and made a run for it on surface.

1 January 1944

My Darling Margaret,

Today is the first day of a new year, and it more-or-less started with a bang. Last week, Christmas, I had meant to write, but as things turned out, as if you won't find out, I didn't. The day itself was only different from any other by an extremely good meal. My thoughts were of you and Nancy about every minute of the day. I tried to imagine just what your Christmas would be like but don't suppose I was very successful. At mid-night Christmas Eve we held one minute of silence for the boys back in Los Angeles and N.Y. City who couldn't get home for leave.

I don't know if I mentioned it before, but I became "qualified" about two or three months ago. We received our submarine combat pins last month also. I don't know if you've ever heard of them, much less seen one, but they are awarded for a successful patrol run. It is a sterling silver pin of a broadside view of a submarine proceeding along on the surface. It's one pin I shall wear. Unlike the ribbons <u>*everyone*</u> *wears, you cannot get hold of the pin unless you have made a successful war patrol.*

Nancy's first birthday will be in a few days and I feel bad that I can't send her some kind of present for the happy occasion. It seems my life has been full of excuses for not being able to send presents for one occasion or another. I always seem to end up by saying 'I hope to someday be able to make it up to you.' I really shall try tho.

I think I missed you last week more than ever before, my darling. To a guy that's in love, life is so very incomplete without his wife near at all times. You just never seem to 'hit on all four.' Even when we had bills and little money, we were always perfectly content with things as long as we were together. Incidentally, one reason I didn't write last week was because of a low mood I was in for a couple of days.

This will be all for today, dear. My love to your mother and grand-mother, as well as you and Nancy.

<u>2 January 1944</u>

Captain received congratulations from Admiral Halsey by radio.

<u>6 January 1944</u>

Made radio contact last night. A light cruiser tow-ing a crippled merchant mar. with two escorts. Have twice tried to get in position to fire but as yet unsuccess-fully. Have little more than enough fuel to get to Tulagi. Still trailing ships.

Balao arrived in Brisbane on 15 January for a normal two-week refit and a brief training period.

16 January 1944

End Second Run.

Fourth patrol, February – March 1944 – 42 Days

6 February 1944

Left Brisbane, Australia for start of 4th run.

On 6 February, *Balao* was underway via Tulagi for her patrol area north of New Guinea, which she entered on the 13th.

9 February 1944

My Darling,

I have found a good spot for the pictures of you and Nancy right at the head of my bunk, on the bulkhead. The trouble is I don't get quite as much sleep 'cause I like to lie awake and look at them. More perfect pictures have yet to be made.

I think after this trip I should be about due to spend a little time in the relief crew. That doesn't mean I'm due to be sent home, so don't get your hopes up. It just means that I've had enough runs in a row, and I'm due to spend a little time in the relief crew before catching another boat. I figure on about two more runs after this one before I can be considered for new construction. Unfortunately they're not sending many Signalmen and Quartermasters back from this part of the world. That means they take the ones with the most runs and the most time out of the states when there is a chance for someone to go back.

I saw a very good "second rate" picture the last time I went to the show that is very good musically. I think the name was "Change of Heart." It started out with Freddy Martin playing a familiar piece of his that I can't remember the name of. One I know you'd love. It had quite a bit of Martin's music, so see it if you get the chance.

I love you so very, very much darling, although my letter doesn't indicate it. Never doubt my love because of that. Just trust in me honey, and someday I'll make you extremely glad you did.

9 March 1944

Dearest Margaret,

As usual, I had planned to write a little more this time out but we were quite busy, and I've had little chance.

I'm pretty sure this is my last run for awhile, and I should have a little time on the beach before making any more. I've gone about as high as possible on this boat, for me, and have passed my point of usefulness, so will ask to be transferred, and can see no reason why I shouldn't be.

12 March 1944 – Same Letter

After spending most of my time at sea this past year makes the prospect of spending a little time on the beach rather inviting. This time I'll be able to look up Ches Jones and a few others I haven't seen for some time.

This run I read a most enjoyable book, one of the best I've ever read, 'The Robe' by Lloyd C. Douglas. If you haven't already read the book, I suggest you purchase it, as it will be a worthwhile addition to a good book collection. I borrowed the book from a new Q.M. that came aboard, who hasn't been long out of the states. I won't say anything about the story 'cause I imagine you'll read it, if you haven't already.

13 March 1944

Margaret dearest,

This is my third attempt to finish this letter, but I still keep my fingers crossed that it will be successful.

This evening I asked to be transferred this time in. The answer was neither a positive 'yes' or 'no' but did tend to be a little more on the 'yes' side. This is one of those situations I wish I were able to talk over with you, Margaret. This is probably a big riddle to you, but I'm afraid it shall have to remain so for awhile.

I wish to God I knew Nancy better. At times it's hard to realize I have a little girl, having seen her little more than I have some strange child in an unknown mother's arms. (It had been a year plus six weeks since he had seen his baby.) *At times I almost forget I have one, then get feeling guilty at such a thought. Many times the knowledge that I have two wonderful girls to come home to has been quite a comfort.*

Well darling, I'm going to close this before another interruption keeps me from completing it. I pray to God for the day we'll be together again.

19 March 1944

Arrived Pearl Harbour.

BEAUTIFUL DAY

The world looks freshly scrubbed today,
The blue skies never brighter;
The trees look prouder as they sway,
The little houses whiter.

I never saw the grass so green,
Or tulips standing straighter,
The birds are busy hatching eggs –
I thought that happened later!

I can't imagine why it is
All things look so much better.
Do you suppose – of course, it's 'cause
Today I got a letter!

Margaret Mabin

Dearest, Dearest Darling … 1944

From Margy to Bill:

25 March 1944 – La Grange, IL

Dearest, dearest darling…..

What a surprise to find in the box a letter from you. I didn't expect one for a week or so at best! And even though you may not have written as often while you were out, as you planned, still it showed definite signs of improvement over other times, and that is very encouraging!

This time I think I worried more than usual. We've been hearing of more submarine losses and just to make matters worse, Frank's wife told me her young brother, who had just been assigned to a submarine, is missing. He was on the Corvina. (I usually don't mention these sinkings to you, but feel, now that I know you'll be safe for awhile that I can discuss the matter without being too emotional.)

At any rate – because I had worried a lot – all I could say when I saw your letter was "Thank God – Oh thank you dear God," over and over. Your letters mean everything to me – especially that first one!

I was sorry you seemed a bit discouraged and hope by now your mood has changed. (Of course I want you to always tell me when you're in a bit of a blue mood. That's what wives are for.)

Of course, even the trouble (whatever it may be – I'm certainly baffled) doesn't seem too important as long as you're safe. Remember that I want nothing from you, desperately, but your return. Everything else is incidental.

It's almost amazing – and yet it keeps happening, to discover how similar our likes are in so many ways, and this time I'm speaking of books. I too loved "The Robe." Belle has it, but since you liked it I may someday get a copy. As you say, it's a good book to keep in a library. I was absolutely enchanted with it. It was a beautiful and inspiring book – yet fascinating reading. There's nothing more restful than good reading or more broadening.

I'm writing this in the afternoon. Tonight I'm going to a dinner party for girls at Barb Brown Flaks.'

I'm a bit concerned over your transfer (though you must know that) in that it might mean you'd have to wait that much longer for a leave and new construction (or won't that make any difference.) I'm just living for the day you'll be here to get acquainted with Nancy. That day when we can start "honeymooning" again, (for it will be that) with our child along.

Guess I'll close now – I'm so happy cause you're sure to be safe for awhile and I love you so terribly much!

Good bye for now my darling –

<u>26 March 1944 – Pearl Harbor</u>

Dearest Marg,

Just finished looking at those pictures of Nancy taken at dad's office. They are very good and natural. In fact just about all the pictures that have been taken of her have turned out good. Not just because she's my little girl, but she does seem to photograph well.

I think she looks an awful lot like you, and gains more than loses your resemblance. I've noticed an awful big change in her size and looks since I was home. The change may be too gradual for you to notice, being with her all the time, but after long spells her pictures come as sort of a shock.

The one picture of mother holding Nancy, with you in the background reading a magazine, is so natural of you. The expression on your face, the way you're holding the magazine, with your purse under your arm, all these I've seen you do every time you come in the office and are waiting for something to be completed so you may go about your business. I love it and can see you turning the pages with those quick jerky movements. I'd like to have a picture of your "knowing" expression when you've caught me in some small lie. In fact there are so many thousands of things I like about you I could probably write a book, and it would be a "best seller" too.

31 March 1944 – Pearl Harbor

My Darling,

I'll start out by mentioning a little about my leave before I forget it entirely. We actually had nine days, not counting a twenty-two hour train ride to and from our destination. The three of us spent a good deal of our money the first four days so the last five days we had to calm down and take things a little easier. The first four days were spent in doing a lot of drinking, and we hardly left our "shack." The reason it was expensive was that most beer and whiskey has to be bought "bootleg." There's a scarcity of both and needless to say quite a demand.

I saw the picture "Crash Dive" and term it one of the best comedies of the year. How I'd enjoy returning to New London after every patrol run. Mangold and I bought a couple of crabs one night, and he showed me how to tear them apart and how to tell what parts to eat and not eat. Enjoyed crab meat very much, especially with a bottle of beer. That's about all I can think of about the leave. My drinking days are over and it's time to get back to work again. Even though costly, it's fun while it lasts. To the days I can have a good time without paying a price for it, at least to a bootlegger.

I love you darling and hope you enjoy hearing me say it as much as I do you, no matter how many times it's repeated. I shall always be with you whether physically, mentally, or spiritually. Raise Nancy to be half the woman you are and you've done all God ever expected of you.

<u>7 April 1944 – Mabin Journal, Written on leave</u>

Sunk four ships. Captured <u>1</u> Jap. Prisoner. Damaged 2. Killed, in cold blood, two Japs on life raft. Dumped prisoner Finchaven, New Guinea. Hauled ass for Pearl Harbor. Got depth charged by Jap plane. Have sighted 64 Jap. Merchant ships in four runs, not counting escorts.

Transferred to Sub. Div. 122 aboard Griffen at Pearl Harbor. Two weeks later transferred to Royal Haw. Hotel for leave and awaiting transfer to states for new construction.

Headline: Submarine Vet, Home on Visit 1944

On April 17, 1944 Bill Mabin reported aboard the *U.S.S. Guardfish* (Flag CSD-82). Nine days later, he was transferred to the submarine base in New London for new construction. Before reporting, he was given leave to see his family in La Grange, IL. While there, the local paper prevailed on him for an interview. The following are excerpts from an article that appeared in *The La Grange Citizen* on May 18, 1944:

> SUBMARINE VET, HOME ON VISIT
>
> SIGNALMAN, GONE OVER YEAR,
> SAW ACTION IN PACIFIC AGAINST JAPS
>
> After more than a year's service as a quartermaster on a submarine engaged in operations against the enemy in the Pacific area, William T. Mabin, signalman second class, is enjoying his first visit in 16 months with his wife and baby, and his parents, the Gordon Mabins.
>
> Much about the submarine service is information that cannot be reported now and Bill was not at liberty to discuss in detail his experi-

ences at sea. But it's no naval secret that he saw a lot of the enemy and went through depth charge attacks and bombings by planes. On the other side of the ledger are some Jap ships that were sunk by his submarine – the exact number can't be told, even though the Japs themselves probably know all too well.

Despite the fact that he wouldn't trade this experience for anything, Bill is frank to state that there isn't a place in the United States he wouldn't rather be stationed than back on a submarine in enemy waters. He doesn't take much stock in reports of veterans returning from combat duty and announcing that they can't wait to get back in it again.

To Report For Further Duty

However, in a short time when his leave is over he expects to be back in the thick of things as his visit here is in connection with a transfer to another submarine. He added that there is a shortage of quartermasters and men trained in this type of signal communications work.

Like others in this service, Bill volunteered for submarine duty upon entering the navy back in October of 1940. After boot training he went to San Diego and then was assigned to a destroyer on neutrality patrol. He served on the destroyer for 14 months, then was on duty at a signal tower in San Diego. Finally his application for submarine training was accepted and he attended school at New London. Later he went to an eastern port, where he was assigned to a new submarine, which was to be his headquarters for the next year. Transferred off the submarine two months ago, he spent one month at Pearl Harbor before coming to the States and then home.

With Australia as their "base," Bill and his crew made four "runs" in enemy zones. During the first two runs, Bill, who was one of four quartermasters on the ship, served as assistant to the chief quartermaster, working in close relationship with the navigator of the submarine.

Put in Charge on Two Runs

On his third and fourth runs he was in charge of the quartermasters, including a signalman first class, who, however, had had no previous submarine experience.

"Submarines are not as crowded as many people seem to think," Bill said. "Although they have a crew of about 70 officers and men, not all of them are on duty at the same time. While some are standing watches, others are having a little recreation. Most everyone has a battle station, however, during actual combat."

As for recreation, there is little the men can do in their spare time. Sleep comes first, said

Bill, and then there is reading and card playing. The submarine has a library and whenever it is in port the men exchange their books for those on another submarine so that they have something new to read on each run. Poker and pinochle are the most popular card games.

Hear Tokyo Rose

There is a victrola with records, but the men quickly tire of the records, he said. As for radio music, some is picked up during the times when the submarine is surfaced and at these times, too, brief news reports are received. Occasionally the men picked up Tokyo Rose propaganda on the radio. But for the most part when the submarine is in enemy territory, the men are keyed up and constantly on the alert for action, with little time for other activities.

When the submarine is submerged during a battle the heat inside becomes intense, said Bill, adding that all possible motors are cut off to eliminate sound and this means the motor for the ship's air conditioning system. At other times this system keeps it fairly comfortable on the submarine even at points along the equator.

No serious damages were inflicted on his submarine on any of the runs, he said, but both the men and the ship were considerably shaken up at times by depth charges.

Encountering 80-Foot Swells

At other times the men had rough going during bad storms. Bill told of one storm that lasted a week and some of the swells were estimated at 80 feet high. Although it is possible for a submarine to submerge and “ride out a storm,” this isn’t done with a strict schedule of operations to be maintained.

Almost completely cut off from the rest of the world during a run, the submarine carries no medical officer or chaplain. If any medical work is necessary it is done by the pharmacist’s mate. On none of the trips was any major medical work necessary. As for a barber, all of the men take turns at it, said Bill.

Commenting on their meals on the submarine, Bill said that the food is satisfactory but much depends on the length of the trip. For mail, the men must wait until they return to port. With a run lasting several weeks, Bill said he and others would find big bundles of letters and other mail waiting for them when they returned.

Now thoroughly enjoying his leave here, Bill and his wife, the former Margaret Miles, and their baby are staying at the home of her mother, Jean C. Miles. He will return to duty on June 6.

Bill Mabin's formal navy portrait. Circa 1941.

Family Life in New London 1944

6 June 1944 – New London

Dearest Marg,

Stu met me at the train and we went out to his house. We just talked, drank beer and then had dinner out. Had quite a nice time and enjoyed Dodie very much.

Stu thinks he'll only have about two more months of shore-duty then will have to go to sea. He expects to go home on leave in about two weeks.

I reported in today and learned I have a Manitowoc boat. I will be stationed here in New London for awhile though. Hope to get more details tomorrow, then will look up Irlandis if I have liberty. They say it's tougher than ever getting a place to live so hope they can help us out.

Miss you terribly.

15 June 1944 – New London

Darling,

I have a little more hope about finding a place. I put in my request for some places they have here on the base for those in transit. You can only hold onto them for a month, but that will at least be a starter. I just found out about them yesterday and went right up to put in my request.

They are two bedrooms and a combination kitchen and living room. There is a stove but no ice-box. They rent for a dollar a day. There is no commissary on the base so will have to make other arrangements about buying food.

Being located right here on the base I will be able to see you more than if you were in town. I don't know for sure if we can get one or not, but I know a couple of guys that did.

Just keep your fingers crossed and be ready to make your train reservations upon hearing from me.

Take care of yourself and Nancy and give Mom and Dad my love.

Bill Mabin found housing for his family, and Margy wrote her mother the following description of what life was like in New London.

<u>24 June 1944 – New London</u>

Dear Mom,

We're certainly happy here & everything has worked out beautifully for us. Nancy has taken everything in her stride – is well acclimated & has been very good, a little less fussy I believe.

It has been raining most of the time since my arrival so Nancy is in a lot. However she was out for a few days & found lots of other children to play with.

There are mostly officers in these houses. Bill insists there are several enlisted men but I have yet to see one outside of Bill. I don't particularly like this set-up as I have to kind of stay by myself. However there's one officer's wife who apparently is not acquainted with the "crowd" & she kept Nancy one day while I shopped. However, she has company visiting so I don't see much of her either.

Nancy, however, lets nothing interfere with her social life. She saw a little girl who appealed to her – watched her go into her house – followed her – crawled up the steps - & then to my astonishment <u>knocked</u> on the door. Out came the little girl (seven years old). They looked at each other for a few minutes & now are the best of pals. She was here most of yesterday but hasn't been over today, perhaps because it is raining. Her father is a Commander –

skipper of one of the new boats. (Nancy's playmate was Sandra Millican, daughter of CDR W.J. Millican, whose submarine *U.S.S. Escolar* (SS – 294) was lost 17 October 1944 in the Yellow Sea on her first patrol. *Escolar's* exact location is unknown as is the cause of her demise. *Escolar* is Michigan's state submarine.)

We had dinner at Irlandis Thursday nite. It was good to see them & they couldn't have been more cordial if I'd been a relative. Nancy had a great time there & was allowed the run of the house which she took advantage of. She probably stayed up too late for she had a bad night. She normally sleeps well & takes her naps in a twin bed – kinda likes it I think.

Bill is very well – has gained weight & seems quite happy. He had hoped for a few days to get a school boat but has now found out that he definitely won't. They are short on quartermasters & he was almost put on a boat to go out sooner, but got out of it. If things go as planned we'll be in New London till September, I think.

Love to Yammy. (Marg's grandmother)

For the next five months, the Mabin family lived a relatively normal family life – first in New London and later in Manitowoc, Wisconsin, where *Lagarto* was under construction.

Halfway Round the World 2005

The most poignant adventure of their lives lay just ahead for my children, John Kenney and Elizabeth Kenney Augustine. The two siblings tried to persuade me to join them on this arduous trip to my father's gravesite in the sea, but I knew the trip would be grueling and I just didn't have the stamina for it.

The trip was indeed grueling. After Beth and John left O'Hare International Airport in Chicago, they would be twenty-two hours in the air before they reached the lovely island of Koh Samui in Thailand. Added to that was ten hours in layovers at airports. It would take eight hours more at sea before they reached the site of *Lagarto*.

John and Beth passed through four airports on the trip – Chicago's O'Hare and airports in Tokyo, Bangkok and Koh Samui. The wait in Bangkok was the hardest. At the time, construction of a new airport terminal was going on, and the Kenney sibs' flights in and out were among the last before the new terminal was finished. [Coincidentally, my brother Tom Chambers was one of the principal architects involved in the design of the new airport terminal.] The substantial time they spent in airports was whiled away in internet cafes and snacking on nachos and beer. In Bangkok, they entertained themselves watching ants carrying away cockroaches.

When they arrived in Koh Samui, they were charmed by the beauty of the island with its thatched huts. They described the scene as a "cross between *Fantasy Island* and *Gilligan's Island.*"

Jamie Macleod met them at the airport, grabbed their bags and took them to their hotel. Never having laid eyes on each other, none of them knew exactly what to expect. They were all a little nervous about the meeting. Although they were exhausted, John and Beth were up for a beer. They found an Irish pub and after relaxing a bit, they all felt comfortable with each other. After a good night's sleep, Beth and John did some sight-seeing and motor-bike riding around the island the next day.

That evening, after the divers had prepared the boat for a trip to sea, the Trident crew held a party. John and Beth called to tell me they had made it safely to Thailand and were about to take off. Invited by Jamie to go along on the trip, the entertaining Steve Burton also chatted with me.

"Hello, Nancy. We are all very excited about the trip. Don't worry about your children; we'll take good care of them," he said, in his charming British accent.

Burton had been the initial contact made by Roy Leonhardt through the internet and was very interested in *Lagarto*. Everyone was excited, and I wished I were there with them. While we were conversing, I heard fireworks in the background. It was a Buddhist tradition to set off fireworks to ward off evil spirits for the trip ahead. They had to go, and I hoped and prayed with all my heart, that the trip to *Lagarto* would be safe and rewarding.

U.S.S. Lagarto (SS - 371) 1944

Launch of *Lagarto* in Manitowoc, WI. 1944.

Lagarto's keel was laid down on 12 January 1944 by the Manitowoc Shipbuilding Company of Manitowoc, Wisconsin. She was launched on 28 May 1944 sponsored by Illinois At-Large Congresswoman Emily Taft Douglas, wife of future Illinois senator Paul Douglas, who at the time was serving in the Marine Corps in the Pacific. *Lagarto,* one of twenty-eight submarines built in

Manitowoc, was commissioned on 14 October 1944 with CDR Frank Devere Latta as her captain. Latta was a veteran of nine war patrols and had earned the Navy Cross while commanding *U.S.S. Narwhal* (SS – 167).

While in Manitowoc, the Mabins lived in a housing complex, reserved for families of enlisted men who were assigned to duty while their boats were being built. The complex was dubbed Custerdale because of its location on Custerdale Avenue. An active social life existed among the sailors and their families. Strong bonds of friendship developed between the Navy wives.

For awhile it appeared Bill would miss going out with *Lagarto*. He was admitted to the naval hospital at Great Lakes, Illinois for surgery while Marg remained behind in Manitowoc.

12 October 1944 – Great Lakes

My Dearest Marg,

They are going to operate on me tomorrow, Friday morning. In fact not three minutes ago, I was informed of such. I almost got two days off to straighten up my personal affairs and get you moved, but now they've decided to operate in the morning.

I will be here at least a month, and maybe longer. There are some that have been here for seven and eight months for the same thing, and on the other hand some that have been here only a month. It just depends upon how it heals.

I think you'd better have your mother or mine come up and help you move. It would be the middle of November, at the soonest, before I'd be home, and maybe even not then.

I know you'll be pretty disappointed at having to give up our place there, but I'm pretty sure I'll miss the Lagarto completely. At least we'll be able to have more time together, and possibly even Christmas.

I'm certainly not looking forward to tomorrow morning and what follows, but guess you're not looking forward to what's ahead of you either.

Give Nancy a big kiss and hug for her daddy, and mentally, many for yourself.

13 October 1944 – Great Lakes

My Darling,

They've decided to operate on me tomorrow, Saturday morning, instead of this morning. It's better for me cause today is Friday the 13th.

The last couple of days, especially now, I've been going nuts just wandering around the ward, sleeping and reading a little, and mostly doing just nothing. It probably sounds like quite a life to you but it drives me nuts. At least after tomorrow, I'll have good reason to lie in bed.

It wouldn't be me, dear, if I didn't bitch. I've gotten used to spending my time with my wife and baby. I certainly wish I was with them now. Even if I had stayed on the Lagarto I wouldn't be seeing much of you in these next three weeks. At least this way, I stand a damn good chance of spending a little time with you in a month or two. Yes, dear, I'm sure this thing has worked out the right way, and we've had a good break.

I certainly do miss you and Nancy, even tho it has only been a couple of days. Can you imagine me writing you two days in a row? The letter I wrote yesterday should reach you by tomorrow, I hope. If I can sneak out of here tonight I'm going to try to call the folks. I haven't written them yet cause I keep hoping to be able to call them.

Maybe next Saturday or Sunday, if you're home by then, you could come and visit me. I'll have had a week to recover by then. If so, you could take the "North Shore Electric" to "North Chicago Junction." After arriving at North Chicago Junction, you'll have to take a street car for about two blocks. This place is about two hours from Chicago.

Well, darling, they've started serving lunch so gotta stop. Every bit of my love to You and Nancy.

Bill's surgery and recovery went better than expected, and he was able to join the *Lagarto* crew, just before she left for war.

Nancy playing amid the laundry in Custerdale (housing for navy personnel), Manitowoc, WI. 1944.

Holding My Grandfather's Hand 2005

The trip to *Lagarto* was not a cruise on the *Love Boat*; but for the Mabin grandchildren, it was infinitely better. For two mid-western-thirty-somethings, John Kenney and Beth Kenney Augustine handled the rigors of an expedition on the Pacific Ocean well. They were on a mission. Before Trident arrived at *Lagarto's* gravesite, there were dives scheduled on other wrecks. Trident MV passengers had signed on to this expedition, not aware until later that this voyage had a more important purpose.

On these early dives, John and Beth got acquainted with the crew and other passengers, a diverse group of people from several different nations. John was seasick from day one, but managed it with pills his doctor had prescribed for him. Beth had some trouble with the food. Anticipating the problem, she stocked up on Pringle's chips, cheese goldfish, candy bars, gummy bears and water at the local Seven-Eleven where, in accordance with Thai tradition, she had to remove her shoes before entering the store.

They shared a compact stateroom, but spent most of their time in a comfortable lounge area of MV Trident, the social center of the boat. When the time came for the divers to go down, the siblings stayed out of the way. They knew that this kind of deep dive could be dangerous without careful preparation.

With fascination, they watched the divers organize themselves, working with dive tables and computers, mixing the gases. The wise-cracking divers became serious and professional when preparing for a dive. They knew that anything less could cause death or serious injury to themselves or others.

Beth Kenney Augustine and John Kenney.

As the dive boat neared the site of *Lagarto,* Trident's crew noticed a shift in the moods of submariner Bill Mabin's grandchildren. Sensing the emotional impact on John and Beth, they were kind, some of them asking if the siblings were okay. Excitement was in the air, but there was also respect for the mission ahead. The American submarine below them still held the remains of those who had died for their country sixty years earlier. The Trident crew was aware of the solemnity of the moment. The sailors entombed below had family who still loved them.

Macleod entered the water first. He tied off the line on the submarine's shears for the others and swam around the sub for a look. The next divers went down in pairs and returned with reports such as "deck gone," "guns gone," etc. The boat was wrapped in fishing nets. Some said it resembled a huge sausage while others thought it looked like a giant mummy. They found substantial damage to the outer hull next to the officers' quarters, but nothing else. The boat lay majestically upright on the ocean's floor.

The divers dove twice that day, with six hours in between for decompression. During that time, they compared notes and discussed what they had seen. Steve Burton told Beth and John that one of the divers placed some Thai coins on the ship as an offering to win favor with the gods. A bouquet of white roses was placed in the periscope opening. The divers were respectful and each found his own way to honor the dead on the lost submarine.

In the meantime, Beth and John waited above. They spent most of this time thinking about the grandfather they never knew. They remembered the stories about him and felt close to him at this time. The parade of divers emerging from the ocean confirmed that the ship below was indeed, as they had believed from the beginning, *U.S.S. Lagarto*. Beth was relieved and happy knowing that she could give me the news confirming

Lagarto's discovery. She told me that while Trident was anchored above *Lagarto,* she felt like she was "holding her grandfather's hand." How Bill Mabin would have loved knowing his only granddaughter felt this way!

At sunset the following day, a gravesite ceremony was held for the submarine's crew. The passengers and crew cleaned up and donned their best clothes. They listened as the Mabin grandchildren read letters, Bible verses, poetry and personal remembrances sent by *Lagarto* families. The hand-woven cross sent by Bess Torgerson, sister-in-law of MoMM1 Caldwell T. Cook, was tossed into the sea. The background music was the gentle lapping of the waves set against a sky that was clear blue. In God's cathedral, the names of the entire crew were read. The service took about an hour. Beth fought back tears, and John choked up, but managed to hold himself together. Trident's crew and other passengers said their own silent prayers.

Stewart Oehl, John Kenney, Beth Kenney Augustine & Jamie Macleod.

Everyone was kind. Macleod's mother, Patricia, had prepared one of her specialties, Shepherd's Pie, as a special treat for the American brother and sister. Beth was thrilled, as she had lived on peanut butter, jam and instant coffee for most of the trip.

The last night at sea was rough. Although uncomfortable, Beth and John reflected on sailing the same sea as their grandfather, whose living conditions were harsh and mission dangerous. Those thoughts put everything in perspective.

After three days and four nights at sea, the MV Trident headed back to shore. On the journey's last morning, I was awakened at 4:45 AM (EDT) by John's phone call. He wanted me to know that the trip had been a success. The divers had found clear evidence that *Lagarto,* in her final minutes, had fired a torpedo and went down fighting. One of the divers had tied Beth's American flag, carried in her suitcase from Chicago to the Gulf of Thailand, to *Lagarto's* periscope shears. Two hundred and twenty-five feet beneath the surface of the Pacific Ocean, America's stars and stripes waved proudly over the lost submarine. When John told me *Lagarto* had gone down fighting and that the American flag flew over her, I felt a surge of national pride that is impossible to describe.

Of course, I couldn't go back to sleep. I got up and e-mailed the other *Lagarto* families the news. At the same time, a message from Steve Burton popped up on my computer screen. It was a sketch he'd made of the sunken *Lagarto,* drawn after he emerged from his dive.

In addition to being a diving trainer, Burton was also an engineer. From memory, in almost perfect scale, he made a drawing of the damaged submarine. I sent this on to other family members as soon as I received it.

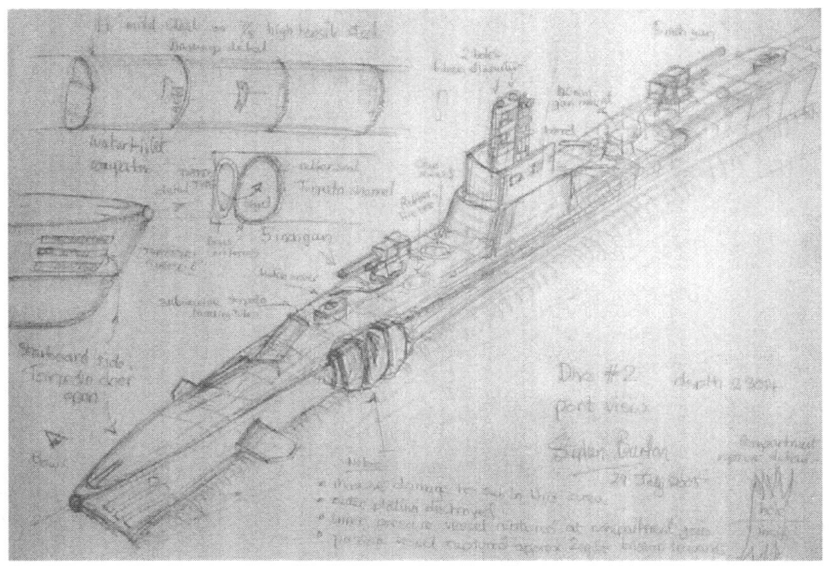

Sketch of *Lagarto*, drawn by Steve Burton after he emerged from his dive on *Lagarto*. 2005.

When my husband saw the drawing, he tried to work out a scenario that might give some insight into *Lagarto's* fate. The sketch showed a huge rupture on the port side, made by a very powerful blast. The strange thing was that only the outer hull of the boat appeared to have been damaged; there was no sign that her inner hull had been breached. This only added to the mystery of *Lagarto's* sinking. However, the fact that the outer door of a forward torpedo tube was open and there was damage from a huge explosion confirmed that *Lagarto's* crew was engaged in battle at the time of their deaths.

For me, this was not only a matter of pride, but a huge relief. Since learning of the discovery of my father's submarine, I had been having waking nightmares. After falling asleep, a few hours later I would wake with visions of the crews' deaths in my head. This left me deeply shaken.

I had never thought about the possible circumstances of the crews' deaths before. But after *Lagarto's* discovery, my father seemed so real to me that I began to feel enormous anxiety thinking about what he and his mates might have gone through. There was no positive way to think about this; they all died. I hoped there had been no operational failure of the sub, forcing the crew to live a long time knowing they were doomed. I thought about the hell it would be to witness their friends die slowly, knowing that the same fate was in store for them.

The findings of the Trident divers showed that, at the time of their deaths, the *Lagarto* crew were doing their jobs and too busy to think about anything else. I was relieved and passed this information on to the other families, who were also relieved.

This whole submarine discovery had acquired the elements of a huge, life-impacting mystery. After more than sixty years of knowing little about the circumstances of my father's death, huge pieces of this tragic puzzle began to emerge. Not in my wildest dreams had I ever imagined that *Lagarto* would be found. Now I knew where she was and that she was engaged in battle when she went down. More than ever, I became determined that the families of the men on that submarine must be found and informed of this news. It also became crystal clear that their sacrifice must be honored. This became my obsession, and I was driven to accomplish these two goals. The other *Lagarto* families shared my feelings, and we forged ahead with fire in our hearts!

Hal and Rae

At the time of *Lagarto's* discovery, very few of her crew's families were known to the Wisconsin Museum. One was the family of LTjg Harold A. Todd. Todd's widow, Rae Kinn, remarried five years after Hal's death and was blessed with two sons – Michael Todd, Hal's son and John Kinn, Jack Kinn's son. Rae, originally from Fort Wayne, Indiana had made her home for many years in Wisconsin. Now in her eighties, Rae was an extraordinary beauty, both inside and out. We became dear friends, and she told me much of her short, but wonderful life with her beloved Hal.

Harold Arthur Todd was born in Louisiana, but spent most of his life in Wisconsin. In 1941, he graduated from Purdue University and worked for General Electric as a test engineer. After the United States entered the war, Hal gave up his automatic exemption from the draft and enlisted in the Navy, volunteering for the Submarine Service. Hal was assigned to the *U.S.S. Lagarto* as a communications officer. Hal and Rae fell in love when they worked together at G.E. and decided to marry. Rae was still in college at the time, but left before graduation so they could spend as much time together as possible before Hal shipped out. They were married on July 16, 1943 in Fort Wayne.

Before being assigned to *Lagarto,* Hal and Rae were able to spend a few months together in Charleston,

SC, Ithaca, NY, and Groton and New London, CT while Hal underwent training for his work on submarines. After a few months in Manitowoc for commissioning and outfitting of *Lagarto,* the Todds spent time together in New Orleans. In Rae's words, "Hal sailed off to the South Pacific, and I sailed off to Fort Wayne." Rae was, by that time, pregnant. Mike Todd was born on March 30, 1945, almost two months premature. Although not the desired outcome of a pregnancy, the early birth meant that Hal received the news of his son's arrival, which he wouldn't had the baby gone full term.

Less than two months later, bad news. In Rae's words, "On May 25, 1945 my doorbell rang, and a man on a bicycle handed me a telegram saying Hal was MIA (missing-in-action). Not Navy personnel, just a drab little man from the Western Union office. It took me about half an hour to get up the courage to open the telegram. I was devastated at the news. Then I decided MIA was less final than KIA. It was close to the end of the war, and the Allies were beginning to liberate all the little islands and atolls in the Pacific, finding hundreds of servicemen. I didn't mourn for Hal; he wasn't dead. He promised me he would come back, and Captain Latta promised he would bring him home. I spent a year in hope and expectation. When the letter came from the Navy Department a year later declaring him officially dead, it didn't mean a whole lot. I had been missing Hal from the day he left, and I was still waiting for him. The Navy didn't give any definite information that the *Lagarto* had been sunk, just a lot of speculation. It was a difficult experience of conflicting emotions that is almost impossible for me to describe. I gave a pulpit bible to Hal's church, something with his inscribed name, showing he had lived. When his father died, his mother put a metal KIA marker next to his dad's grave for Hal. His father's company, Wisconsin Motors, in West Allis, organized an American Legion Post named Harold A. Todd, Jr.

He had such an impact on my life it is hard to believe I only knew him for three years. He was very special – handsome, charming, romantic, bright, funny and delightful. He was a musician and won state awards in high school for French horn and coronet, and he was student band director at Purdue. And he was a fabulous dancer! We both loved ballroom dancing. We both loved to sing, and we harmonized on many old tunes. I have often wondered how different my life would have been had the *Lagarto* not been lost."

A few years after Hal's death, Rae and baby Mike moved from Indiana to Wisconsin so Mike could be near his Todd grandparents and Uncle Wes, Hal's brother. When Rae married Jack Kinn in 1950, Hal's parents were very supportive. They even gave the new couple a wedding breakfast and spent every other Christmas with the Kinns as long as they lived. When Rae's son, John Kinn, was born, the Todds treated him as their own. Rae loved the Todds very much and remained close to them.

Rae had a happy second marriage. Jack Kinn was an attorney and taught Business Law at Marquette University. He was a go-getter and put himself through college and law school, repairing and selling Johnson outboard motors on Wisconsin's Okauchee Lake. Shortly after their marriage, Jack Kinn purchased a small marine business in Oconomowoc. The Kinns had many happy and productive years operating Kinn Motors Marine in Oconomowoc, working and rearing two sons. After Jack's death in 1985 and the sale of their business the following year, Rae sold her home on the lake and moved into a condo. She kept busy at the Oconomowoc Public Library, first as a volunteer and later an employee. In addition to her two sons, Rae had three Todd grandchildren: Chris, Kate and Amy.

"Life has been good to me," Rae said. "I have no complaints or regrets, just a nagging wonder of what direction my life would have taken if the *Lagarto* had come home."

Rae and I have talked of many things since the discovery of *Lagarto* and have become good friends. She is bright, beautiful and very dear. The discovery of *Lagarto* has brought many surprises. One of the best is the closeness of the *Lagarto's* families. We share a terrible but profound bond. But we have also become a new family of sorts. This, I believe, is in itself a tribute to *Lagarto's* crew. Submariners, especially in times of war, are very close. It is fitting that their families have now, sixty years later, also become close. We are a new family.

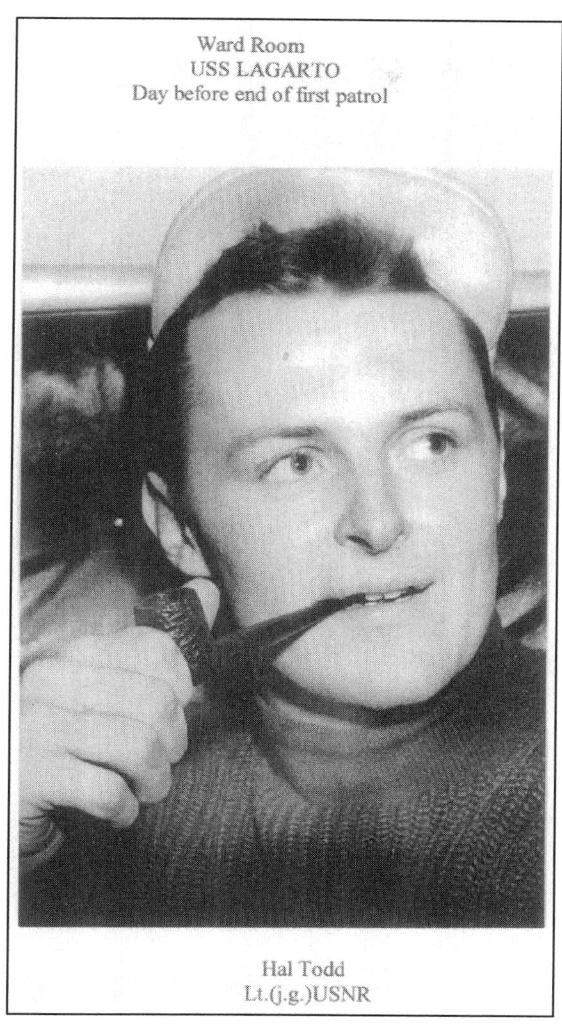

Ward Room
USS LAGARTO
Day before end of first patrol
Hal Todd
Lt.(j.g.)USNR

Lt. (j.g.) Harold Todd on *Lagarto*. 1944.

Letters from Panama 1944

Lagarto, as many submarines built in Manitowoc, was transported down the Mississippi River to New Orleans in a floating dry dock. Most of the crew, having been granted leave to see their families, joined the boat in New Orleans. From there, she headed to Panama, escorted by the submarine chaser SC-512. On 17 November, *Lagarto* began her shakedown, training the crew on the new submarine and checking for any potential problems with her construction. This lasted until 5 December 1944.

Hal Todd's letters to his wife, give his view of this wartime adventure.

3 November 1944

Darling Lil Beebee Doll,

This is proving to be a very interesting trip – in spite of the fact that I would certainly much rather be with the mother of my sturdy little family. It has been strictly no strain these last couple of days, although our first night was rather rugged as far as watch-standing was concerned. Sure have had an interesting time, however.

I am Acting First Lt., Acting Torpedo & Gunnery **(officer)**, along with the Communications – and have learned quite a bit just since we left. Ham **(Lieutenant Hamilton B. Joslin)** and Al **(Ensign Allen G. Brewington)** and I are getting along fine, lots of laughs.

Well, Beautiful Dream Girl take good care of yourself and Mike **(Mike was Hal and Rae's unborn child at the time)**. I miss you something awful – and I've been away for such a short time by the calendar. What will it be like when I've been gone for months & months?

13 November 1944

Darlin' Lil Beebee,

Things are going along smoothly. We have not been bombed, strafed, or menaced by any zoomies 'cause we can see them before they see us, and also, we are escorted.

I believe you know I have the 4-8 watches. They aren't bad, in fact they're damn fine. That's the watch that makes the dives and surfacings. It's nice, too, because I'm up there to see the sunrise and sunset, get plenty of fresh air and sunshine, and lots of experience. Up there about 0430 when we're riding along in the middle of the phosphorescent streak, and the white water whips across the main deck and froths around the gun, and there's nobody up there but you and me and God, I look up at the Little Dipper and the North Star (the Big Dipper is below the horizon now) and Orion and Cassiopeia and think about how we used to climb up on the bridge model on the hill back at the sub base and look at those same stars, and court a little, and have a cigarette. Dammit! How I miss that – and you! I can't even have my cigarette anymore on deck, but I can sure dream about you and do.

18 November 1944

Darlin' Little Girl,

Today has been a very memorable day for me...I have seen things my father helped build, the hills he blasted, and the valleys he flooded, along with the help of General Goethals. It's hard to tell you the pride I feel in his work which has been so important in world trade and the prosecution of a war. **(Harold Todd Sr., an engineer, worked building the Panama Canal.)**

Last night I made liberty in a place which is very quaint. I bought something for you just for the fun of bargaining with the Hindu shop keepers. I'll mail what I bought as soon as I can.

Today we anchored for awhile in a lake and all hands and the Captain **(CDR Frank D. Latta)** went over the side for a swim. Sure was great.

Tonight I may get a chance to go ashore in a city where the folks used to live. It will be the last one ashore for a couple of weeks, so don't worry about mail for awhile, Sweetheart.

You're a great lil' gal, Darlin,' and I love you and miss you an awful lot. It will be some while before we'll be able to be together again and finish planning for the future, and every minute hurts like hell inside. But meantime, I'm just thanking God for the swellest, loveliest little wife a guy could ask for. Wish you were here or I was there.

Joint POW-MIA Accounting Command (JPAC) 2005

While I was delighted that my children were taking the trip of their lives to Thailand, I continued to be frustrated. It had been six weeks since *Lagarto* had been found, and except for a nice article in my local newspaper and the Springfield, MO *News-Leader,* there was nary a mention of it in the news. The Navy seemed disinterested and declined to communicate with anyone on the boat's discovery.

As we found the families, and I made the calls, I asked each *Lagarto* family to contact their United States Senator with a request for the Pentagon. That request was for the Navy to acknowledge *Lagarto's* discovery and to consider holding a memorial service for her crew. Everyone felt this was reasonable, as this was done whenever the remains of a member of the military, from any war, had been recovered. I had personal knowledge of this. The airman husband of one of my mother's friends had been MIA for fifty years when his plane was found in a thick forest in France. His remains were identified and returned home. An official ceremony at Arlington cemetery was held with his whole family present.

The branch of the government/military responsible for this was JPAC, which is the Joint POW-MIA Accounting Command. This branch of the military used teams of forensic anthropologists to research, recover and identify the remains of anyone thought to have been missing as the result of a war action. After the identification had been made, the remains were returned to the families for a burial with full military honors.

JPAC is noble and fascinating. It is located on the Island of Oahu in Hawaii. Its present structure emerged from the Army Central Identification Laboratory in Hawaii and the Joint Task Force – Full Accounting. Combined in 2003, they became JPAC. JPAC's website stated:

> Commanded by a flag officer, JPAC is manned by approximately 400 handpicked Soldiers, Sailors, Airmen, Marines and Department of the Navy civilians. The laboratory portion of JPAC, referred to as the Central Identification Laboratory (CIL), is the largest forensic anthropology laboratory in the world.

It went on to state:

> On average, JPAC identifies about six MIAs each month. To date, the U.S. government has identified over 1,300 individuals. The search for unaccounted-for Americans starts with in-depth research. JPAC historians and analysts gather information such

> as correspondence, maps, photographs, unit histories, medical and personnel records about POW/MIAs from many sources. At any given time, there are more than 1,000 active case files under investigation.
>
> JPAC's recovery missions can last from 35 to 60 days, depending on the location, terrain and nature of the recovery. Teams often work in jungles, rappel cliff-sides, climb mountains, and ride on horseback, boats, or trains to reach sites.

This would not be a job for the faint-hearted. Suffice it to say, the research and recovery work involving our American military is very arduous and dangerous. Even after remains are recovered, the work has just begun and can take years to complete. Remains must be thoroughly examined and correlated with historical evidence. Only when a case is completed and the identification is positive is the deceased next-of-kin notified.

Many are still missing from all of America's wars. The greatest number of those, approximately 78,000, are from World War II. The next largest number comes from the Korean Conflict at approximately 8,100.

While JPAC was notified of *Lagarto's* discovery, there was a huge obstacle. The crew of *Lagarto* died at sea. Naval tradition considers the sea a proper gravesite, and they do not engage in recovering remains. Several years ago, the U.S. Congress adopted laws forbidding any attempt to enter a sunken U.S. war vessel, as that vessel is considered a grave. This is a good law, as it deters tampering with gravesites of those American military who died at sea.

However, the frustration of the *Lagarto* families had more to do with the fact that the discovery of a missing submarine with the entombed remains of 86 American sailors had just been found, and we believed these men should be acknowledged and honored. To the best of our knowledge, only the families and other interested individuals were involved in doing that. Most of us wanted our loved ones to receive at least the same respect as those other heroes who died on land, rather than sea.

We thought we were alone in this desire. We had no idea what was going on behind the scenes.

November News from *Lagarto* 1944

Mabin - 19 November 1944

My Darling,

I hope to soon be able to sit down and write you and the folks a fair size letter. I received three from you and one from mother today.

I've thought about you and "the little guy" so much. Everything you write about her, I try to visualize. Don't fail to keep me informed on everything she does and says. This time, unlike the last time I was away, I am fully conscious that there are three of us now instead of just you and I. Nancy became quite a major part of my life while I was home. I so wish she'd wait 'till I got home again to start growing up.

I can't quite believe I'm to be away from you and Nancy for so long. It just seems like I'll be seeing you in a few days, and this is just a slight inconvenience, like my time in the hospital, and we'll be together again. I sure wish it were that.

Thanks for those clippings about the Illinois-Michigan game. I heard where Illinois lost to Ohio State last Saturday also. I guess I'll just have to pin my hopes on their next year's team or their basketball team this year.

Well darling, guess I'd better get a letter off to the folks.

Todd- – 21 November 1944

Dearest Lover Bunny,

Hello again, Sweetheart. Gosh, I didn't think it was possible to miss a person and long to be with her as much as I do you. Honest, Honey, there's such a doggone ache in my heart when I think of .....how much fun we used to have and will again when I lick these bums.

So Mike kicked you, huh? Rough little b-bum.

Say, what's all this about "Joey?" I think "Joan" is a nice name for a little girl, but I do not go for "Joe" or "Joseph" for a boy. "Mike" was O.K. for me, Darlin. Please understand that I will not be disappointed if it turns out to be a girl; on the contrary, I will be quite happy, 'cause I know – being her mother's daughter – she will be the loveliest little lady in the world, except for her mother.

Have to go on watch now, My Darlin...

Todd – 22 November 1944

My Dearest Darlin,

Surprise! I find I have time to write again – twice in two days!

Well, lots of things have happened since my last letter: – I had my first dive, which was pretty fair, and I got the boat ready for getting underway this morning. I had the deck until some dope in a tin can cut across our bows and the Captain took over the conn (navigational control of the vessel).

Another thing – I have never had any deck (i.e. been in charge of the boat while underway) alone – but yesterday they sent me up to relieve **(Lt. Robert)** Ruble without even an "aye," "yes," or "no." So far as I knew they didn't even know whether I could give orders to the wheel and engine rooms. But there I was – just me, and the lookouts and the big gal below me, slashing thru big waves. Much fun.

Had a bit of excitement yesterday...Al dove the boat with the conning tower hatch open – I was in the conning tower with the Cap'n and Lloyd **(Irving)** and the quartermaster. When all the water started coming in, the Cap'n ordered the conning tower hatch between us and the control room closed. Quite a sight I'll grant you, to see all that stuff pouring in. Luckily we didn't go too deep so the water didn't get too high on us. The best part, as far as I was concerned, was that I wasn't scared or nervous. In fact, it had a very calming effect after the battle surface. My first real crisis – no, my second: my first was the day we almost broke up.

We went into an anchorage last night and had some movies – Joe Brown & Judy Canova in "Chatterbox." Next time will be "You Were Never Lovelier," dedicated to you.

Todd – 23 November 1944

Dearly Beloved, (Has been running thru my head ever since the movie)

Just came below after seeing Fred Astaire and Rita Hayworth in "You Were Never Lovelier," and am in a very mellow mood. Just picture us…the crew sitting around the fore deck, the screen tied to the forward gun platform, the music soft and low, palm-covered islands around us, a soft, warm breeze blowing gently by, and the moon high over the islands; I was sitting there watching Astaire and Hayworth, but dreaming about the loveliest girl in the world. And now I'm very pleasantly tired, 'cause you and I danced every step that they did.

The mail came today and brought me your second letter. Darling, your letters, which have always meant so much are coming to mean so damn much more, now that they are our only tangible connection. I have our picture from the court of the Two Sisters posted on the overhead looking down not a foot over the head of my sack. Every night before I turn off my light I look at it, and after dark; it's just like you were here with me.

Todd – 24 November 1944

Darling,

Was today a lolla palooza! Everything went wrong. I got jumped on all day by about everyone. Just one of those days, I guess.

I've seen it happen in the movies, but I never thought I would be the guy who stood and watch(ed) everyone else get the mail. For heaven's sakes, Sweetheart, get some mail out here before I jump ship and come on home. I gotta know what's going on at home. Please, Darling.....for Mike.

Mabin – 24 November 1944
My Darling,

I've now received about four or five letters from you since leaving home, and I've never enjoyed rereading letters so much in my life. It's beginning to dawn upon me that I won't be back home in a few days, but I keep trying to believe I will. Your letters help greatly.

Being able to build or buy a house, with no down payment, after the war, is a good deal. I think that part of the "soldiers and sailors act," like most of the other parts has to be done within two years after discharge or you lose the benefits. Anyway, two years after I'm discharged I should have a steady job and income. Owning our own house seems like something out of this world, something that only other people can have.

I want you to send me an itemized list of everything Nance gets for Christmas, with her reaction to each. This was the Christmas I really wanted to be home. I pray to God I can be with you both the next one. This is only the fifth Christmas in a row I've said that. The next one will be the one she'll talk of Santa Claus tho, so let's mark Dec. 25, 1945 as our big day.

I'm afraid my letters can't be a bit newsy. I'll just have to comment on the things you write. If I was allowed to say what I pleased, it would probably still hold no interest for you.

Todd – 30 November 1944

Dearest Darlin,

Hey Honey! I'm in love!! I just got your letter written Thanksgiving, and for some reason I think it's the best I've ever gotten – it's just exactly the way I want your letters to be. When I finished reading it, I had the mellowest feeling, and my heart felt like I could love everybody in the world and still love you and little Mike more than anybody ever had been loved before.

The mail boat came alongside just at sundown and we got our letters and took them to our private holes. When I finished yours – I read it about three times, I guess – went up on deck (we're anchored in some islands) and sat on the deck gun under all this tropical moonlight. I sat there for about an hour, feeling homesick for our apartment or Quonset hut and missing my favorite gal like all hell. I thought about all the things that have happened to us, and all the marvelous times we'll have when this is over. It's things like that that keep a guy going.

Now about "Thanksgiving." We forgot about it out here – one day being just like the next – so we didn't join you in your prayers of Thanksgiving – officially that is. On Friday the Captain read a proclamation saying we would have Thanksgiving on Nov. 30 and signed it "Franklin D. Latta," which you see is today.

Lest I forget – Bob Ruble fell overboard yesterday in a shark-infested area when we were going at full speed, but we got him back aboard all in one hunk. Another half minute and it would have been too late. Such a business.....

Well, Lil Nell, I have about four hours to sleep tonight, so I'd better go. Maybe I'll see you tonight in one of your new fraternity dresses. It's a date?..... Damnit, Sweetheart, I'm all eaten out inside from missing you so much and wishing I could put my arms around you and kiss you right on your lovely little chops.

Goodnite, Darlin.

The Chicago Tribune 2005

Back in the U.S., the *Lagarto* families were riding an emotional roller coaster. We were frustrated by the apparent lack of interest in *Lagarto's* discovery by the Navy and that her discovery was being ignored by those we thought would care most. We made our own plan. We knew that generating media interest was crucial.

The first major newspaper to write about *Lagarto's* discovery was the *Chicago Tribune*. I had lived in the Chicago area most of my life and had a few contacts with that venerable publication. After some gentle badgering, the paper agreed to send a reporter, Kelly Kennedy, and photographer, Charles Osgood, to meet with John and Beth upon their return from Thailand. In the first week of August, an article with photographs appeared on the front page of the paper's METRO section.

The *Tribune* article was published while I was in Chicago visiting my children. It included my e-mail address, and responses poured in from all over the country. Much of the mail was from veterans (including a man who served on *U.S.S. Baya, Lagarto's* partner in the Gulf of Siam) and relatives of those in the military. Since the *Chicago Tribune* had nationwide circulation, responses came from states as far-flung as California,

Rhode Island, Texas, Pennsylvania, Florida, Indiana, South Carolina, Iowa, New Jersey, and Georgia, as well as, of course, Illinois. The message from Newport, RI came from a Professor with the National Security Decision Making Department of the United States Naval War College expressing his warmest regards and sending the families his prayers. The New Jersey note was from a member of the Federal Aviation Administration who said: "I was a sub sailor in the 70s, so perhaps stories such as your father's hit home a little more. Just wanted to say I am happy your family has found closure and express my gratitude for your father's service and sacrifice. Our country owes an immeasurable debt to the ordinary citizens who fought in WWII."

One of the messages was a direct link to *Lagarto*. It was from a woman whose father served on *Lagarto's* first patrol. It read, in part:

My father served on the Lagarto. The Lagarto had 2 deck guns. For protection, the sailors were instructed to put cotton in their ears while the deck guns were engaged. Unfortunately, the cotton fell out of Dad's left ear while firing one of the deck guns. ...He did not leave the deck and continued to fire the gun. ...Later he began experiencing severe pain in his left ear. ...The pharmacy mate gave him some medication but it did not relieve the severe pain. He did not want to report his condition to Captain Latta, for he knew he would be disqualified from submarine duty. He realized he had no choice but to report his condition. He was released from duty on the

Lagarto. Two hours after his dismissal, Lagarto went on her last voyage. My Dad was devastated when he heard of the sinking of Lagarto; his new friends and acquaintances were all dead! All those young lives gone.

Dad was diagnosed with deafness in his left ear. He was assigned to the Proteus, a submarine tender.

As I was recently viewing Steve Burton's sketch of the wreckage of Lagarto, I immediately took notice of the 2 deck guns. While researching through my Dad's papers, he noted that Lagarto was one of the 1st submarines to actually have 2 deck guns. (*Lagarto* was one of only three American submarines to have two 5-inch deck guns. The others, *U.S.S. Sennet* and *U.S.S. Haddock*, were CDR Latta's wolf pack, under his command as part of Operation Detachment involved in the Iwo Jima invasion.) *My Dad, age 80, recently passed away, missed the news of the finding of the U.S.S. Lagarto.*

The most unique message came from Karen Lusson King of La Grange, IL:

Dear Nancy,

I read with great interest and sadness the moving article in the Tribune about the recovered WWII submarine and your lost father, Bill Mabin. I can only imagine how difficult it must have been growing up not knowing what had happened to him.

I wanted to write and tell you that the name "Bill Mabin" has been a bit of a mystery to me for years now. I say this because I live in La Grange, and carved in the cement of our garage floor, front and center near the door, is the name "Bill Mabin," in large capital letters. Also, in a corner of the garage are the initials "BM." Ed and I have lived there since 1998, but we bought the house from my parents, who moved there in 1973. I was 14 years old then. I can remember quite clearly looking at the name Bill Mabin in the garage floor with my father soon after we moved in. We could only speculate who Bill Mabin was. Our house was built around 1927, according to my dad, and the cement in the garage is the original foundation.

After Ed and I read the article, I called my mom since she volunteers at the La Grange Historical Society. She told me that Bill Mabin never lived at this address as far as she knew.

Either way, I wanted to tell you about your father's name being etched in the cement. I'd be happy to drop off a rubbing of the name to your son, who Ed says works in La Grange, or send one off to you. Or if he would like to come see the name, we'd be happy to show him.

I hope you are well up in Michigan. Ed sends his best. I know it was 60 years ago that your father's submarine was lost, but it strikes me that there is no statute of limitation on grief. Our deepest condolences to you and your family.

The following day, I went to see Karen King. We went out to her garage, and I saw the name Bill Mabin scrawled on its cement floor. In the scheme of life, it is such a small thing, but so human and so tangible. My father's family lived on the next block, and Billy Mabin might have had a playmate who lived in King's house. I suspect the dark-eyed eight-year-old was invited by a friendly neighbor to forever memorialize himself in that humble spot. We'll never know.

Nancy Mabin with her sons, James and William. Circa 1925.

But seeing this childish scrawl of my father's name touched me, and tears came to my eyes. King became emotional too, and she hugged me as we both cried.

Feeling a little silly, I joked about the improbable marker and told Karen this meant she could never replace her garage floor.

After I left the King home, where my father (as a little boy) felt so real to me, I thought of the irony of two mysteries being solved. First, *Lagarto's* location and then the Bill Mabin name in King's garage floor. Life is so very, very strange!

Tragedy in Panama
1944

In December, Chief Machinist's Mate Pat Cole died of coronary thrombosis while *Lagarto* lay at Saboya Anchorage off Perlas Island, Panama.

***Lagarto* cleared Balboa, Canal Zone on 9 December and reached Pearl Harbor on Christmas Day 1944.**

<u>Todd - 5 December 1944</u>

Darlin' Lil Nell,

Aw, Honey, before I say anything else, let me tell you how very damn much I love you and miss you I'm honestly at a loss for words to tell you how much you mean to me, and how much more you are coming to mean every day ...

I guess just about everything has happened to us that could happen. I told you about Bob Ruble going over the side, didn't I? Along with that, **(F1 Clark R.)** Byrer, a motor mach striker, fell down a hatch when we were clearing the bridge and busted his arm, but good. The destroyer operating with us sent a doctor over, and he took Byrer into the Naval Hospital.

But most disturbing of all, Pat Cole, the oldest chief we had aboard, went off watch Saturday morning and went to the chiefs' quarters and died. Coronary thrombosis, the doc said. We transferred his body to the destroyer which took him back to where my folks used to live. The funeral will be tomorrow and we are all going. We finished our training and got back in this afternoon after being afloat the longest time in my brief Naval Career – or rather, to be more accurate, away from civilization longer than I have ever been before – excluding Cornell. First, let me say, this dope is not to be discussed with anyone connected in any way with the Lagarto – including wives – except our respective folks, nor is any information about our movements or anecdotes. Even tho they may mention things to you, if you think the dope may in any way contain information of a military value or content, please pretend ignorance. This includes Pat Coles' death.

The Captain let everybody make approaches and fire a torpedo. Surprisingly, for all concerned, my fish hit the target 10 yards forward of the middle of the target, which was a little better than any of the others did, except the skipper. Lloyd's hit 50 yards aft. We all got hits, by the way. In fact, all the time we were at sea, we only missed with one fish of all we fired, which, according to the powers that be, is little short of miraculous.

Todd – 7 December 1944

My Darling,

...Yesterday we had the funeral for the fella who died; it was really an impressive thing, being military. I'll never forget standing on the side of that slope, the chaplain reading the word, the marine guard with their snap and precision, the palm trees moving slowly in the hot wind, and the sun glaring down on the many identical markers at the head of each mound.

You know, I'm proud as hell to be part of the submarine force. You don't realize how much it's respected by the other Branches until you get ashore and meet guys from the other ships and bases. I can't help sticking out my chest and pushing my head up and my chin out just 'cause I'm lucky enough to be part of it. We got a real fighting ship – or will have by the time we make our first patrol. We've had some tough luck, but it's made us a better boat. She's my boat and I'm proud as hell to be on her.

This is our third night here – and so far I haven't had the duty... the first night I stayed aboard and squared away my publications preparatory to turning them in. The second, Bill & Ham & I went to a Hotel for dinner – "Blini au caviar, Russian salad, noisette of Beef chateau Briand, etc." – went to a movie and got back about eleven-thirty. Tonight I filed and sorted a two-foot stack of correspondence that the mail truck brought over – mail that had accumulated since 14 October. It's now 0115, and I'm whipped.

<u>Todd – 9 December 1944</u>

Well, Precious, this is it. Today seemed a long time away back in August in Manitowoc. But it's what we've been training so hard for. Now looking forward to the day when directions are reversed.

I'm afraid you're going to be...disappointed come Christmas time: with the exception of the little package I got for you about six letters ago, I only had time to buy for you two other items. ...The only chance I had to do shopping was when ships' service – which was fairly nice, but had little selection – opened at 9 AM this morning...

<u>Mabin – 9 December 1944</u>

Darling,

It's been several days since I've been able to write, and this letter is being written in the early hours of the morning when I should be in bed. There's been a lot of work to do of late.

From your letters, it seems Nancy is progressing quite fast, and is becoming the little lady. It's been just a month since I was home and it's hard to realize the changes that can take place in that time, not only in Nancy, but in all of us.

I had a little bit of luck in a "game of chance" last night (even though both knees are sore as a result) and will try to send you a little Christmas money in the morning, if I am able to get a money order. Wes (SM2 Wesley Shackelford) *has done quite well by himself, along the same lines, in the last month, but last night was my night. I won back all I'd lost in a previous encounter, and then some, so hope to get that money order off so I can stay ahead of the game. Don't worry darling, I'm not throwing all my money away on gambling. Last night was the first I'd done in three weeks and I couldn't have lost enough to worry about if I'd lost all I had.*

I certainly do miss you honey. I can think of so many ways that I could do much better if I were home now. Of course I'd probably do the same foolish things over again after I'd been home a week, but I don't think quite so often. Those six months were the best of our married life yet, and there will be so many more for us after another interval of time.

Well darling, I can hardly keep my eyes open, and I'd like to get a letter off to the folks if I can stay awake long enough.

All my love to you and Nancy.

Bill

Bound for Pearl Harbor 1944

Letters from Hal to Rae on *Lagarto's* way to Pearl Harbor:

10 December 1944

Beautiful Li'l Doll,

...So it's snowing, huh? Won't you join me? I go up on the bridge in the early morning or late afternoon and stay until the sun rises or sets bareheaded, with no shirt, and wearing a pair of shorts and sandals. The moon has sure been pretty and bright the last two or three weeks, too – reminds me of us on the training conning tower on the hill in New London – except, most important, you aren't here. Aw, Honey, I want so very much to hold you close to me and feel your soft, lovely hair on my cheek and hang a honey on your beautiful chops!! Tonite, maybe?

11 December 1944

Rae Darlin,'

...Time is sure going quickly, surprisingly enough, in spite of our routing; I honestly believe I have more work to do than anybody on the ship, which leaves me sort of beat up constantly. They wake me at 0330 to go on watch at 0400. I usually grab a cup of coffee and get up there about 0345. Off at 0800, after a dive or two, and battle station drill, and get breakfast at 0801. (Notice the time elapsed between relief and chow is just enough to permit me to fall down the hatch to the control room, bump my head on the water tight door leading to the forward battery, wash the salt out of my beard, comb the barnacles out of my "butch" hair cut, and trip over the Captain into my seat in the wardroom.) During breakfast I look over the night's radio traffic and give some to the Captain. About this time my eyes are closed longer than they are open, so I hit the sack for an hour or two, hit the deck for a drill, then back in the sack until lunch, after which I communicate until time for watch at 1545. Al relieves me for chow about 1830, then back to work until 2000. I go below, relying on the law of gravity to get me there, as usual, and take care of various communicated odds & ends. About this time I am painfully brought to realize that as yet today I haven't visited the library and take care of that too. Upon completion I am staggered to find I have all the time from 2145 to 2200 as my very own, so I write you...

<u>12 December 1944</u>

My Darling Rae,

Boy – it sure is rough out here – quite a few of the crew and officers have been sick. I haven't as yet – in fact, I think I got my sea legs now, 'cause I feel pretty good. It's so rough, though, that this afternoon up on deck I noticed that when we were in the trough (the area between two wave crests), I could look up and see the crests of the waves on either side about six feet above my head. And I was about twenty feet above the water line. When we were up on the crests I could damn near see Guatemala or Mexico.

At this point in the war, Bill Mabin had served the four years for which he had originally enlisted.

Found in his personnel file was the following notation made by CDR Latta.

This was the extension that cost him his life.

12 December 1944:

Retained in service beyond normal date of expiration of enlistment (which would have been 24 November 1944) in accordance with ALNAV 155-41 and BuPers C/L No. 158-42.

14 December 1944

My Darlin Beebee,

Honey, do I feel good!! The Captain showed us a letter written by Captain Johns – four-striper, Commander of Squadron who came aboard a couple of weeks ago for a visit and inspection. The letter was to the Pacific Fleet Admiral, and guess what, Ol' Trace **(Todd)** was in it! The letter commended Bill **(Mendenhall)** for his fire control work and me for my plotting – said each of us was "outstanding." How about that? It also said as a communicator, I was "excellent. Will be a good submarine officer. Has the right spirit." So I feel pretty good.

...I started to tell you the other night about this watch-standing business on the bridge... At night it's really something. I guess you've heard that there is a lot of phosphorous in the water, especially in the Pacific. In the daytime it makes the water alongside the ship look like frothed up milk, but at night it has the same satiny-smooth- silveryness that your wedding dress had when you came down the aisle on July 16. As I say, when the water is disturbed, it glows with a luminescence, which, at times, can be very disturbing. The other night I suddenly noticed two silver streaks coming at us on the starboard bow, but just as I was about to give the alarm (I thought they were torpedoes) they swerved and paralleled our course and disappeared. We figure it was caused by two porpoises racing for the bow, then turning away. You think I haven't got gray hair?

16 December 1944

Boy! Did we have fun yesterday!! I think I told you the J.O.'s (junior officers) – Lloyd **(Irving)**, Al **(Brewington)**, and myself – are taking all the dives that come on our respective watches. As mine is the "DIVING WATCH," I have to make all the "trim dives," or the ones that trim the boat for the day. I think I'm getting about twice the experience they are – although they laughed at me and kidded me the first couple of times 'cause I didn't do so hot – but I kept thinking "O.K., me lads – while you're having your chuckles, I'm getting the experience, and one of these days things will look different." Sure enough, yesterday was the day: after I got my trim, they put me thru the mill, giving me orders to do things I had never seen done – although I'd heard of them – things you wouldn't believe if I could tell you. I guess it was about the most fun – along that line – I had ever had. It gave me a sense of something I've never experienced before, and exhilarating feeling, no end. Then, when I came up on the bridge after I had surfaced, the Cap'n said, "fine dive, Hal." I felt like a million.

Bless me if I'm not getting to feel like an old sea dog. I'm beginning to really like this business. The ocean is a wonderful thing – deep blue topped with the purest white spray, but big and powerful as it is, a bunch of little guys can lick it, and in so doing, derive from it the same swashbuckling, adventurous feeling that Eric the Red and Magellan and Cook had when they sailed "with the wind in their teeth and a stout full rigged mizzen-mast at their backs." No kidding, Sweetheart, when you're standing on the weather deck with your foul weather gear flapping and the salt spray running down your cheeks and the seas breaking around your legs, your feet wide apart and your knees slightly bent to take up the rolling and pitching of the ship, you have a spirit unconquerable and strength unlimited. (Lots different from Lake Michigan.) The ship, too, is no longer just a welded mass of metal and gismoes but is something alive and friendly that shrugs off the buffeting of the heavy, ponderous seas and smashes back with a force that sends them reeling away on both sides.

I guess all this sounds melodramatic, but I've tried to picture for you what a guy feels and thinks when he's out here getting farther and farther away from the girl who is now his whole life – present and future, and most of the past – out here only because there's the enemy who needs a damn good kick in the teeth and is gonna get it.

<u>18 December 1944</u>

Darling,

Last couple of days have been tough, nothing to be worried about, however...We're really shaping up – everybody is pulling together.....

All small difficulties have been ironed out and we're living together like brothers, or real comrades in arms. For instance – Lloyd is a great guy. Swell attitude, good worker, and a fine fella to have around. We work well together, helping each other out.

You develop quite an affection for these guys in the crew, too. We've weeded out the few parasites, and the ones we have left are the best. It's queer, and a little hard, to know the first names of all the men, but yet not be able to call them by it. For example, you know that in a few minutes one lookout, Bill Moss, will be up to relieve another, **(Robert C.)** "Hoot" Perry. He comes up, goes aft, and you hear, "What say, Hoot? How's she look?"

"Morning' Bill Boy. Yeah, she's all clear. Guess I'll go below and grab me a BIG cup of Joe."

Then "Hoot" comes over, and he knows my name is Hal, but he says, "I've been relieved, Mr. Todd, I'm going below." And I say, "Aye, Aye, Perry," but I want to say, "O.K., old fella, good job. See you at four." But I can't. Such a business.

22 December 1944

Sweetheart,

This will be short. The last couple of days haven't been too hot, as far as I've been concerned. I've had some bad luck with my dives and I'm afraid I've dropped numerous red points along the way. But it's not too bad – everybody has had almost the same bad luck; what we all need is a few good night's sleep and a little relaxation.

We've sailed for 13 days now without even seeing another ship or airplane – we don't even know if we're in the right ocean. I still like this Navy business, though.

Wish I could be with you and the folks to decorate the tree, but I would settle for just being able to kiss you, Darlin' – I love you awful much...I can still feel where you were in my arms when I kissed you goodbye in New Orleans. That won't ever go away.

Request to the Navy 2005

By the end of August, more than twenty *Lagarto* families had been found. We began to formulate a plan to deal with the Navy.

As each family was located, their input was sought on what they considered a reasonable request to make to the Navy. All felt that we asked little, considering we all lost loved ones in World War II. However, the response from the Navy continued to be nil.

We kept going, and each family was anxious to know how they could help. I had learned that a request to the Pentagon had to be made through an official source, so I urged them to contact the senators from their states. Almost all did, and some contacted their congressmen as well.

Responses trickled in via their members of congress. They were identical form letters, with only our names changes (and sometimes misspelled). They came from the Naval Historical Center (NHC), an essentially civilian organization overseen by a naval official. The form letters sent to the families indicated they would not become involved. This attitude shocked me.

In a September 2005 e-mail to a reporter for a major news publication, I wrote:

In the past 3 months I have communicated with all the family members we have found so far – 22 out of 86 crew members. The emotions have been overwhelming, and the families are so glad to know what happened. Not knowing is worse than anything, and the *Lagarto* children have grown up with both the loss of their fathers and unanswered questions. The sailors' parents died not knowing their sons' fate, the widows who are now elderly (and many no longer alive), the brothers and sisters and grandchildren all still feel their loss. Those of us who know what happened are finally finding some peace.

As the families speak with each other, we grieve not for ourselves, but for those young men who didn't have these past 60 years. I think how proud each of those sailors would be if they knew (they probably do) how much their families still love them. They are not forgotten.

That being said, I believe, as do most of the other families, that the Navy must get involved. So far, they have been mum on the subject, and to my knowledge, no one from the Navy has contacted a single member of any family. Attempts to contact them through our elected representatives have been responded to with platitudes that do not apply to this situation...

On the same day I wrote a letter to officials at the NHC. In this letter, I stated I understood that when the remains of servicemen killed in war were found, they were brought home, and a special service with full military honors was held for their family. A friend, who lost his father in France, participated in such a ceremony just ten years earlier.

I pointed out that we were not asking for the submarine to be raised or the 86 separate remains be identified, as that would be long and expensive, if not impossible. After speaking with other *Lagartos* thus far, we requested the following of the USN:

1. Issue a clear and unequivocal statement, which would include the news media, acknowledging that *Lagarto* had been found.

2. Assign a naval representative to be a liaison to the families to help us find others. As the families were found, the Navy should notify them of *Lagarto's* discovery.

3. Participate in a ceremony/memorial service, complete with full military honors, for the families of the submarine's crew.

We believed this was a reasonable request. Letters to family members from the NHC stated that "Additionally there is no plan to notify the families of the crewmembers of *Lagarto's* apparent discovery. The Navy notified the families when the submarine was initially lost in 1945, and unfortunately notifying families 60 years after the loss would be impractical."

We did not believe it was impractical to give the submarine families peace of mind in knowing where their loved one rests. We believed this was a matter of decency for the Navy. I pointed out that while *Lagarto's* crew may not be family to them, they were the Navy's men.

The Last Christmas of Their Lives 1944

Todd - 23 December 1944

My Darling Wife:-

I have just come off watch and will try to get this off before I fall apart.

Gosh! I sure wish I could be home with you, Honey. We all go around saying we don't mind being away from home and it's not so bad, but it's just to buck up everybody else. We aren't fooling anybody, though – in reality, about the most important thing to us in the world is to be home with our wives and families during this season of the year. Every time we hear Bing Crosby or somebody sing Silent Night or White Christmas on the radio, it's like somebody sticks a knife in your heart.

But this will be the last Christmas I'll spend away from you, Darlin' – you won't be able to pry me loose from here on out.

Remember the Christmas tree and bell you gave me to bring with us? I'm going to have the messenger put it up in the crew's mess on the 12-4 watch. We got some kids on this vessel who haven't been away from home on Christmas before, and I think the stuff will perk them up.

Tomorrow, being Sunday, I gotta have a Christmas service. I have the calendar or program, or whatever it is, all typed up – has on it the words to hymns they know the tunes to, and some responsive reading. I'm going to give them the Christmas Story – again, but that's what they want..." **(Todd was assigned to be the ship's chaplain.)**

Todd – 24 December 1944

Rae Darlin,'

A very, very Merry Christmas, Lil Nell!!! The very best in the world to the finest little wife in the world. I wish I could tell you in different and colorful words just how much I mean that, and just how much I love you and want you to have the best in the world, Honey, but I can't; no matter how I try, it still comes out the same way: All the love I have is for you and every day my stock of it doubles........

I've been thinking about names for the baby, should Mike turn out to be a girl – in fact, I've thought about it a hell of a lot. ...... How about Susan or Suzanne? Suzanne Burgess might be O.K. or Susan Brooks. The Captain was helping me out the other night – he thinks Nancy is a good one.

Or how about Carol Lynne, or Joanne: (I sure like those double n's, don't I). Adrianna is sort of unusual – what would we use for short, "A?"

What ideas do you have, Sweetheart? Just thought of another – how about Wynne – but what's the full name? certainly not Winifred.

Gosh, Darlin,' I want to know so much about Mike – don't leave out even one little detail. Is there anything I can do? Yeh, I know, "I've done enough already." Sure wish I could be there to take some of the load off of you. Good night, Beautiful Beebee.

Todd – 25 December 1944

My Dearest Beebee,

Mele kalichamacha, Sweetheart!! That's the appropriate way of saying "Merry Christmas" to a beautiful little girl – the lovely little girl is the best wife I ever had.

I rather enjoyed Christmas – in fact I had a damn good time – at least as much as circumstances would allow, said circumstances being the fact that my lil Nell was "there" and I'm "here."

When we hit the dock there was big Ol' Wes **(Todd – Hal's brother)** as big as life, with Willy Brown. Wes had a Jeep, and the three of us were going out for Christmas dinner, but of course I had the duty, so he and Will went out and ate. I was a little disappointed, naturally, but it was short-lived, 'cause the mail came aboard, and there were 15 letters for me, 11 from my beloved, beautiful Beebee!!! Darlin,' I've already read them so many times that the writing has come off in lots of places. That was the best – no, the second best – Christmas present I could get. All the good news about the apartment, Mike, furniture, and most important, that you are in great shape, and still love me a little bit. That was wonderful!

So a little later Ruble found out that he would have to stay aboard to work on his fish (torpedoes) and offered to take my duty for awhile. The three swishes that went past him were a Brown and two Todds on their way to the Marine Bar – and Christmas supper at the Marine barracks. And so it came to pass after all. How about that? What a night! I was back aboard, at least materially, by 2200, but we sure had fun. Lots of bourbon and coke, lots of laughs. Met all the fellas in Likes' Squadron – damn swell guys, almost as swell as submariners.

Well, Sweetheart, go to sleep thinking this: there may be a lot of ocean between us, but I could get to you in 40 hours if you needed me physically; and I'm right beside you when you need me immediately.

The last Christmas of Bill Mabin's life wasn't quite so enjoyable. It was his fifth consecutive Christmas away from home.

<u>Mabin – 29 December 1944</u>

Yesterday got quite a bunch of letters which was the best Christmas present I could receive under the present circumstances. One of your letters was postmarked the 19th, which was quite recent.

Spent my usual Christmas, as of the last four years, only probably the most unXmas-like of them all. Wes (Shackelford) *and I stood in line here on the base for an hour and fifteen minutes waiting for our turn to get a couple bottles of beer, only to have the beer shut off when we had about ten men to go. I didn't bother to go ashore either yesterday or today, even though I rated liberty. You have to wait for everything you do or everywhere you go. If I were in the states, I'd wait all day in line for one beer at home, but not in this place. You probably little realize just how good your husband is when he's away.*

Nancy's progress seems quite remarkable in so short a time. God! How I'd love to hear her little voice or feel one of those little kisses of hers, to say nothing of yours. It's very flattering to hear from you the small ways Nancy seems to remember her daddy, but I'm 'fraid she'll soon forget she has one.

I just interrupted this letter long enough to refill my pen and see a three-hour movie. It was "Since You Went Away," which I think you mentioned as being quite good, and it was. Quite long, and a little sad, but very good. I'd forgotten what a good actor Joseph Cotton is.

Tell the Harry McDonalds their Christmas card was not mailed a bit too early, in fact it arrived Christmas day, and I appreciated their remembering me. It's funny how one appreciates small things when away from home.

...Incidentally, Bill Reno was transferred. He has a trick knee and will have to have it operated on. We've had a few leave the boat, but none of the rest you know. A Chief died suddenly of a heart attack while laying in his bunk. Pat Cole was his name, and he was a hell of a swell guy. Don't believe you ever met him.

It's late darling, and I've quite surpassed myself with the length of this letter. I love you a terribly lot my darling.

The day after Christmas, *Lagarto's* crew began a period of training and availability. During this period, a second 5-inch deck gun was installed, and special armament installations were made to the submarine. The special training and availability period concluded on 23 January 1945. In the meantime, Todd and Mabin continued to write their wives.

Todd – 26 December 1944

Rae Beebee,

Morning, Sweetheart... you sure look pretty today, Honey – just like you look every morning when I wake up and every night when I sack in (Pretty soon this picture better turn into the real thing).

Lloyd got word today of the arrival of his son and heir – he sure is a happy fella to know that Connie is O.K.

Haven't seen Wes since last night, of course. We're going to try to get together New Year's Eve...I will probably get very jovial toasting my lovely wife and her accomplishments, and various and sundry details.

Except for going to the air base with Wes, I haven't been off the base...I'm afraid I may miss the famous places in the towns around here...oh well, I'll probably be back.

Todd – 27 December 1944

Lovely Beebee,

This may be the "vacation-land for the elite," but I guess I'm not elite. As per usual, I haven't been able to do any shopping or carousing except the first night in. I'm on the base all day, then come back to the boat and do the shipyard work.

Oh yeah – remember I had the duty Christmas? Well, six days later, when comes again my duty, it is New Year's Eve...Was I bummed!!! But old Al offered to take the duty for me that night so I can go to the Marines' Brawl with Wes & Willy – offered all by himself! How times have changed. So I'm going to take him up on it – which means I'll have the duty Friday instead.

Your description of the apartment – "our" apartment sure sounds great. Your description of it makes it seem like I've been there a lot and know it by heart. I'm glad you're having such success with your furniture shopping.

Todd – 29 December 1944

Dearest Rae,

Got your 20th and 21st letters today – poor Beebee; you need old H.A.'s shoulder to lay your little head on when you feel low. Any time you feel like that, Sweetheart, you just tell me about it. While I'm awful sorry those crotchety old spinsters are inconsiderate, I'm glad to hear about it, 'cause it's just like I was home – hearing the unpleasant stuff with the good.

I'm gonna turn the tables on you: I feel lower than a snake's belly myself. I guess I've told you (ten times or more) that I've been working pretty hard since I've been here, getting my stuff in shape, staying aboard at night, and taking the duty for the other fellas, while they took trips around the island, or went out shooting, or knocked off early about 2000 and went over to the club for a bout. But there was a method to my madness: I wanted to get about twenty-four hours off to go out to the Marine Air Station and play tennis and golf with Wes, and he was going to take me up. Well, Our Boy (Captain Frank Latta) won't let me go – won't even let me have an afternoon off. No good reason, just says "we may get underway in a few days." Certainly! I know that. I also know that if I don't get it tomorrow, I won't get it until after the first patrol. And Wes won't be here, then. As far as I'm concerned he can take his communications and jam it.

I'm sorry, Honey – I'm in a rotten mood.

The First Day of the Last Year of the War 1945

Todd – 1 January 1945

My Darlin,'

Please forgive me for not writing yesterday or Saturday and forgive the brevity of this letter...we have been so damn busy that I just haven't been able to work it in. And because I've been up for about 36 hours, I'm afraid I won't be able to write very much or very coherently.

I want to thank you Sweetheart, 'cause Christmas came to my house day before yesterday. I'll write in greater detail later, but suffice it to say that I sure appreciated the box with the candy, fruitcake, cards, etc. And Honey, those pictures of you and Petey **(Todds' dog)** almost did it...I love you so much and you looked so cute and lovely I almost deserted – I want to be home with my Li'l Nell awful bad! This is killing me!

Todd – 2 January 1945

My Darling Beebee,

Boy! It sorta scares me when I realize that before the month is over we will undoubtedly have had contact with the Japanese – and from then on we'll be the terror of the seas! Basically, I guess I'm not too brave – I'd rather be home with Beebee than go looking for trouble, as I said in my last letter. But on the other hand, we've trained so damn long now that it's sorta like a challenge to see how good our systems are.

Then, too, the quicker in, the quicker out and home again.

Thirdly – and I don't mean to be idealistic – when the Japanese get toned down, everybody in the world will be able to go back to somewhat the same life as we were living five years ago – home, work, family, parties, etc., and above all, a little peace and quiet. That will be one of the happiest days of my life, the day I come home.

Have you thought of any other combinations of names for Mike? If you could think of a good one, I'd like possibly to use "Wesley" as a middle name, or a first name if you could work it out. I'm still undecided about the "Junior" business – I don't particularly like "Harold Arthur Todd III," but when you get right down to it, it's sort of a heritage or something. What do you think about it?

And if little Mike turns out to be a girl, I am again at a loss. To me, the loveliest name in the world is a three-letter one that looks like Rae. Don't you think you could work that in? Oh, woe is me...I don't have enough time anymore to think very long about the situation. I'm afraid you're going to have to do most of the work.

Saturday they gave me off from 1300 to 1600 Sunday – how about that? I spent it all out at the Marine Air Station with Wes – played tennis, billiards, swam, had numerous cans of Milwaukee Beer and a lesser quantity, but not too lesser, of Park & Lilford Bourbon. Very restful. Haven't seen him since, but hope to see him again.

A few nights ago, we went into a famous city and to a famous hotel, which I will tell you about after censorship has been lifted; we didn't stay overnight – just looked...

Good night, lovely Beebee – sleep tight and pray for us a little.

Mabin – 4 January 1945

Dearest Marg,

I finally received your letter about Nancy's Christmas today. I certainly wish I could have been there. I've tried to picture it many times but your letter greatly helped. What I would have given to have seen her expressions and actions on that day. Now that the day has passed, I guess I can dismiss it from my mind for another year. Incidentally, are you planning a party for Nancy's second birthday?

To answer a couple of your questions, yes you may dispose of those letters from Jean (a former girlfriend of Mabin's). *I lost any thrill from them years ago. You and mother seem to be the only ones to get any enjoyment out of them, so do what you please with them.*

I have a bit of news that may be of interest to you. Bob Peterson made Quartermaster 3/c and I made Signalman 1/c, the first of January. Now you may look your friends and relations in the face, even if it did take me four years to do it. I've reached my peak now, so you and your mother may no longer worry about my lack of ambition while in the Navy.

I'm hoping to get over in town to get birthday cards for both Nancy and Dad, but if I don't it's for reasons for which I have no control.

I love you and Nancy more than anything in the world, so take care of each other, and someday I'll be able to take care of you both.

All my love to my two best girls.

My Darlin' Darlin
1945

Todd - 5 January 1945

My Darlin' Darlin,

...the program I got on the wardroom radio is giving out with a number of the songs of the last few years. Right now some tomato is singing "And the Angels Sing." They already have played "You'd be so nice..." and "Black Magic."

Don't think that life as a communicator is as bad as I picture it in my letters & "cartoons" – I get my share of time ashore. I usually spend it over at the Marine Air Base with Wes – in fact they give me a quota of three bottles of beer a week from their commissary. But all my parties are with them at air base with Walt Shaw and Bill and Al & Lloyd Irving at the sub base BOQ, so don't worry about my morals.

Which brings up a point: Beebee, you know that you won't have to worry about H.A. and any feminine entanglements. I guess you've heard stories about how some of the guys cut loose on parties in the various ports they hit and go pretty far with the women they pick up. Well, a good part of them are true. Some of our own guys do. But the way I look at it, when I come back to my Beebee – both of them – I want to be able to look them in the eye and know that there's nothing on my conscience about being unfaithful or unfair in <u>any</u> way. To be perfectly frank, the reason I won't be unfaithful is not because of convention or laws or because I don't have the urge (you know the kid); it's because I'm not going to do anything that will in any way mar the wonderful life we've had together by cheapening any part of it. When

Old Trace comes home to his li'l wife, he'll be untainted. You're for me, Darlin,' and nobody in the world can or will take your place in any way at any time.

Todd – 6 January 1945

Darlin Li'l Nell,

I can hardly wait to get home so we can have our second honeymoon (might look sort of funny to have Mike along – people might not understand – do you suppose?). Maybe we can arrange it so we can finally get in that vacation in a cabin in the North Woods and do some fishing and courting – some of the former and lots of the latter.

You know, I was thinking today about the little bar of soap and box of tooth powder you sent in my Christmas box. On the surface they are plain, just everyday necessities. But to me they mean a great deal more; I guess it's hard to imagine that they could be symbols of home and peace where guys named Hal & gals named Rae can brush their teeth together before they go to bed. Maybe my imagination is working overtime, but I never fail to think of that every time I take that little box out of the cabinet...

Mabin – 9 January 1945

My Darling,

Lately your letters have been coming in no particular sequence. One day I'll get a couple of recent ones. Then there will be a lapse, and I eagerly await fresh news. Then I'll get a couple of old ones. No fault of yours, of course, and I enjoy every letter no matter how late, but it's like reading a serial, or seeing one in the movies when we were kids. You eagerly await next Saturday's continuance of the thrilling adventure, only to find it's installment #2 that you had missed, when you thought you were going to see installment #5 and find out the solution to last week's abrupt end. The only difference is your letters are all fresh and good and seem to have you stamped all over them. (No darling, I haven't had so much as a beer for several days.) Maybe someday I shall get real romantic in a letter and let my love for you really flow out on paper the way I wish it could. I feel it but I can't write it.

Well darling, my letter came a little easier tonight, although when I first sat down I didn't think I'd be able to write more than a few lines.

Gathering Steam 2005

The press was becoming increasingly interested in the *Lagarto* story, and we were grateful. After the first press report was published in the *Leelanau Enterprise,* the *Suburban Life,* a local newspaper chain published in suburban Chicago, wrote an article on *Lagarto,* and Bill Mabin's connection to the submarine. This story was initiated by an old friend, Chris Ganschow, who had once reported for the newspaper but was then a member of Congressman Dan Lipinski's staff.

Soon after these stories appeared, journalist James Goodwin did a series of articles for the *News-Leader* newspaper in Springfield, Missouri, which were the means to finding three Springfield *Lagarto* families. In August, the *Chicago Tribune* did their article, written by Kelly Kennedy. With the exception of these newspapers, little interest in *Lagarto* was shown by the media.

The inquiries trickled in. One of the first was an e-mail sent by Bill Engle, the public affairs reporter for the *Richmond* (Indiana) *Palladium-Item.* He was looking for information on *Lagarto's* S1 William G. Moss. Engle had been contacted by former Richmond resident John Balmon, with the news that *Lagarto* had been found and had a local connection; Balmon and Moss had gone through submarine school together. Bill Moss had grown up in a large family in the Indiana town, and Engle didn't anticipate a problem in finding relatives. He was wrong.

The difficulty in tracking down *Lagarto* relatives was typified by the story of Bill Moss. Although the Moss family had been a large one, it had virtually disappeared from the area. Moss was unmarried at the time of his death, and his parents were deceased. His siblings had either left Richmond or were deceased, as well. Engle did find one sibling who, sadly, was too incapacitated to be contacted for information. Engle kept going anyway and based his article on memories of Moss related to him by the sailor's friends. The article ran, and an amazing thing happened.

Sue and Jim Hill, who lived in nearby Lynn, Indiana, read with astonishment, the front-page story in the *Richmond Palladium*. Sue Hill, who was eight years old when her uncle, Radioman Third Class (RM3) Glen E. Halstead died on *Lagarto*, couldn't believe her eyes. She and her husband made a trip to the news office of the *Palladium* to meet with Engle. The paper wrote a follow-up story on Glen Halstead, another *Lagarto* casualty. Fortunately for the Halstead family, relatives still lived in the area where Glen had grown up, and Sue remembered him well.

Sue Hill and I had a long telephone conversation. She adored her young uncle and loved playing with him. He was never too busy to have time for his little niece. Halstead had many friends, and girls thought he was adorable. Hill remembered the day at her grandparents' farm when they saw a dark car driving slowly down the road toward their home. The adults seemed to know what was coming. When Hill's grandfather went to greet the military vehicle, her grandmother fainted. She will never forget that day.

Hill put me in touch with her brother, Larry Halstead, and he expressed the family's eagerness to help. They pledged to write their senators.

Preparing to Go to Sea 1945

Todd – 10 January 1945

My Darling,

I hope you'll forgive me, Sweetheart, for being delinquent in this letter-writing…We've been so damn busy getting ready, I've hardly had time to turn around. We've had an awful lot of work to do. Last night, however, I took off – the Captain gave me the ship's car – and went out to Wes' outfit's beach party. They are leaving soon – Wes on the 21st – and they sure are having a good time.

About 12 of the 27 fellas had dates; most were American, some were natives, some were Japanese Americans. Wes & 2 of his roommates and Willy Brown and I sat in the sand, singing, watching the moon come up and drinking beer. I sure got homesick for you, my Beebee. I couldn't help remembering the beach party you and I and the Mendenhalls and Jim & Dottie had on Labor Day. How I wish we could do it again – real soon.

Hot dope!!! Bill Mendenhall is exec, and we have another married academy man on board as engineer. The crew is really working together now – doing a wonderful job. ……Now this is really the fightingest boat in the fleet – we hoped before, but we know now – our training record bears that out.

Todd – 11 January 1945

Hi Honey,

I just reread your last five or six letters – I had to, cause I didn't get one from you, again...- I'm sure lonesome for you. If only Uncle Sam would let me go home for just 24 hours before we go out...It's funny, Wes and I leaving on the same day.

We gave a party for the crew – a "luau" they're known around these parts – but I didn't go on account I got lots of stuff to do. It was at a native park, and was complete with beer, steaks, and native hula dancers.

We are tied up alongside a tender and I had to move the ship aft to get some gear aboard. I had to laugh, 'cause they still haven't let us J.O.'s (junior officers) handle the ship (although now that Bill Mendenhall is exec we may get a chance) and the first time I had to handle it was when I was all alone. A couple of Captains and numerous commanders were leaning over the tenders rail watching the proceedings which didn't ease my mind. But we got aft O.K.

Mabin – 11 January 1945

Darling,

To go back a few days ago, I met a guy while drinking beer, purely a routine bar conversation that only starts because there's nothing else to do. He knew both Jim Clarke and Jim Lightbody. He was also from York High School, in the same graduation class I was. A graduate of Harvard U., but not an officer, surprisingly enough. Still probably the thing that endeared him mostly to me was the fact that he remembered me running track at both La Grange and the U. of Illinois. God rest his soul. ...What a feeling to have someone remember you for some slight accomplishment you attained a few years ago.

I also ran across Jim Dennehy yesterday, my old chief from the Balao. It was good to see him and he likewise seemed glad to see me. He and Charlie

Anker were best friends on the Balao. (MoMMC Charles Anker was also lost on *Lagarto*.)

Darling, I've got to quit and shouldn't send you this messy thing, but I'm going to if only to show you how much I love you. (I have had a few beers tonight.)

Todd – 12 January 1945

Sweetheart,

Well, we don't have too long here in this place – we're all getting our odds and ends straightened away, that is, the guys who have odds & ends are.

Today I mailed a box with a little present for Mike's zeros birthday which I got at the local ship's service. It's blue only because that's the only color they had; if it turns out pink would have been more appropriate, just pretend it is. (By golly, I'd almost rather Mike will be a girl, 'cause she'd be such a cute li'l gal on account of her mother.)

I'm going over tomorrow to get the hot dope on how you can best notify me of coming events. (Some say "this way" and others say "that way.")

I'm also enclosing a little note to Mike. Guess you better read it to him – don't imagine he'll feel like using his eyes for a week or two.

About the car – I'd say we better store it up (put on blocks, take out the battery, drain the radiator, etc.) unless Dad thinks parts will be poorer and/or more expensive after awhile. If such is the case, I'd say get it fixed when we can financially. Only as a last resort, sell old Hessy. Do Not Drive her the way she is. I'll write Dad about it.

Baby Names and Other Important Matters 1945

Todd – 12 January 1945

My Darling,

Because of time limitations I'll have to get this off now – at that it'll probably be just about on time.

Though the sentiments on the inside of the card are very apropos, the appearance of the card is a little more gaudy than I normally choose; I wasn't the guy who chose it, however. I was just hitting the sack the other evening when Taylor, my 2nd class technician, came in and said, "Mr. Todd, I know you don't get much chance to go downtown, so I bought a valentine for you to send your wife – if you want it..." That really got to me – I didn't expect anything like that from such a rough and tough fella like him.

Todd – 14 January 1945

I spent most of the day in water up to my knees or waist – the water was either coming up inside my pants leg or out my pockets - who's got pockets? – or vice versa. As of a couple of days ago, I am the sight-setter on the deck gun – the big one – and we had a couple of gunnery runs today, hence the high degree of personnel saturation. It's more fun than I've had for a long time in the Navy – war gets more interesting every day.

It sure is a problem, this naming progeny...I'm afraid I've run out of ideas. I'm afraid that there won't be enough time, anyway, for you to answer this letter so I would get it before Mike arrives, so last minute changes may be possible, if you get any good ideas. (I'm afraid this is a pretty stilted letter – everybody hates to see me with a minute to myself and they keep bringing up a lot of interruptions.)

To get back, if Mike is "he," I like Michael Wesley or Michael Burgess, or a similar combination. I don't really know how I feel about H.A.T. III – I'd like to have my son named after me, but the names themselves aren't so hot.

"Calvert" could be used both for a boy and a girl – Janie's and also my Grandmother's...

Did I ever say I didn't like Christopher? "Chris" would be a good nickname – just so it isn't "Kit." I keep trying to figure out what she would be called when she gets up to high school or college age. Along that line I like Nan, etc. – I think I listed them in a letter written on our way across.

So to sum up – I would like to have <u>him</u> named after his old man, if only the names were different – although "Hal" isn't a bad nickname. "Michael Wesley," or "Michael Burgess," or combinations, possibly with "Calvert."

I would like to have <u>her</u> named "Becky Brooks" (would the first name be "Rebecca?" (Ouch!) or something like "Nancy Rae" or "Christopher Rae." If only we could get down together and figure it out.

I love and miss you 24 x 60 x 60 times more now than I did yesterday at this time.

<u>*Mabin – 16 January 1945*</u>

Dearest Marg,

Shall write a couple of lines before the movie starts, then maybe I will have some new thoughts on my mind.

Received the candy and razor blades from Nancy yesterday, and certainly treasure anything she does, writes or says. I'm 'fraid you're just flattering me by telling me the ways she remembers me and the things she says, but I sure love to hear it. Of course with the mother she's got, she's bound to be a little smarter than the average child. I sure wish I were home and we could give her a little brother.

Just came back from the movie on the tender, "Dark Waters." I'd advise you not to see it. Slightly weird and a little depressing if one's in the wrong sort of mood.

You mentioned "There Goes That Song Again" in a recent letter. We have that record by Russ Morgan. I wish you'd get it. It's damn good.

Darling, I'm sure glad I have you and Nancy to think about. The last time I was away it was almost you alone that occupied my thoughts, 'cause I really didn't know Nancy at all. I'm so glad we had a little girl. It's hard to imagine us having anything but a girl. A boy doing the things Nancy does just wouldn't be so cute. With little girls you give and receive the kind of love you can't get from little boys.

Nancy's already two years old, and I've had less than six months of her life with her. Can't you just keep her two years old 'till I get home again? You two have sure made an impression on the old man.

Engaging the Press 2005

By October, our efforts to find families were slowing down, but other things were going well. Norma Bishop, the Executive Director of the Wisconsin Maritime Museum, was making plans to hold a special memorial service for *Lagarto,* and the Manitowoc and Wisconsin State SubVets were eager to work with the families on a memorial ceremony.

Due to the forward moving plans, it was more important than ever to find as many families as possible to share in this occasion honoring the *U.S.S. Lagarto.* We were determined to find many more – hopefully all – of the families before the ceremony in May 2006. But we had hit a wall, and Karen Duvalle and I discussed a new approach to find the missing families – the press. We believed that the press would be interested – if only because we had such a great story. Based on the articles already published in several papers, which had helped us find some families, we knew that more enthusiastic journalists would be willing to work with us. We made a plan.

Duvalle, the whiz researcher, created a list of newspapers that served each of the *Lagarto* crew's home town. I wrote the press release and e-mailed it to contact people on Duvalle's list. Each press release was individualized with the name of the missing crew member(s) from their circulation area. We sent these press releases out in mid-October and waited for the results.

Press Release
The *Pekin* (IL) *Times* –

WORLD WAR II SUBMARINE FOUND
After 60 Years, *USS Lagarto* Location Known
Local Man Was Member Of The Crew

For 60 years, the families of the crew members of the USS LAGARTO have not known what happened to this submarine, lost just weeks before the end of World War II. According to a 1946 letter written by James Forrestal, then Secretary of the Navy, the submarines, USS LAGARTO and USS BAYA, had made plans to attack an enemy convoy in the Gulf of Siam. "The BAYA proceeded on ahead of the LAGARTO about fifteen miles and was driven off by alert radar-equipped escorts. The BAYA had no further contacts with the LAGARTO," said Secretary Forrestal in a letter to Margaret Mabin, the wife of crew member SM1 William T. Mabin. He also said, "In view of the strong probability that the submarine sank during action in enemy-controlled waters...I am reluctantly forced to the conclusion that he is deceased." The letter from Secretary Forrestal was the last correspondence received by families on the presumed fate of LAGARTO's crew.

Eighty-six men went down with the boat, and for six decades the site and circumstances of this loss were largely unknown. RICHARD LOUIS FISHER of Pekin was a member of that crew.

This past May, almost 60 years to the day, the USS LAGARTO was found by commercial divers in the Gulf of Thailand. The boat was sitting upright in 225 feet of water and was found to have been engaged in battle to the end. The British divers did an assessment of the condition of the boat and found a large rupture in the portside bow area, apparently made by a depth charge. An open torpedo tube revealed that a torpedo had been fired. The LAGARTO had gone down fighting. The crew of the USS LAGARTO is no longer missing.

Through the efforts of the Wisconsin Maritime Museum, numerous US Submarine Veterans' Organizations, and individual family members, 29 families of the 86 crew members have been informed of this discovery. After 60 years, it had been a daunting task to find everyone and let them know where their loved one rests. If you have information on family or friends of MOMM1 Richard Louis Fisher, please contact Karen Duvalle at the Wisconsin Maritime Museum by e-mail at kduvalle@ wisconsinmaritime.org or toll free at 866-724-2356. You can also contact a LAGARTO family member, Nancy Mabin Kenney at nancykenney11@yahoo.com. The goal is to find every crew member's family to inform them of this important event. A memorial service at the museum will be held in May.

Similar press releases were sent to local and major newspapers and/or their websites all over the country. A few of them were *The Arkansas Times, The Baltimore Sun, The Boston Herald, Vicksburg Post, Denver Post, Rocky Mountain News, Atlanta Daily, Santa Fe Mexican, Toledo Blade, Cleveland Plain Dealer, Tulsa World,* and *Philly News.* Karen Duvalle and I contacted the appropriate news outlets and hoped for the best. Within days, we got results.

Before They Leave for Battle: Letters to Their Wives From a Lieutenant and a Signalman 1945

Todd – 18 January 1945

My Darlin' Darlin,

I've certainly been neglecting you in the last few days, Honey, please forgive me. We've had it a little easier these last two days, and I've spent almost all of my free time catching up on lost sleep, although I think I could sleep a year and still be behind.

I left the boat last night and went out to the air station to see Wes. (Bill Mendenhall said I could come back about noon.) We shot the breeze for awhile, then hit the sack, expecting to play a little tennis today after he came back from an early hop. I got up at six and watched the six on them take off. About 0930 I went out to watch them land – five of them. Guess who had cracked up? But all the guys said his plane looked O.K. after he was down and they were sure he was all right, even though they couldn't see him. They were right. However, he came in an hour after I left, perfectly O.K. Those guys are nuts. That flying is dangerous.

All my Love, Ace

P.S. We have little to do but load and shove off.

Mabin – 18 January 1945

Dearest Marg,

Not a thing of interest has happened since my last letter to you, so for the moment I'm stumped for something to write. As long as I have the time and opportunity, though, I shall at least address an envelope and insert these few lines so you'll know I'm thinking of you.

It has dawned on me, as of late, that my letters may have shown too much of an interest in "the little guy" and not enough in you. Such is not the true condition of my mind though. I love you both with all my life. It just happens that Nancy is the biggest thing you and I together have ever had, and when I write of her, I write of you and our great happiness. This explanation is becoming involved and getting a little out of hand, so I'll just drop it here and go on thinking how wonderful you both are.

Your mentioning of your "thought waves" in your letter today, and your description of how you felt also brought quite a warm feeling to me. It was almost as if I was with you. I also have a vivid memory of many times only you and I lived.

Todd – 23 January 1945

Dearest Li'l Nell,

I'm awfully disappointed that I won't be able to make this a long newsy letter, but I have so damn much stuff to do – last minute stuff – that it looks like I won't be able to spend as much time on this as I'd like.

The main thing is that we're really a hot-shot outfit – just capable as hell of taking good care of ourselves. We got lots of potent reasons why we're coming back, and if we got anything at all to do with it, we're gonna come back in a blaze of glory.

So don't worry about old Trace...just remember that he's out "somewhere" on the biggest adventure a guy could have (not necessarily the most important one to him in terms of his lifetime) having a big time, and piling up anecdotes to tell Little Mike.....

I'm awfully glad you had a good time in Milwaukee, Beebee. Mom wrote and said you made her mighty happy just being there in the house, to say nothing of going downtown with her. She sure enjoyed going through all the baby gear with you, too. And by the way, old Dad thinks you're the finest li'l gal in the world (he should tell me?) and says he couldn't have done a finer job in picking a wife himself.

Well, my beautiful favorite girl, I'll be praying for you and Mike every day – lots of times a day. If I could only be there to let you cry on my shoulder when you want to and brush my teeth with you, and comb your hair when you want me to, and kiss you when I want to, and cut cards with you for the first one in...I love you tremendously, Lil Nell. Excuse me while I go blow up a few ships.

Mabin - 23 January 1945

My Dearest,

It seems like there are so many things I should say to you in this letter, but I know I'll fall far short. In fact it will probably be full of small trivial things that would be better not written. Anyway, the money order may be worthwhile.

You know, I had a very funny wish this evening concerning you. I was watching a movie, a very second rate one that I've forgotten the name of, and I got to thinking how I'd like to be at a very scary movie with you. One that would make you grab my hand and arm real tight and hold on. I got to thinking about it so strongly, I could almost feel you next to me clutching at my arm and turning your face away from the picture. I used to complain about it a little to you, but I sure wouldn't now. I'd love it. There are so many things I would no longer complain about, if only I had the chance not to complain about them.

I know, my darling, there's no need for me to say "take care of our Nancy," 'cause there's no one that could take as good care and make her as happy, as you could. Just give her a little extra love for her old man. Then someday I'll be able to do some of the things for our daughter that most little girls expect from their fathers.

Doing Their Duty
1945

January – March 1945

The *U.S.S. Lagarto* (SS-371), accompanied by the *U.S.S. Haddock* (SS-231), departed Pearl Harbor on 24 January 1945, escorted initially by *PC-486.* Releasing their escort four and a half hours out, the two boats proceeded in company, conducting dives and drills daily and acting as targets for each other on alternate days. Ultimately, the pair reached the Marianas on 4 February, exchanging recognition signals with friendly planes as they neared Saipan. Escorted in by the infantry landing craft *LCI-677* on 5 February, *Lagarto* moored in a nest alongside *Angler* (SS-240) as she lay alongside the tender *Fulton* (AS-11) in Tanapag Harbor. *Haddock* also moored alongside.

In the ship's log, *Lagarto's* CDR Frank D. Latta wrote this in his REPORT OF WAR PATROL NUMBER ONE.

(A) PROLOGUE

U.S.S. LAGARTO commissioned at Manitowoc, Wisconsin, on 13 October 1945. Departed New Orleans 12 November 1944 for Panama. Training period 20 November – 5 December 1944, Captain John G. Johns,

USN Training Officer. Departed Balboa 9 December, arrived Pearl Harbor, 25 December. 26 December – 25 January, Training period, Captain Jesse L. Hull, USN, Training Officer, and special availability for accomplishment of following items –

- Installation of additional 5" gun and two 40mm mounts.
- Installation of two additional topside ready lockers.
- Installation of eight topside mounts for .50 cal. Machine guns.
- Installation of low pressure blower silencer.
- Installation of two Ion Exchangers.
- Installation of holding down stop for fully rigged out position on pit log.
- Installation of TDC speed having and range doubling adjustment.
- Installation of hydrogen elimination circuits in both torpedo rooms.
- Installation of whip antenna, two wing antennae and accompanying shear valves.
- Installation of APR, VHF, SCR equipment.
- Installation of booster blower in hull ventilation supply (aft. battery).
- Accomplishment of ShipAlt SS265A5 (design change in bow and stern plane hydraulic rams).
- Accomplishment of ShipAltSS239K-A (Modify roller supports in torpedo tube shutters).

- Accomplishment of OrdAlt2057 (Provide safety latch actuated by breach mechanism).
- Altered small arms magazine to accommodate additional 5" stowage, bringing total 5" capacity to 220 rounds.
- Repacked stern shafts twice.
- Replaced circulating fresh water cooler on number 3 main engine.
- Replace port propeller (Reported as "singing" on Panama Bay sound test).

(B) NARRATIVE

Officers attached as of 24 January 1945

• Commander F.D. LATTA	9 patrols
• Lieutenant W.H. MENDENHALL	3 patrols
• Lieutenant A.H. KEENEY	none
• Lieutenant W.R. SHAW	3 patrols
• Lieutenant R.T. RUBLE	none
• Lieutenant L.G. IRVING	none
• Lieut. (jg) H.A. TODD	none
• Ensign F.L. AUCHARD	none
• Ensign A.G. BREWINGTON	9 patrols

Chief Petty Officers attached as of 24 January 1945

• H.D. ANDREWS	CT(PA)	6 patrols
• F.D. TURNER	CGM (T)	6 patrols
• C.N. ANKER	CMOM (PA)	6 patrols
• W.L BRITAIN	CRM (AA)(T)	7 patrols

- J.R. JOHNSON 7 patrols
- G.A. PRICE 7 patrols
- R.B. SPAULDING CPhM(AA) 3 patrols

In addition to these 16 officers and chiefs, there were 70 enlisted men in *Lagarto's* crew.

Exhaustion
1945

Todd - 31 January 1945

My Darling Favorite Girl,

Holy Smokes!! Will this ever stop? Every time I breathe a sigh of relief 'cause we secured from doing something that takes a lot of time (in this case, finishing training) something else comes along that is just as grueling and time-consuming.

I've had seven hours sleep in the last 60 hours – in fact, I haven't even undressed for 48 – and no let-up in sight for a couple of days, at least. To top it off, we have about a 30 knot wind and awful heavy seas, and consequently, lots of fellas are sick...Ruble, Lloyd, Art (Keeney – new Engineer), and Bill, among the officers – and Les (Auchard) our new radar officer...which is rough on tempers. I had a headache for the first couple of days out, but now I feel pretty fit. When I get up on the bridge, I just feel tough and enthusiastic as hell, in fact. Just an old Sea dog at heart, I guess.

By the way, we have a photographer aboard who is taking still and moving shots for a movie they are going to make about submarines – he's taking pictures of all the officers in various phases of "Our Day." He's going right into the forward areas with us. Boy! Are we gonna get him some shots!!

Today – incidentally we're almost half-a-day ahead of you – we will pass within 60 miles of a Japanese-held island on our way to a place we took from them. Come to think of it, I think you saw those movies about three times.

Mabin – 5 February 1945
My Dearest Marg,

Surprise! I don't expect you thought you'd get a letter this soon from me, nor did I think you would. I may be able to write one more soon, but if it doesn't arrive soon after this one, just go back to holding your breath for a spell.

*Pete (*Bob Peterson) *kind of took advantage of me tonight. I came up to the conning tower to write about two hours ago and found Bob just finishing his letter. We've been discussing all the problems of the world, and even mentioned our wives now and then. It ends up that it's after midnight. His letter is finished and mine's just begun. This keeping up with the next guy in writing, because the wives may compare notes on just how many letters they've received, keeps me stepping.*

I saw (name cut out of letter) *today and had quite a chat with him. Don't know if you remember him or not. Also saw another kid who used to be on the* (another cut out). *I've seen several former shipmates since leaving home. They're spread around quite a bit.*

Good night, my darlings. Will say my nightly prayer for you both.

Newspaper Searches North and South 2005

Within days of sending out 43 press releases, we began to hear from reporters. The first to respond was Sam Knowlton, a journalist with *The Vicksburg* (Mississippi) *Post.* He called me and wanted to do a story on YN2 Charles W. Breithaupt Jr., who grew up in that town. Knowlton had done some digging of his own to find Breithaupt relatives, but had little success. Once again, Karen Duvalle and I were reminded that many of the next of kin would never be found. Knowlton thought it was a good story anyway and hoped it would help us find some relatives of Charles Breithaupt.

On October 11th, an article appeared in *The Vicksburg Post* and said, in part:

> "A memorial service for a World War II submarine crew that included a Vicksburg man has run into some snags, mainly that the U.S. Navy has not yet confirmed the discovery of the long-lost *U.S.S. Lagarto.* Charles Woodson Breithaupt Jr. of Vicksburg, believed to be a graduate of St. Aloysius High School, was one of 86 men on the boat when it disappeared in combat in the Siam

> Gulf, now called the Gulf of Thailand, in May 1945..."
>
> "At least one other Mississippian, Walter Jackson Rutledge of Tupelo, also died aboard the *Lagarto,"* ... "No direct family members of either he or Breithaupt have been located to inform them of the memorial service..."

The day after the article appeared, Duvalle and I both received phone calls from A.J. Breithaupt, one of Charles's brothers. He followed up with an e-mail that said in part:

> "I read an article in *The Vicksburg Post* yesterday regarding your attempts to identify the family of members of the *U.S.S. Lagarto.* Charles Breithaupt (nickname "Pug") is one of my older brothers. I was about 10 years old when we received word that his sub was missing. After World War II ended my mother did receive information from the Navy that an exchange of info with Japan indicated that my brother's sub was in the location that a Japanese ship claimed it had probably sunk a US sub. But there has not been actual confirmation. Also, earlier this year I had received info, from friends surfing the net, about

the discovery of a submarine, possibly the *Lagarto,* by a Thai diving group. I would be interested in any further info you are able to obtain and keep us informed about the possible memorial service. I mentioned to you that I have an older brother who lives in Odessa, Texas. I will also keep him informed."

The day after we received this note, Duvalle heard from Charlie Breithaupt:

"It was by accident that I found out about the article on the *U.S.S. Lagarto.* Charles Woodson Breithaupt was my uncle. He has a lot of family in Mississippi and other states still alive. ...My father, Ernest Breithaupt and Charles joined the Navy together. My dad was a Navy pilot. I have a lot of my uncle's keepsakes including his Purple Heart given to my grandmother. I was named after my uncle and grandfather..."

Later in the month, Duvalle and I received an e-mail from Lisa Howeler of the *Morning Times* in Sayre, Pennsylvania. She said she had found a niece and three nephews of S1 John Leslie Williams. Their names and addresses had been provided to her by an out of town gentleman, and she had not yet contacted them. She stated, "They would be John's sister's grandchildren," and indicated they were probably the only family members left.

Tragedy 1945

Tragedy struck *Lagarto* and *Haddock* on February 6th. An automobile accident on Saipan resulted in serious injuries to two of *Lagarto's* more experienced officers – Lieutenant Walter R. Shaw, a "mustang" (commissioned from the enlisted ranks), veteran of three war patrols, and Ensign Allen G. Brewington who, like Shaw, was a mustang but a veteran of nine patrols, including one in *Haddock* for which he earned the Silver Star. Additionally, the mishap also incapacitated three of *Haddock's* officers, including her skipper, Commander John P. "Beetle" Roach, who was a Naval Academy classmate of *Lagarto's* commanding officer. Consequently, Lieutenant Robert J. Williams (five war patrols) and Lieutenant (jg) Walter B. Phelps (four war patrols) arrived by air from Guam, reporting on board *Lagarto* on 7 February to replace Shaw and Brewington.

The following notations were taken from *Lagarto's* captain's log:

<u>6 February 1945</u>

2130 Automobile accident injured Comdr. J.P. ROACH, Lt.(jg) E. BOSTROM, Lt.(jg) P.C. TEACHEY, all from HADDOCK, and Lt. W.R. SHAW, Ens. A.G. BREWINGTON, from LAGARTO.

Transfer Lt. Shaw's and Ens. Brewington's records and accounts to SubRon EIGHT.

Todd – 7 February 1945

My Beebee,

It's awful late, Honey, but I had to write you this letter – not only because I wanted to, but also because it was an absolute necessity. You may hear that two of our officers met with Miss Fortune. This letter is primarily to prove it ain't neither one me. They were injured on the beach, not the boat – could have happened to anyone. To be honest, if I hadn't had the duty I might have been with them…

Darling little gal, it will now definitely be a long time between letters. I'd like to tell you all about the big way I love you and talk about a name for our little girl Beebee, if such be the case. That is the most important thing to me personally, but I gotta be sharp because tomorrow the safety of a lot of men and a boat may depend on me.

Pray for us, Honey. (And I'll pray Awful hard for you). Don't worry – we have lots of luck.

Todd - 7 February 1945

Dearest Lil' Nell,

Seems like every time I write "just one more letter," because something has come up, something else comes up. Here it is again…(This has gotta be short – gotta get this off before they take in the gangway.)

I guess you just must be in a sort of despondent stage, my darling – it's supposed to be normal. Don't let it get you down. You have a tough fight ahead, and I wish like all hell I could be there with you – but I can't and we can only do our best where we are.

All my love, for some time to come.

P.S. Walt may not live, and Al is all knocked up and won't go out with us. Do not write to Pat or Max first.

Underway on 7 February 1945, escorted by the motor minesweeper *YMS-426,* "Latta's Lancers" – *Lagarto, Haddock,* and *Sennet* (SS-408), part of Iwo Jima's "Operation Detachment," headed for the Bonin Islands to destroy Japanese picket boats. Releasing *YMS*-426 at midnight, *Lagarto* decoded a dispatch a little over two hours into the mid watch on 8 February communicating the sad news that Lieutenant Shaw had died of injuries suffered in the automobile accident on the 6th. At noon the same day (8 February), while *Lagarto* mourned the loss of one of her officers, CDR Latta informed the wolf pack that its being behind schedule would not permit coordinated practice firing.

<u>8 February 1945</u>

0000 Released escort, formed task group in line of bearing, increased speed to 17 knots.

0223 Decoded ComSubPac dispatch notifying us of the death of lieut. Walter R. SHAW, U.S.N.

<u>9 February 1945</u>

1200 Latitude 20 – 55N, Longitude 137 – 47E.

1647 Number 2 main engine out of commission with 2 broken head bolts.

<u>10 February 1945</u>

0235 Number 2 main engine back in commission.

1002 HADDOCK reported sighting a periscope at 2000 yards to westward. HADDOCK turned away, other boats being to eastward were well clear. Contact unconfirmed by OOD or C.O. Did not send contact report.

1200 Latitude 26 – 04N, Longitude 137 – 35E.

In a letter to his wife, Lt. William Mendenhall, *Lagarto's* executive officer wrote:

8 February 1945

"I have been busier than ever the last couple of days, and I can see now that I will continue to be throughout the patrol. It looks good though and you'll be hearing about us...

...Needless to say the loss of Walt and Al has left us in a pretty unsettled condition. We got a couple of nice replacements – both good eggs and good submariners. Actually we now have more experienced officers on board than we had before. However it has disrupted our organization somewhat and it's too late now to do much training. Just think out of 8 officers who went to New London for training only four are left, the skipper, Hal, Lloyd and me...

...We have been too busy to get any news the last couple of days. The last I heard the Russians were 35 miles from Berlin and we had Manila. Those were big developments. I wonder if the Manitowoc radio station announcer puts any life into his voice when he reads the 'Distance to Berlin' now"...

The Pekin Daily Times: Richard Louis Fisher, MoMM1

On the same day the article in *The Vicksburg Post* ran, I received an e-mail from Jared Olar, a staff writer with the *Pekin* (IL) *Daily Times*. He was asked by his editor to see if he could find any surviving family of Motor Machinist Mate First Class Richard L. Fisher. Olar's search became one of the most intense of all the reporters looking for *Lagarto* family. It began with good, old-fashioned shoe leather, and Olar described the search to me in a series of fast and furious e-mails.

His search began by visiting the Tazewell County Courthouse in Pekin. There he saw three war memorials – one inside the courthouse with the names of all the Tazewell County's veterans who served in World War II, the second outside inscribed with the names of those killed in WWII, and the third memorial stood on the lawn outside the courthouse; they were several tall black marble monuments, engraved with all the county's fallen soldiers' names, branch of service, and date of death.

In the courthouse, Olar looked up Fisher's birth certificate and searched for information indicating possible siblings. This effort bore little fruit. In spite of this, Olar said he would continue the search and keep me informed.

Later that day, I sent Jared Olar the following response:

> You have quite a task before you. I would be happy to help you in any way I can. The information we have on MoMM1 Richard Louis Fisher is extremely sparse. I do not believe that Mr. Fisher was married, so there won't be any descendants. You can only hope to find siblings, cousins, or nieces and nephews. ...We are having difficulty finding many families for just this reason – they do not have descendants.
>
> However, you may find classmates or friends in the area who knew Mr. Fisher. The story that develops may become something you don't expect.
>
> ...Hopefully your article will have amazing results. At the very least, it will be a great tribute to an area man who gave his life for his country. ...Just a couple of tidbits. ...MoMM stands for Motor Machinist's Mate, and the 1 is first class. This means that Mr. Fisher was very experienced in his area of expertise. ...Illinois had many men who lost their lives on *Lagarto*. They were from Pekin, Tunnel Hill, La Grange (my father), Mattoon, Rockford, and Chicago. ...Let me know if I can help you further. Good luck!

Two hours later, Olar replied. In the County Clerk's Office, he found the names of Fisher's parents and birth records of his siblings. His next tasks were to get a copy of Fisher's high school yearbook, primarily to find a photo, and then look for Fisher's siblings to find out when and to whom they were married and who their children were.

I wrote Olar an early-morning e-mail at 5 AM:

> Wow! You are quite the genealogist! I just recalled that a good friend of mine, who is the president of the La Grange Historical Society, told me that the historical societies in the area can help. It's kind of an exciting project – engaging all sorts of people in the search. You may be surprised with what you come up with. We've had good luck with the high schools.
>
> I noticed that Pekin is close to Peoria. Do you think Bradley Univ. might be interested in doing research? Just a thought. Good luck...

That afternoon, Olar responded with an update. He planned to contact their historical society and later talk to someone at the high school about their old yearbooks.

He had already searched the marriage records of Fisher's siblings, but found nothing. He also couldn't find a death certificate for Fisher's father, but did find one for his mother. He then went to Lakeside Cemetery to find Minnie Fisher's grave, but their records didn't show where her burial plot would have been. Olar was told that either the cemetery's records were incomplete or she was buried in an unmarked grave. Records for the old part of the cemetery weren't that good, they said, and that's where Minnie would probably have been buried.

However, Lakeside Cemetery did have records of the burial of a George T. Fisher, who died on February 28, 1934, assumedly Richard's father. Olar's task that afternoon was to find that grave and see if other relatives might be buried nearby.

It was a busy day for Jared Olar, but he achieved success. He found the graves of Fisher's parents, two of his sisters, and an unnamed baby. They were all part of the Fisher family plot with a very nice grave marker displaying names and dates. Next to the marker was a weathered American flag placed there by the United Spanish War Veterans.

Olar kept going. He went to the Pekin Community High School but didn't find anything on Richard Fisher.

I responded to this latest piece of information:

> If the trail goes cold, have you thought of writing the story as sort of a community mystery? Here's a family who lived in Pekin (and died), and no trace can be found! Somebody must know something.

Olar responded that the newspaper was going to run a big story on Richard Fisher, even if they couldn't find any family or friends. He thought the story might be read by people who remembered him.

He contacted the Navy to find out when and where Richard Fisher joined up. He also searched the paper's archives for a death notice on Fisher. That effort had a successful outcome. An obituary in the *Pekin Daily Times* read:

> Richard Louis Fisher, MM1c, U.S. Navy, has been listed MISSING IN ACTION on April 15, (sic) 1945, following the announcement that his submarine, *Lagarto,* was missing and presumed lost.
>
> The 24-year-old Sailor made his home with his brother-in-law and sister, Mr. and Mrs. Alva Manhusen, 1523 Center Street, Pekin, Illinois, until entering the Navy in August, 1940. In June of the year he graduated from PCHS. Fisher was on the *USS Nevada* before the war broke out, and he later was stationed for a time on *USS Indianapolis,* which was sunk on July 30, 1945.
>
> Fisher took sub training at New London, Connecticut, and was assigned to the sub *Lagarto,* newly commissioned November, 1944. His last letter to his sister was written March 27, 1945, and the family believes he may have been lost since April.

> Richard Louis Fisher was the son of Mr. and Mrs. George T. Fisher, both deceased, and the following brothers and sisters – Fred C. Fisher, storekeeper 2/c, Admiralty Islands, Capt. George J. Fisher, U.S. Engineers, New York, Mrs. Walter J. Stanley, Chicago, Mrs. Frank Wonder, Miami, Florida, Mrs. Ralph Hoppe, Peoria, and Mrs. Manhusen, Pekin, all survive.

This obituary gave Olar a lot of information, and he expanded his search for the relatives, many of whom were last known living in distant states.

The next e-mail I received from the dogged reporter was filled with news. He checked the high school library and discovered that Fisher had indeed graduated from Pekin High School in 1940 and was listed under the heading of Camera Shy Seniors.

Olar's big break came when he found the death notice of Richard's older brother Fred, which ran in the *Daily Times* on January 8, 1996. The obituary listed his survivors; two of them, Judy Kluever and Carol Lawson, still lived in Pekin. In fact, Judy Kluever was married to a former City of Pekin employee. She remembered Richard Fisher coming home on leave from the Navy and her mother, Ruby Theodora (Fisher) Manhusen, receiving the 1945 telegram stating the *Lagarto* was missing and presumed lost. After his mother's death, Richard lived with his sister Ruby, who became his surrogate mother for the rest of his teens. Judy Kleuver said

Richard was "ornery," and thinks he broke his nose in a boxing match while in the Navy.

Kleuver's cousin Glen Bolander, son of Fisher's sister Myrtle, was also reared by her mother, Ruby Manhusen. Bolander remembered Fisher best; they were close in age and became companions. Kleuver told Olar that her sister, Carol Lawson had the family photo album, which had photos of Fisher.

Jared Olar found that the Fisher family had been prominent Pekin residents. Richard Fisher's father had built numerous homes in the town, and a street and subdivision bore the Fisher name, as well as Jerome St., named after Richard's brother George Jerome.

Olar wrote a wonderful article that covered several pages of *The Pekin Daily*. The perseverance of reporters like Jared Olar touched our hearts, and they became invaluable allies in our search for *Lagarto* relatives. And more were to come!

The Navy - Pearl Harbor 2005

With so much interest from the press, we *Lagartos* were thrilled and encouraged to keep going. There was a lot ahead of us.

The only regret I had was that we still hadn't connected with the Navy.

It was maddening. As a result of this frustration, I fired off e-mails and made phone calls to everyone I could think of to get help in getting through to the Navy. As each *Lagarto* family was found, always asking what they could do, I gave them the names of their state's U.S. senator and suggested they contact them for help. We were developing a large number of supporters from *Lagarto* families, their friends, and folks who contacted Karen Duvalle or myself through reading the newspaper articles.

The break-through came on November 3rd. As fate would have it, I was suffering from the flu and was taking a nap. Things always seem to happen when I try to nap.

Lt. Commander Jeff Davis, the Public Affairs Officer for the U.S. Pacific Fleet Submarine Command in Pearl Harbor, called me. He introduced himself and told me how interested the Navy was in the *Lagarto* story. He informed me that on the upcoming Veterans' Day ceremony at the Pearl Harbor submarine base, there would be a special tribute to *Lagarto.* Every year at this time, all submarines lost in WWII were honored at the submarine base. However, with this exciting news of *Lagarto's* discovery, it was decided to give the submarine some extra attention. LCDR Davis advised that if the families would like their own wreath laid at the ceremony, the Navy would be happy to include it. He gave me the name of a florist, and I ordered a wreath with red, white (orchids) and blue flowers in it, along with a blue banner that read "With Reverence and Respect from the *Lagarto* Families." Commander Davis also gave me the phone number of the Navy Office of Casualty Affairs to see if they could shed some light on the *Lagarto* matter.

LCDR Davis couldn't have been nicer or more helpful. He reassured me that the Navy was very interested in *Lagarto* and would be glad to help with the memorial service we were planning in Manitowoc the following May.

The next day I received another call from Pearl Harbor, this time from Chief David Rush. He called to interview me for an article for a Navy publication. I then made a call to a Lt. Sanchez, the contact given me by LCDR Davis. We had a pleasant conversation, although we were both rasping and wheezing the entire time we talked. His cold sounded worse than mine.

At this point, I felt much more at ease with the Navy and was happy with the interest and involvement of LCDR Davis. I had worked for months to get the Navy's attention, and at last I heard from them. It pleased me to know that the Navy was interested in *Lagarto* and would henceforth be a partner of some sort in the submarine families' goal of honoring her.

Momentum
2005

Momentum started to build in our quest to find *Lagarto* families and gain support from the Navy. LCDR Davis and I began to build a rapport with each other. He made me feel comfortable in knowing I could contact him whenever I needed to.

There was a lovely Veterans' Day Ceremony in Pearl Harbor and LCDR Davis sent me a video and a copy of the program, as well as a copy of the remarks made at the ceremony by RADM James Beebe. Those remarks included mention of *Lagarto:*

> "Just this past May, a British wreck diver named Jamie MacLeod was diving in the Gulf of Thailand when he came upon an awesome sight," Beebe said. "Resting on the seabed about 200 feet below the surface, in crystal clear water, sat a submarine. After cross-referencing it with war-time records, his team concluded that it was likely the *USS Lagarto.*
>
> "*USS Lagarto* was a Balao-class boat, one of 28 produced during World War II by the Manitowoc Shipbuilding Company in Wisconsin. On April 12, 1945, it left Subic Bay in the Philippines with 86 souls onboard bound for the Gulf of Si-

am, where it rendezvoused with USS Baya and got into position to attack a Japanese convoy. On the night of May 3, 1945, as the convoy approached, Baya was detected and driven off. But nothing was ever heard again from *Lagarto*. It was supposed to dock in Australia at the end of May...but it never arrived.

"After the war ended, Japan released records showing that it had sunk a submarine at the same time and same place as *Lagarto's* last known position. And so, *USS Lagarto* joined the solemn list of those boats lost during the war...one of the 52 boats still on patrol. For the family members, their worry and uncertainty slowly turned to sorrow and grief. But as with all who lost loved ones in war, they also had a great sense of pride in knowing that the loss was not in vain...rather, it was in service to our nation.

"I mention the story of *USS Lagarto* for two reasons. First, of course, because it is current news – something that many of you have likely read about recently – and something that has brought a much needed sense of closure to the families of the men who were killed aboard her.

"But I bring up *Lagarto* for another reason as well. You see, when Jamie MacLeod and his team were inspecting the wreck earlier this year, they noticed something. On the port side, the middle torpedo tube was open. And the torpedo inside was missing. Though we can't be sure, it certainly suggests that the torpedo had been fired...and the *Lagarto* went down fighting.

"I believe that is indicative of all the submarines that served in World War II. Under the most perilous of conditions, they stayed focused on the mission. They were ready to go down fighting if need be...and sadly, many of them did. But they were successful in their mission...and for that our nation is eternally grateful..."

This gesture on the part of the Navy was a balm to the nerves of the *Lagarto* families and was appreciated.

Gratifying as well was the discovery of more *Lagarto* families. We heard from the nephew of TM3 Walter E. Hinken, who lived in Michigan. Hinken's nephew spoke with reverence of his uncle – and his father – who both served in World War II. He said that the knowledge of *Lagarto's* discovery had given their family great comfort.

On November 12, I received an e-mail from Ray "Chic" Eads, a close friend of S1 William H. Jordan, Jr. of Charleston, West Virginia. He said:

Dear Nancy,

I have just discovered the *Lagarto* has been found. For 60 years I have wondered how my best friend, with whom I enlisted in the Navy in 1942, died. His name was William H. Jordan, Jr. He was a S1c

> on board the *Lagarto*. My eldest son was named after Billy. It is really wonderful to know that at last there is an answer to where he is. I always knew he died fighting for what we both believed in. I am one of the lucky ones for whom they died. I made it back from N. Africa and Sicily and managed to spend a weekend with Billy in New London before he left there. That is the last I heard from him until his Mother informed me of the loss of the *Lagarto*....
>
> My condolences and deepest regards to you and all the other families."

Gradually more and more *Lagarto* families were hearing of the news and contacting Karen Duvalle and myself. We knew that with the Christmas holidays around the corner, there would be a lull in our momentum, but there was no question we would stay on top of our goal to find more families. We needed to do more to find other families.

On December 2, a cold, snowy evening, Michigan U.S. Senator Carl Levin braved the icy weather and ventured into Leelanau County for a visit. He held a town meeting at the Leland library, and in spite of the frigid night, the room was packed. Senator Levin was accompanied by his Traverse City Regional representative Harold Chase, with whom I had spoken earlier about the *Lagarto* situation.

I realized that many constituents wanted to speak to Senator Levin that night, and I worried about my chances of connecting with him. As Senator Levin wound up his remarks, I wove my way through the dense crowd to get closer to the door. As he made his way outside, I hurried after him. I felt guilty about pursuing him as he was overcoatless and probably tired from a long day and anxious to get home. But Carl Levin was a gentleman, and when I told him who I was (he had been briefed on the *Lagarto* situation), he took my hand and gave me his full attention. After a short conversation (it was really snowing hard by this time), I gave him some information I had prepared and asked him to look it over. He assured me he would, expressed his condolences on the deaths and bravery of *Lagarto's* crew and left. I felt reassured that he was sincere, and I was right.

VALENTINE

I've looked and looked, sweet love of mine,
Hoping to find a valentine.
That's nice enough to send to you.
But absolutely none will do.

Superlatives must "super" be
To say half what you mean to me;
The sweetest songs still understate
Exactly, dear, how well you rate.

For years and years you've been my life,
And Heaven let me be your wife.
Mere printed words could never say
How much that means to me each day.

Somebody's way of making money –
A stranger's bleak "I love You, Honey" –
Neat little words placed on a line,
A cold and sterile Valentine.

Margaret Mabin

Operation Detachment 1945

In January 1945, many in the military believed the war was winding down.

Lagarto's first mission was her most important – and most dangerous. *Lagarto, Sennet,* and *Haddock* were part of a "wolf-pack" under the command of Commander Frank Latta. The wolf-pack was dubbed "Latta's Lancers." The submarines were part of "Operation Detachment," which was devised for the capture of Iwo Jima. Their assignment: a submarine sweep to clear the carrier route of picket boats.

According to *United States SUBMARINE OPERATIONS in World War II,* written by Theodore Roscoe and published in 1949:

> "A double sweep was designed – one group of sweepers to clear the path for the aircraft carriers, and a second and smaller group to create a diversion by sweeping an 'off the trail' path...The diversionary sweep was assigned to 'Latta's Lances' (sic) – *Haddock, Lagarto,* and *Sennet* under Commander F.D. Latta, captain of *Lagarto.*"

The submarines were specially equipped for this operation – including a second 5" deck gun. *Haddock,*

Lagarto, and *Sennet* were the only submarines in the Navy that carried the second 5" deck gun.

Roscoe said, 'Latta's Lances' – the diversionary sweepers – were instructed to attack the pickets with gunfire, but not to sink them until they had time to send out a radio alarm. By this stratagem, Latta's wolf-pack would decoy the enemy to the area it was sweeping – divert him from the scene of the main sweep. The 'Lances,' it may be observed, were to take hold of the thorny end of the stick. And the thornier it was – the more enemy aircraft and A/S (anti-submarine) vessels they attracted to their area – the better it served the devices of 'Operation Detachment.'

Latta's wolf-pack began its diversionary sweep on the morning of February 11 at 0800. Striking the picket line in broad daylight, the 'Lances' rattled against the pickets and created a fine uproar. In the process they sank two picket boats. The diversion was a complete success."

LATTA'S LOG

11 February

0800 Entered assigned patrol area. Formed line of bearing, searching for picket boats.

1200 Latitude 30 – 16N, Longitude 139 – 16E.

12 February

1200 Latitude 30 – 00N, Longitude 139 – 16E.

1615 Sighted four B-29s, contacted two of them by VHF and received dope on picket vessels.

2300 HADDOCK made contact. Ordered SENNET and LAGARTO clear while HADDOCK determined contact to be two small vessels, speed zero. With excellent SCR communication, outlined plan to other skippers as easily as if we were in the same wardroom. Ordered SENNET to westward, maintaining contact with LAGARTO by SJ. LAGARTO maintaining contact with HADDOCK by SJ.

13 February

0002 SENNET in contact, targets still lying to, apparently not alerted. Ordered HADDOCK to break off contact and formed line of bearing on SENNET.

0415 Began opening out to westward.

0540 Heading in on surface toward last known position of targets, in line of bearing, communication, outlined to both skippers a plan previously proposed by Comdr. Porter. Ordered HADDOCK with no 5" ammunition remaining, to remain in contact with targets while SENNET and LAGARTO opened to westward as before. SENNET and LAGARTO to attack at dawn with gunfire and HADDOCK make submerged torpedo attack at close range. Ordered HADDOCK to be in position by 0640. Formed line of bearing with SENNET to north and stood to west.

<u>14 February</u>

0550 Began easterly approach for attack. No likelihood of bright eastern sky today, all heavy gray overcast and seas less favorable to gun firing.

0605 Stations for battle surface.

0647 Opened fire on right hand vessel, range 5600, swinging right to bring both guns to bear. Cold seas washing over gun crews. Target return fire heavier than yesterday, but targets slower getting underway.

0700 At 4100 yards, all 5" ammunition expended from both SENNET and LAGARTO, no full bodied torpedo explosion as had been expected. Broke off attack and retired to southward. SENNET reported one man wounded by shrapnel, several holes in superstructure. Targets had been hit repeatedly by 40mm and 2 or 3 hits by 5".

0800 Detached SENNET to proceed to assigned patrol area.

1200 Latitude 30 – 18N, Longitude 135 – 42E.

1515 Ordered HADDOCK to proceed to patrol area HEARTH until 21st while we patrol ROASTER, then to shift areas. LAGARTO remaining in this area to LAGARTO guide, SENNET left and HADDOCK right flank, spacing 3000 yards. Planned to close to 7000 yards, then turn right about 50 degrees, to put seas and wind in most favorable position and still close range. SENNET to take northern picket, HADDOCK southern, LAGARTO to direct fire to larger or whichever one appeared to be offering most opposition.

0620 Manned battle surface stations.

0723 Opened fire. Japs began jabbering in high gear on 4475 KCS! Target nicely outlined against red eastern sky. Photographer in happy daze of "Oh boy, Oh boy!" See Gun Attack No. 1.

0739 SENNET hastened sinking of second burning picket boat with a couple of rounds of 5" from close range. No survivors. Formed scouting line and continued search.

1131 Lookout sighted Jap "BETTY" crossing our stern, heading for HADDOCK. Dived. Heard several explosions. Stayed down for lunch.

1200 Latitude 30 – 00N, Longitude 135 – 54E.

1258 Surfaced.

1900 Received contact report from HADDOCK.

1930 Exchanged calls with SENNET by SJ, ordered SENNET and LAGARTO to close HADDOCK. Our choice of direction is biased, neither boat having had a sight in two days. Porter and I agreed on a compromise.

2249 Contact with HADDOCK by SJ. When within range of good SCR transmit tonight.

2200 Cleared ComTaskGroup 17.13 dispatch 140615 to ComSubPac.

The two Japanese vessels sunk by Latta's wolf-pack were *No. 8 Kotoshiro Maru* and *No. 3 Showa Maru.* They went down with all hands. Although *Sennet* reported one man wounded and damage to her superstructure, *Lagarto* came out of the fierce battle unscathed.

Excerpts from executive officer Bill Mendenhall's letters to his wife:

14 February 1945

The Lagarto has now been tried in battle and I might say conducted herself creditably. More specific than that I cannot be. It was an experience I will have to tell you about in my next morning report.

The skipper and I work very well together I believe. That is not much credit to me because I believe anybody could work well with him. But any decision we have to make, he always discusses with me and respects my judgment. This exec. Job is a sweet one just because of that. You are 'in' on so much of the planning that it makes for a much more interesting time.

I still feel guilty not standing watches but the skipper has said positively that he does not want me to. Because when the heat is on, he and I have to be up all of the time. But even with that, it certainly makes for a much easier time of it at sea.

We are actually pretty well along on this patrol now, and so far it hasn't been half bad. But the thought of many months ahead when I will not see you is awfully discouraging...

17 February 1945

You are undoubtedly as excited over news of the carrier strikes over Tokyo as we are. It seems truly now as Churchill said prematurely six months ago 'Victory is everywhere.' Some of us are beginning to get hopes of being home for good this year. I hate to let myself hope that in one way, and yet in another it helps to keep me going...

...We have only heard scraps of news from the Crimean conference and so do not have any idea of what has been announced. From the repercussions I would guess that the decision about Poland hasn't satisfied everybody by a darn site...

19 February 1945

I imagine that everybody at home is agog now with the news of the Tokyo raid and the landing at Iwo Jima. We certainly are. The wardroom radio has been going all day with the news. It is something to hear the enemy broadcasts and then ours...

Because *Lagarto's* crew could not tell their families about their part in the Iwo Jima invasion, most of them didn't know the role the submarine played in "Operation Detachment."

Some fifty years after that famous historic episode in the Second World War, my mother applied for a copy of her husband Bill Mabin's war records. It wasn't until she received that report that she had any idea that

Lagarto had played a crucial role in that decisive Japanese invasion.

Cleveland Plain Dealer 2005

Of the thirty-two states represented by *Lagarto's* crew, the state of Ohio lost the most men. In 2005, their families were spread across the country, but during World War II, ten Ohio men who entered the Navy lost their lives on the ill-fated submarine. On October 12th, I received a quick response to my press release from Tom O'Hara of the *Cleveland Plain Dealer.* Mr. O'Hara sent me a short e-mail to let me know that the newspaper was considering doing an article on *Lagarto.* A day later, I received another message from Elizabeth McIntyre, then Assistant Managing Editor of the paper's Metro section, saying the paper had assigned a reporter to look into the matter further.

The next day, Karen Duvalle and I received e-mails from reporter Donna Iacoboni saying she was writing a story about the *Lagarto* crew from Ohio. Right off the bat, she had plenty of questions. Duvalle and I were ready for her, and a lengthy exchange of e-mails transpired between the three of us for a month.

Donna Iacoboni, as Jared Olar and the other reporters, did her homework and tried to find families before the article appeared. She visited war memorials in the Cleveland area and contacted high schools, city directories, probate court records, and the Western Reserve Historical Society. She came up dry.

Be that as it may, she wrote an article that included the names and home towns of all the Ohio men lost on *Lagarto,* and we all hoped for the best. It said, in part:

> Friday was the first Veterans Day that the families of 86 men who died aboard the WWII submarine *USS Lagarto* knew where the men are buried. At sea. At the bottom of the Gulf of Thailand.

In the article, she mentioned that ten of them were from Ohio and asked that anyone related to the men contact the Wisconsin Maritime Museum. They were:

Lloyd Raymond O'Hara, Cleveland
Louis Jerome Lynch, Cleveland Heights
Lloyd Gordon Irving, Cleveland Heights
Clark Richard Byrer, Canton
Joy McDowell Marriot, Columbus
John William Kneidel, Dayton
Gerald Allen Price, Elida
James Northrup Gerlach, Oregon
Albert Kirtley, Springfield
Raymond Edward Reichert, Toledo

Karen Duvalle and I knew the families of two of the Ohio men, but as a result of this article, we were soon to know more.

RT2 Lloyd R. O'Hara

After the article about *Lagarto* appeared in the *Cleveland Plain Dealer,* Karen Duvalle was contacted by a woman named Betty St. John. Betty was a good friend of Lloyd O'Hara's as she went to school with him and was his date for the senior prom.

Betty became close to Lloyd's mother after he died. Lloyd's mom was widowed when her son was twelve, and he was an only child. Lloyd was all his mother had. This necessitated hard work for Mrs. O'Hara. She went to work at a company that made upholstery for cars, where she operated heavy-duty sewing machines. Since she didn't have a car, she walked everywhere, including work every day.

When the building with her little apartment was sold, she had to find another place to live. Mrs. O'Hara bought a small house with her son's death benefits and felt very guilty about it. Betty assured her that her son would want this for her.

For a long time, Mrs. O'Hara kept the hope that her son might still be alive, possibly on an island somewhere. One day, the *Plain Dealer* published a photograph of some men on a raft. Mrs. O'Hara was convinced her son was one of them. She asked Betty to go to the newspaper office to see the original photo. Betty found, of course, that Lloyd wasn't the man in the picture.

Over the years, Betty and her family stayed close to Mrs. O'Hara, who became a grandmother to Betty's children. They celebrated all the holidays together. Betty had become Mrs. O'Hara's family after her son was gone. There was no one else.

Seeing the article about *Lagarto's* discovery was a huge shock to Betty. She never thought the submarine would be found. Betty lamented the fact (as all the *Lagarto* families did) that Lloyd's mother was not alive to learn the news of her son's final resting place.

Quiet Danger
1945

For the better part of the next ten days, *Lagarto* dealt with the routine of being a submarine at war. On the 17th, 19th and 20th of February, Japanese BETTYs were sighted, necessitating dives. On the 18th, the officer on duty thought he saw a periscope, but nothing came of it. Radar picked up an enemy, and *Lagarto* dove. There were also mechanical glitches with some communications equipment, and the No. 1 main engine went out of commission. These problems were quickly repaired by communications officer Hal Todd and chief radioman, Wardour Britain. Latta wrote in *Lagarto's* log "Caught up on all serials during night."

On 21 February, Hal Todd got a chance to write his wife:

<u>Todd – 21 February 1945</u>

Darlin' Li'l Nell,

Here I go, neglecting you again. This going on watch for four hours sure takes up your time. Couple that with doing normal communications work, taking enlisted men through the boat to qualify them, and trying to learn something myself, and you have a pretty full day. (Our watch standing is on for four – either at dive or surface, four hours decoding, then off for sometimes six, sometimes eight.) Oh, yeah, we sleep once in awhile, too. I've averaged about five or six hours in twenty four since we left – never have gotten more than 3 ½ hours at one time.

The longer I work on this qualification, the more there is to know. I think by the end of April or May I will be able to go through a qualifying board....I sure as hell hope so, so you can wear your dolphins **(insignia worn by those qualified as submariners)**.

I just realized I've been spending all my letters telling you my problems, when you – we, that is – have a bigger one coming up and I haven't said much about it. Mike, I mean. I've never wished for anything more in life... **(than to)** be with you while you're going through this big thing that's so important to us. I guess I wouldn't be much good, but just to be there where I could watch out for you and take care of you....would sure help a lot. I know you must get lonesome at times and sometimes a little scared. You're being so damn brave and light-hearted about it, and it's made me love you more – more than I thought possible. ...Just remember that I pray for you every chance I get...

When I get back, I'll never again leave you in the lurch like I did this time, heel that I am. I'm going to do so many things for you, that you'll think you're queen of the world. As far as I'm concerned that'll make it unanimous.

The best part about it is that it won't be too long to wait – just think, I've been gone a third of a year already – a third of a year since I kissed the most wonderful favorite girl in the world good bye in front of the Roosevelt in New Orleans. And there's always the possibility of getting home sooner than we expected. Keep your fingers crossed.

Action! 1945

Theodore Roscoe related in *United States SUBMARINE Operations in World War II* that there was heavy action in the South Pacific at this time, and *Lagarto* was part of it. According to Roscoe,

> ...*Lagarto* (Commander F.D. Latta) stepped in to make it a record anti-submarine month for the American undersea arm. The A/S bout came as a sequel to the diversionary anti-picket boat sweep which *Lagarto* had led two weeks before. ...There, off the Bungo Suido on February 24, *Lagarto* sank a small freighter. Not long afterward she spotted a Japanese submersible. Day-periscope attack resulted in a whacking hit.

Notations in Commander Latta's log show that 24 February was indeed a very busy day for the *Lagarto* crew:

<u>24 February</u>

0619 Dived for submerged patrol off OKINO SHIMA.

1000 Photographed OKINO SHIMA.

1050 JP contact and sighted top of ship, range 5000 yards.

1058 Identified ship as Japanese RC Class submarine.

1113 Fired four torpedoes. See torpedo attack No. 1. One torpedo reported running erratic, ordered 150 feet. This was an erroneous report as all four torpedoes later tracked down to target, however, we were below periscope depth.

1117 Torpedo explosion. Target screws stopped.

1118 Torpedo explosion. This interval greater than maximum firing interval, later analysis showed this torpedo to be number 2, and detonating against OKINO SHIMA.

1126 Heavy underwater explosion like collapsed hull.

1150 All clear by periscope.

1200 Latitude 32 – 38N, Longitude 132 – 35E.

1346 Sighted 7 planes, similar to (unreadable) flying in long column to southward, distant about 5 miles.

1602 Distant depth charge.

1716 Seven distant, heavy depth charge explosions, preceded by pronounced click. Nothing in sight through periscope. Hope HADDOCK is not paying for our attack.

1904 Surfaced.

While the next day did not produce the same violent action, the turbulent sea could not have made it easy for the crew.

25 February

0627 Dived for submerged patrol off VAN DIEMEN STRAIT. Seas very heavy, depth control difficult. Rolling 8-10 degrees at 80 feet between observations.

1045 Conducted Diving Services.

1200 Latitude 30 – 52N, Longitude 131 – 19E.

1834 Surfaced in very heavy seas.

Harold Todd found time to write his wife:

Todd - 25 February 1945

Dearest Beebee,

Well – things are turning out quite well – better than we had expected. It's the same old wheeze, of course – "I'll tell you about it after this is over." Wish I could tell you now, 'cause I know you'd like to cut in on the dope, but I'm sure you understand.

It sure has been rough these last couple of days – never know what to expect. The guys are bearing up remarkably well, considering everything. A little more nervous, perhaps, and not quite so heavy, but morale is high.

It is quite a strain, at that...when you're submerged, you're comparatively safe, but still listening for every little thing. On the surface, it's a "damsite" more strenuous. When you have the deck, you go nuts trying to keep your eyes open for everything. Porpoises are torpedoes, and their fins are periscopes, and every dark cloud either hides a plane or makes you think there's one there. Even a harmless little bird flying along damn near makes you jump off the bridge. The phosphorescence of a wave turning over – not the female kind **(Women in the Navy during World War II were known as Waves)** – looks like a torpedo wake or the bow of a ship. But just so long as porpoises stay porpoises, and fins stay fins, we'll be happy.

We do have lots of things to take our minds off the situation – like last night we made fudge (imagine Lloyd and me wrestling to see who got the pot to lick, then both of us eating out of it like a couple of ten year old brothers.) It'll be great to knock this off, though, and get back to my darling little wife.

Routine War Time Danger 1945

Not all days were filled with fighting, but they were full of danger, no less – as Commander Latta's entries in *Lagarto's* daily log showed.

<u>26 February</u>

0612 Dived for submerged patrol off BUNGO SUIDO.
1140 Sighted tops of four ships, battle stations submerged.

1155 Identified ships as small wooden hull light draft, picket vessels, similar to those attacked by gunfire early in patrol. Estimated draft about 3 feet. Considered not worth torpedo expenditure. Pickets were in column, tracking at 12 knots.

1200 Latitude 32 – 40N, Longitude 132 – 35E.

1215 Sighted two more picket vessels, on same course, trailing other four. Photographed nearest one (2500 yards).

1234 Nothing following these lads, secured from battle stations.

1815 JP reports usual twilight pinging and screws, nothing sighted.

1839 Surfaced.

1958 Began transmission of LAGARTO FOUR to ComSubPacAdComd.

2100 Completed transmission.

<u>27 February</u>

0620 Dived for submerge patrol off BUNGO SUIDO.

1200 Latitude 32 – 33N, Longitude 132 – 17E. Radar officer worked over APR gear while submerged today with result that we were never long without an APR contact throughout the night. Only those which might conceivably have a bearing on the sighting of the midget submarine are reported in this narrative.

1844 Surfaced.

1850 APR contact 156 mgs., tried swinging ship to obtain maximum and minimum signals and thus determine direction of contact. Efforts proved fruitless, decided it was shore-based radar, sweeping across and occasionally settling on us.

2025 APR contact 154 mgs.

2039 O.O.D. sighted an object showing a distinct wake, which he described as similar to the conning tower of a midget submarine. Range estimated varied from 500 to 1200 yards, bearing on starboard bow. Turned toward and increased speed to flank. Nothing further seen or heard. We had been zigzagging by Arma Clock in brilliant moonlight and fairly calm sea with only occasional white-caps. C.O. did not sight object.

2111 APR contact, 155 mgs. – and so on through the night!

For the next few days, CDR Latta's log entries show routine activities. They mention a few plane sightings – and the dives that followed. On March 5, the log states:

1111 Sighted a plane, SD contact 17 miles, did not dive.
1135 Sighted plane, about 15 miles, did not dive.
1200 Latitude 32 – 19N, Longitude 133 – 26E.
1254 Sighted floating mine. Case was a rusty sphere about 30" diameter, studded with 6" horns. Carbine fire only chipped off rust flakes. Sank mine with .50 Cal.

Occasionally the monotony of being constantly on vigil was broken. On March 13, while on submerged patrol off VAN DIEMAN STRAITS, CDR Latta notes:

0732 Sighted about 30 small, single-masted, Marconi rigged sail boats. They were about four miles off the beach and looked very much like a racing regatta rather than fishermen. Their sails were unusually clean and white.

Then things got interesting. At 0612 on 14 March, *Lagarto* sighted a submarine through her high periscope, and began calling *Haddock* on the SCR. At 0648, however, *Lagarto* sighted another submarine on an opposite bearing. "One of them," Latta later recounted, "is probably enemy – but which?" The log entries contine:

0703 Established voice communication with HADDOCK, identified her as first submarine contacted and advised her of second contact. Enemy submarine tracking on base course 165, speed 12, bearing 146 T. HADDOCK has four engines to our three. Directed her to make end around and when in favorable position to attack. Tracked enemy all morning, gradually improving bearing. Identified her as I-class submarine. HADDOCK's four engines are not sufficient to overtake us making full on three. Looks like we may be able to make first attack. Bearing on enemy at noon had decreased to 125 T, base course 170, speed 12, range about 9 miles.

1200 Latitude 29–54N,Longitude 133 – 59E. HADDOCK found a few more turns and began to pull ahead rapidly.

1235 HADDOCK reported she was beginning attack. Wished her luck and told Comdr. Brockman we would continue tracking. I planned to continue to pull ahead and if enemy neither sunk nor alerted, to attack after HADDOCK had had sufficient time to complete an attack.

1255 Number 2 main engine back in commission – several hours too late. We needed that engine badly this morning.

1301 Ahead of enemy. Slowed to 12 knots. Planned to give HADDOCK 45 minutes to reach her firing point, then to reverse course, dive and attack when good contact was regained.

1325 Reversed course, increased speed. No explosions as yet.

1334 Sighted submarine – but it is HADDOCK. She reported contact lost 45 minutes after diving, believe Nip sub had dived or made radical change of course. Formed scouting line on westerly course toward assumed enemy track (distant 13 miles), then 010 for one hour (reverse of enemy base course), then retired along enemy base course.

1540 Began transmission LAGARTO TEN to ComSubPac.

1847 HADDOCK suddenly enveloped herself in a huge brown smoke screen and turned away. She reported SJ contact at 11,000 yards. We paralleled her course, own radar screen blissfully clean of any contacts save HADDOCK.

1855 HADDOCK reported contact was friendly, and call that of SEGUNDO. I doubt identity. SEGUNDO should be off CHINA COAST. May be RONQUIL, as there are only two digits difference in their calls.

1931 After final talk with Comdr. Brockman and mutual well-wishing, took departure and set course for previously assigned route to SUBIC BAY.

2015 Began transmission. LAGARTO ELEVEN to ComSubPacAdComd and ComSubPac.
2105 Completed transmission.

Lagarto joined her escort, *Douglas A. Munro* (DE – 422) an hour into the morning watch on 20 March, and after anchoring for a sound test in Subic Bay, moored alongside the submarine tender *Howard W. Gilmore* (AS – 16) to commence a refit. She returned from patrol "clean and shipshape with a minimum number of material defects." In spite of this assessment, *Lagarto's* logs show otherwise. Throughout the first patrol report, CDR Latta mentions engine and radar troubles on several different occasions:

16 February - "EMC out of commission."

20 February - "No. 1 main engine out of commission to renew liner."

4 March - "A new high in radar technician's reports to the bridge – this from the APR watch, 'It came in again, went out again, all clear on SD!'"

14 March - "No. 2 main engine out of commission with 2 broken head bolts."

15 March - "Number one main engine out of commission with what appears to be leaky liner.....Number one main engine back in commission having replaced liner. There

is yet life in the engineers' force, even if the engines can't take it."

16 March - "Number 2 main engine out of commission with two broken head studs."

During this time period, Rae Todd received the following letters (undated) from her husband:

Dearest Beebee,

What a misnomer "Pacific!" Somebody ought to send Balboa back to school for the meaning of the word.

In spite of hell and high-water – and those two terms are really accurate – this little ship is still slamming around in A-1 shape. We're all hale and hearty, except for appetites, our morale is higher than hell, and we all want to go home.

Hey, Darlin,' you ought to give a look at your old Tracy – about 15 pounds lighter in the right places, a few more crinkles around my eyes, and feeling tougher than hell. I had a real butch hair cut – one that made my Charleston cut look like a musician's bob – and it's grown just the right amount now. You could have a lot of fun running your fingers through it. I'm for it!!

I had a beard and mustache – both red as a barn – but by popular vote, they disappeared one day. Oh well, they itched awful, anyway. I keep telling myself I wouldn't have worn them home anyway.

Hi there, Li'l Nell,

I'm on watch now, waiting for some messages to come in so I can break them.

Boy! Will we be glad when this run is over! This didn't turn out to be much of a glory run, but it certainly had its moments. The first part of the run was pack full of thrills and chills **(clearing the carrier route of Japanese picket boats, preparing for the invasion of Iwo Jima)** and we did a pretty good job on it, but the rest was just full of chills.

I can't make this as lovey-dovey as I'd like, cause there are numerous amounts of spare radiomen here in the shack, looking all around and trucking on down. I won't be able to finish this on watch, so when I get all by my lonesome (except for your pictures) I'll really cut loose and tell you what I want to.

Gotta get back to work now, Darlin'...I'll finish this just as soon as I can...by the way, things are looking up along qualification lines...no definite dope yet, however.

Tis now two days later than the above, I think. Lots has happened – can't tell you about it yet, but there are some pretty good anecdotes.

Golly, Darling – let's end this awful thing and let me go home to my Beebee where I belong. (This is a lousy way to earn a living – has anyone ever told you? Not submarines – they're still 4.0 A-1, but this whole nerve-wracking business of watching and listening and hoping and praying and sweating.)

My Dearest Darlin,

I'm very mellow again tonight, Sweetheart. I have just come off watch, during which time I did a lot of reminiscing about the past two or three years.

Every once in awhile I would sing to myself, and almost every time it would turn out to be "You'd be so nice to come home to."

And then, of course, I'd get around to thinking about food and my favorites. First naturally, is my Beebee's fried chicken and noodles. I could almost taste them, just like being back at our Quonset Hut at chow time. When I get home I want to eat fried chicken and noodles for a week.

Darlin Rae,

This little vessel is pitching and tossing so damn much, you probably will have no little difficulty in translating.....

She is almost finis, now – this patrol....The guy that figured out how long we could stay out sure did an exacting job – one more day and I would be stark, staring mad.

It's hard to visualize just what goes on and why it's a strain, but you find out awful quick when you make a run.

It's not making attacks that's the strain – hell no, you pray for them to give you something to release energy you stored up. It's building up to them. If you've never spent a day during which you just had time to do the things you must do if you worked like hell, you'll find it hard to understand this. And when you put four or five such days together consecutively, you really get worn down.

I know I came as close to a nervous breakdown – or "battle" fatigue – as a guy can without actually having it. When I'd come off watch, I'd be tingling, and as I picked up my coffee cup, my hands would shake so much I could hardly hold it. And everyone in the ward room would be the same way. If someone dropped anything in the forward compartment, we'd all jump up and spill coffee all over the place. What a rat race!

We're sure looking forward to this rest period. It won't be the hilarious party rests that some of the fellas have talked about, but anything that gives me a chance to sleep anywhere will be a boon.

Les Auchard – a new officer we picked up at one of our stops before this run – and I have a program laid out with a view toward bettering our beat-up physical conditions. It includes lots of sack, boxing, football, running, and general calisthenics – but we've left plenty of time to write at least one letter a day to our dearly beloveds. After what happened to Walt and Al, we've all decided to go pretty much on the wagon – and by the way, I'll sure be interested to know what you heard from the other wives.

To his wife, Bill Mendenhall wrote:

28 February 1945

Today I was thinking that this war has been going on for such a long time that it almost seems like the natural order of things that I have to be away......And sometimes it seems as if it will just go on and on. Of course, it won't but it does seem that no matter how overwhelming is our might, and no matter how hard we hammer them, somehow they are able to fight on and on for months.

But doggone it we have got to get this thing over and soon! The progress in the last year has been terrific and just as fast as can be expected, but there still seems to be such a long road ahead.

Last Entry in War Patrol Report Number ONE

0500 Joined escort, U.S.S. MUNRO (DE1422).
1100 Anchored for sound test, SUBIC BAY
1300 Alongside U.S.S. GILMORE (AS16) for refit.

R & R In The Philippines 1945

The war was winding down, but there was still danger in the Philippines. The following are excerpts from letters home by *Lagarto* XO Bill Mendenhall:

4 March 1945

As usual, a lot of spare time is spent sitting around and talking about what we are going to do after the war. Les Auchard, one of the new officers on the boat, is really set. He has a job teaching math at the small Nebraska college he graduated from. He will also be assistant football coach. The college gives them every summer off with pay, provided they either teach, travel, or study one summer in three. He is a real nice fellow, a lot of fun, intelligent, eager, and clean cut. This post-war set up of his sounds ideal.

23 March 1945

I cannot, of course, tell you where we are, and it is too bad because you would be interested. There isn't much in the way of recreation, in fact I have done nothing yet except have a few beers, see two movies, and try and get the crew situated and as well provided for as possible.

24 March 1945

The food for us this time has not been bad although we don't get any fresh food, even during this period. It's just a problem of supply and actually we do darn well, so much better than any of the other services. But gosh what I wouldn't give to sit down to one of your salads. Isn't there some way to send me a head of lettuce? I haven't seen a real head of lettuce for three months at least.

27 March 1945

Actually the half-enjoyable things are kind of few and far-between around here. I have been working just as hard during my 'rest' period as any other time. But none of that particularly worries me. The lack of adequate recreation facilities for our very fine crew does though. But whatever, and we might as well resign ourselves to it. The heck of it is that all during our rugged training and repair periods and patrol, up to now I have held the prospect of this first rest period up to them as a reward. Actually they are all pretty good about it.

Mabin – 19 March 1945

Dearest Marg,

It's about that time I sit down and prove I can still write. I was fortunate enough to get in that letter about a month ago, so the time between letters shouldn't seem so long to you. It's sure been a long trip for me though.

I should have a couple of weeks leave coming up in a few days so hope I'll have plenty of mail to read then. That will be the only thing I'll have to do on leave. These leaves aren't what they used to be. If there's beer I'll be satisfied but I have my doubts about even that.

I was sorry to hear about Nancy's playmate, Sandra, losing her father (CDR William Millican, captain of submarine *U.S.S. Escolar*). *I didn't know him except by sight. One of our officers, Mr. Shaw, lost his life and Mr. Brewington was in an automobile accident awhile back. It was quite a surprising shock. The loss of Lt. Shaw was the loss of a very valuable officer.*

I sure hope I receive some pictures of you and Nancy when I get in. These past four months plus have undoubtedly brought quite a few changes in our little guy. She sure makes you wonder how people can possibly exist without children of their own.

When the war's over I hope it won't be too long before we can afford another. These periods at sea sure give one plenty of time to think.

For almost six months I'd almost forgotten there was any kind of war going on. Now the damn thing's in my back yard, my front yard, and throughout the house. God! For the day I'm with my wife and baby, and the only war there will be, will be the one I start myself.

Well, my darling, in a few days my letters should start coming regular again for awhile. I love you very much, honey.

Todd – 28 March 1945

Dearest Beebee Darlin,'

I had the duty two days ago. When I got off yesterday morning, Les and I got our canteens, helmets, side arms and packs and started out. Using PT boats, native bancas, and US Army trucks and automobiles of all description, and finally the Wild Blue Yonder Boys' winged craft, we got to the big city in this place. What utter ruin! It makes you sick to see the devastation of what had once been beautiful buildings, statues, and homes. The Japanese dynamited and burned everything as they left last week.

But we enjoyed the experience. We teamed up with two damn

swell zoomies, one of whom had been there a few days ago. The four of us (imagine the combination – two fly boys and two so called (by the air corps) "bravies" – walked all over the place once and rode through it twice. Hitch-hiking there was better than anything back home.

We walked down what was left of the streets and found that the native stores and cafes had miraculously bloomed out of the ruins. I bought you two handkerchiefs with your initials embroidered on them. I will try to send them to you before we shove off.

It's surprising that these people can be so clean...Along about sundown they get all cleaned up and come out in crisp white linen blouses and what we used to call "polo shirts" and white trousers and skirts. Some are barefoot, and some have clean white and polished saddle shoes. But all are clean and neat, in spite of their past hardships.

They are apparently awfully glad to have us there, as who wouldn't be after what they went through? They walk down the streets, give you a big Pepsodent smile and say "Good morning, sir." They're only too glad to stop and talk with you. Even the littlest kids can speak English-American as well as I can.

The four of us slept on cots in the patio of a beautiful home – only slightly damaged – guarded by the native vigilantes, who are up all night and sleep all day. We woke up in the morning and looked over at the hill where we could see the artillery banging away and the shells flashing.

The next day, after we had eaten and seen American ex-internees, we walked out to the airfield where there was a hell of a lot of bombed and burned and strafed Japanese planes. (A couple of days before, a zoomy stuck his head in one and a Japanese shot him. But the Japanese are all but flushed out now.) There was a plane warming up on the runway, and Les stuck up his thumb. Damned if the pilot didn't tell us to climb in! He flew us right back here. The Zoomies are great fellas.....

Todd - 30 March 1945

Darling Sweetheart,

I just received your letters 51 & 52....Thank the Lord you're feeling so much better - I've been awful worried. Take it easy, now from here on out...I'll be pulling for you all the times. I still have the letter you wrote that I'm supposed to read when he gets here - but when? I'll read it along about May 10, if I haven't received any word, unless you rather I'd wait until I hear?

Darling, you write such marvelous letters - just what I need. I only wish I could tell you everything that is in my heart. I must be a disappointment 'cause I don't do better, but please remember the guy who fell so completely and everlastingly in love with you, realizing that he got such a good start loving you and doubling and tripling that love every day, every hour. I may not be able to write it, but nobody can feel it more.

Mabin – 30 March 1945

My Darling Margaret,

I haven't used your full name for some time. I like it too, only sometimes forget it belongs to you. In fact our next little girl shall be a Peggy.

I have two hundred dollars in money orders that I shall enclose in this letter. A good deal of it, I must confess, was formerly my shipmates' money. That makes three hundred home this time, but unfortunately I won't be able to count on my shipmates every time in. Next time I probably won't be able to send any.

I received the finished print of our "little guy" yesterday afternoon, and now she lies on my bunk looking up at me as I write. That alone is enough to make one feel capable of doing big things in this world. She's my first real success in life, coupled with my most wonderful wife. That's more than enough to make up for all my failures. And I'm hoping that's a good indication for our future.

As far as my past preference for brunettes is concerned, it's strictly a young man's idea that passes with time. I've become quite a fancier for natural blonds. I always have liked the natural ones and only became prejudiced because so many were artificial. My wife and daughter are natural, and as such are my preference. Does that help any, my darling?

For the last week or so, we've been living in a screened-in barracks on the beach. We have our beer in the afternoon, and it's amounted to more than four cans 'cause some can't drink any, and a few others are stopped at one or two cans. Needless to say, I don't fit in either class, so I'm happy. The rest of my time is spent sleeping and quite a bit of pinochle playing. It's a restful life.

Well, darling, I must send this back on the next boat to the tender or it will have to wait until tomorrow to go out.

The following letter was written to Bill Mabin by Ed Stuart, his best friend in the Navy who was also best man at his wedding three years earlier. Although it was written more than a month before *Lagarto* went down, Bill missed receiving it. It was returned to Stuart marked "Unclaimed." Stu must have given it to Margy, as it was found among her other old letters.

Ed Stuart - 26 March 1945

Dear Bill,

Mind you I'm not writing cause I owe you a letter. No, not that, inasmuch as I can't owe someone who I don't hear from. But I love you for it Joe – no news is good news.

Now to get down to the purpose. Want to wish you a very happy anniversary and remind you that it is about that time....For both your sakes I sure do wish you and Margy could be together. Perhaps next year. Maybe we can all get together and throw a party to end them all.

Well guy I've found another home. Shall never know why I get all the breaks. No kidding, this is another Crosby (the destroyer they served on together at the beginning of the war) *Didn't think there were any more four stackers left but here I am putting up with the same old shit. Tho we have a skipper that can run a ship just like "K-Willie." He is really a swell guy and a real sailor. Only a Lieut. at that.*

Had a date with Jean McDonald (Margy's cousin). *She is really one peach of a gal. Very much like your precious Margy. We had a darn swell time and one long talk. She sure thinks a lot of you Junior. Why I don't know.....*

This is about enough for one who doesn't write. Margy says you're a lousy correspondent and I agree.

Best wishes on going into your fourth year, Pop.

Ed Stuart and his wife Dodie lived on the west coast, and my memory is vague on the times I saw them. However, I do remember the last time I saw Stu. I was in high school, and he stopped by to see my mother. They had a nice visit, and I saw Stu to the door. He looked at me rather awkwardly and appeared to be trying to say something. Finally, he delved into his pocket and pulled out a five-dollar bill, which he thrust into my hand. He turned quickly and hurried down the sidewalk to his car before I had a chance to thank him. I noticed there were tears in his eyes.

I was confused by this and told my mother what had happened. She told me that Stu loved my father and was devastated by his death. She said I reminded Stu of my father and he was very moved by seeing Bill Mabin's child. She thought Stu wanted to give me something but didn't know what to do. The last minute five dollar bill was his way of doing something for me.

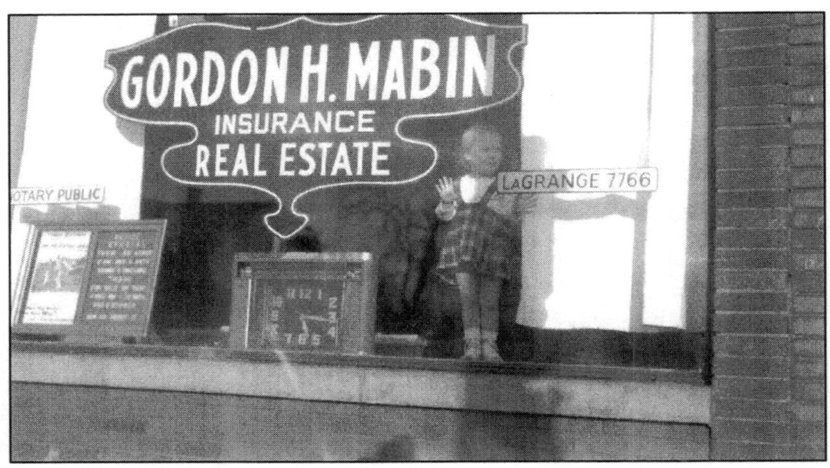

Nancy Jean in window of Grandpa Mabin's real estate office. 1945.

The Last 33 Days of Their Lives 1945

On 30 March 1945, Rae Todd gave birth to a healthy, but 2-month premature, baby boy.

Todd - 1 April 1945

Darling Lover Bunny,

Boy! Are we having fun out here – a real rest, something I've needed ever since we shoved off from N'Yawlins. But let me bring you completely up to date.

We've moved over on the beach to a rest camp. "Rest" they call it. Sailors guard the place all night because it seems the Japanese come down out of the hills on raids every now and then for water & food. One guard was killed the other night and numerous shots were fired.

But in spite of it all, we are really enjoying it. We have an "officers' club" where we can get ice-cold Budweiser & Miller beer, and two fifths of liquor a week. We have a baseball field the Seabees made, and we've got swimming in the bay and marvelous chow. And, Sweetheart, we live in QUONSET huts!! They are big and airy and about ten feet from the water. I'm sleeping like a log...

It's great relaxation for the guys. Lloyd Irving hasn't budged off the (sub) tender because he says it's "too primitive." Maybe he's scared the Japanese will get him.

We've had a lot of fun going through the native villages. The houses are all clean and built of woven bamboo and thatched roofs – all very orderly.

The other day we stopped and watched some kids playing in the road. I guess all the little fellas the world over play the same way – until they get trained otherwise. I took out a piece of tropical chocolate and cut it up and gave it to them. They beamed and politely said "Thank you." Then I saw some older people smiling from a house and went over and gave them some. Across the road was another house where about seven girls – from about 14 to 20 – were leaning out the window and laughing. So we walked over there to give them some. There was one little girl with dark brown eyes, long black hair, golden brown skin and a very attractive smile showing unbelievably white and even teeth. I gave her a pack of Dentine. With that, we turned to go out of the yard, leaving them laughing and giggling like a bunch of cute little high school sophomores.

Just as we left the yard through the bamboo fence, a boy named "Joe" (found out he was 20, although he looked 15) who had been beaten up by the Japanese a couple of times, came up and asked us confidentially, displaying a wide smile, "You want to go upstairs?" It didn't dawn on me for a second or two, and then it suddenly hit me! Les and I both spun around and stared, our mouths wide open. But sure enough, they were prostitutes!! I told Joe, "No thanks – we have a long way to go." So he sticks his little puss up to my chest and says, still laughing (these people always laugh) "Whatsamattah? Y'Bashful?" That did it! Here we are, on the other side of the world from home, and some little guy no higher than my I.D. dog tag around my neck asks me if I'm bashful in the best Brooklynese! Les and I got out of there quick.

It seems that 98% of these girls are devout Catholics, but the other 2% are the business girls – the whole thing is called "Pom-Pom." But we got away safely.

Wally Spies came in a few days ago – big old reunion. He says for you to come on out and take care of us, to which I add my second.

Crutch is on the KETE (which was lost sometime between March 20-31 on her way to refuel at Midway).

Oh, yeah, our run was successful and I can now wear the combat pin.

Todd – 4 April 1945

My Darling,

Did I tell you that I'm to be Asst. Engineer next run – this one coming up – and possibly (don't let on that I got the word on this) Chief Engineer the run after that, if Art gets transferred. When I think about not having to communicate during runs or when we get in, I sure feel elated.

Mabin - 4 April 1945

My Darling Marg,

I've had a little interruption for a couple of days, so I'm again behind on my letter writing. I took a little trip to see part of the country. One can see the same thing in the newsreel, but the impression doesn't last as long as it does when you see it.

Well, back to the "salt-mines," so to speak. The vacation is over and back to work. It's been rather a dull leave but was interesting for a day or so. Maybe my next one shall be more of the "leave" type.

Nancy seems to have become so much more of a little girl instead of a baby. I so often wonder how she'll react and treat me when I come home again. I hope she really feels I'm her father and not just a strange man that seems to come and go. Undoubtedly my connection will be vague to her, but I pray I'll someday become her favorite father.

Naturally a late picture of her will be forthcoming at the end of my next run. She can change so much in that time, and I don't want to miss any change. Another must is a good picture of you. You haven't had one taken since the first time we were in New London. I also have a wife I like to show off.

I've had such a queer good feeling every time I think about you lately, especially today. I can't explain it further than that. I want to go to bed and lie down and just enjoy the feeling. Maybe I shall be able to figure it out tonight. Anyway, it's good and I like it.

Leave us not tarry any longer on this cold paper. To bed where my thoughts and dreams may seem real and be uninterrupted. I know I shall dream of you tonight.

Then – letters from Bill Mendenhall:

4 April 1945

Kirtley (StM1 Albert Kirtley, the steward for the officers' mess) is just bringing me a dish of ice cream with some frozen blueberries on it. Not bad for way out here. It is funny, we are always complaining about our chow and we eat so much better than anybody else in the service. Other fellows are amazed when they see how we eat, our living conditions, officers' club, etc. Da glamour boys of the service, dats us. It's just that in the beginning of the war submarines were doing practically all of the damage and got all of the breaks. And we have held on to them.

6 April 1945

You asked for pictures – and this is what you get. That is the same character on the right in that cribbage game. Incidentally, you can tell that picture was taken early in a patrol because there is fruit on the table.

The news tonight contained about the best news I have seen for many a day – the cancellation of the Russ-Jap Peace pact. If the Russkys come in with us when the European War is over, the thing is going to be a matter of months. Lloyd and I had talked about that very thing the night before last, and I made the statement that I did not think it would ever happen.

About the pictures again – the single one of the skipper I want for the photograph album. The pipe he is making is a bright green one, which he makes only once a year on St. Patrick's Day. Holly (Latta's wife) gave it to him.

I wish you could have been around the last couple of days, because if I do say so, as I shouldn't, the landings I made were pretty good. It's really fun to handle this ship anyway, and when the landing turns out pretty good, I feel wonderful.

The talk that Lloyd and I were having the other night about the war was a good one. We both said that as we read the news dispatches every night, we see our homes getting closer and closer all the time. We all want to be in those homes with you we love so much, that every 500 yard advance seems to be helping each of us personally.

I really gave the boys a workout today, and I am satisfied the way it turned out. We are actually a darn good ship, and everybody on board is pretty happy. If it weren't that we had wives, daughters, families at home we love so much, this wouldn't be a bad life."

Todd - 6 April 1945

Darling Beebee,

Les & Joe Pash – a new officer we just got to replace the one who replaced Walt – and I have been displaying pictures of our wives and we got ourselves so homesick we all shipped out the writing materials and proceeded to write our O.A.O.'s.

You know, Sweetheart – we really do have a marriage that no one else has. I constantly think of you as my "girl" whom I'm still courting rather than just the gal who cooks my meals when I'm home.

What I wouldn't give to snuggle up to you tonight and feel your tenderness near me and your soft hair on my shoulder…It won't be too long, Darling – just hang on…

Todd – 8 April 1945

Beautiful Beebee –

Two more letters from you! And the last was dated 28 March!! This mail service is terrific – but then, they take care of their boys in subs.

Golly, Honey, I'm on pins and needles…has Mike appeared? Am I a father? How I wish I could be there to hold your hand and take care of you. It's lots easier to fight a war than to be away from my little gal.

Beebee gal – having you tell me you're "awful proud of me" makes me want to go out and lick what's left of the Japanese fleet all by myself, just for you. I'll never get any medals, but you can bet your boots I'm breaking my neck trying to get this over with in a hurry so I can come home to you and our single bed so you can lay that lovely head on my shoulder and we can sleep for years & years & years.

You can wear the big dolphins now. **(The dolphins were a pin configuration that could be worn only by a submariner after he passed stringent tests. It was highly prized, and often the dolphins** meant more to the sailors, both officers and enlisted, than any other medal they received. Wives and mothers of the submariners had their own dolphin pins.) Soon I'll be qualified good and sound before you get any more. I can't wait till I can put on those dolphins you gave me on Christmas, Oct. 7, 1944.

I guess by now you've seen the error of your ways in saying "it's good to know...you're sleeping in a good big bed..." We slept on cots under mosquito netting! But it was a real rest doing just what we wanted and going anywhere we could get to. Les & I saw a lot of real interesting things and had a lot of excitement. By the way – a photographer took a picture of Les & me in our infantry fighting gear – helmets, side arms, carbines, packs and field shoes – with dust. If I ever run into him again I'll get you the picture. He said he'd entitle it "Those blood-thirsty submariners."

Bill Mendenhall's letters describe the experiences and outlook of a Naval officer in the last stages of World War II:

7 April 1945

Today was sort of a Christmas. We all received bundles from the Red Cross – candy, cigarettes, cards, a book, toothbrush, soap, writing paper, etc. The bags are real good looking, and it was a darn nice thing to do. It is sort of a shame though to give them to us, because we are supplied so darn well with that sort of stuff. Rather it should go to some Marine or soldier in a foxhole whose PX is not within 20 muddy miles. But they make us all feel pretty good.

The whole darn thing can't last too much longer. I am William Optimistic Mendenhall these days and am predicting the collapse of Germany in April and the surrender or complete neutralization of Japan within six months after that. Of course my predictions get so mixed up with my hopes that they are not much good. I've got to get home and get some home cooking – I am down to 135 lbs.

8 April 1945

Today was sort of a rugged day – and I am not sure that I did so well, in my own job and organizing other people's work. For one thing I lost my patience once and that is one thing for which I used to criticize Hank. But tomorrow is another day and perhaps everything will go better. Right now I am kind of tired and discouraged.

My Darling Marg
1945

<u>Mabin – 9 April 1945</u>

My Darling Marg,

Yesterday's mail was sure a joy. Your letters sure make me feel like quite a guy. Surprising how much more one appreciates those kind words out here than he does at home. Flattery doesn't exist, and justly so, but I soon come down to earth when my letter reading is done and I get back to my present position. Thanks honey.

I don't think I ever did answer your question about the Lagarto launching picture. The Lagarto is the one that is autographed. I don't know what boat the other one is. If you have an extra one, after giving the folks theirs, Jim may want one.

I think you were smart in buying that typewriter and getting it fixed. (Just spilled water on this but won't rewrite it cause I want to make the second show).

My luck in gambling has dropped a little lately, but I've already sent home more than I drew this time in, so I'm ahead of the thing. After I've sent home $1000 above that, I shall go for a car when I get home. I may not reach that goal, but at least I'm half way to it. Five hundred dollars in five months is a better average than I expected. Of course I've been no place where I can spend money. Friendship has no place in these games. We all like to send money home for that day it will do us some good. God knows, I'll grab mine when I can do it honestly. Do I sound tough? I wish I were, and I might get more than a bald head out of this Navy.

Pete is waiting for me to finish so we can get to the show in time to get a good seat. Much love my darling, Bill

Margy Mabin never heard from her husband again.

Margy and Nancy Jean Mabin in La Grange, taken ten days before *Lagarto* was lost. Nancy was 2 years, 4 months old. 1945.

Dearest Wonderful Beebee 1945

Todd – 11 April 1945

Dearest Wonderful Beebee –

You did it!! I knew you could you Darling little gal! And golly, Honey, I've been walking about 3 ft. above the deck ever since I got the word.

We got our last mail today. The last I had from you was dated the 29th in which you said, "Any day now." For the last three days I've been on pins and needles, as you can well imagine. When the mail came, there was only one letter from Mom – the other guys didn't get much either. We were all sorta disappointed when finally I got to reading Mom's letter. I certainly wasn't prepared for the news, in spite of the fact she'd started out "Dear Daddy," and in spite of the fact she said I had "a little son," it wasn't until the second paragraph that I came to. They are working feverishly now to patch up the hole in the hull where I went through the overhead.

When I finally came back below, I remembered that, by golly, I did have a letter from my Beebee, at that!! So I took out the letter you wrote in the Roosevelt just before we left. I didn't open it right away, though. I sat there and fondled it for a couple of minutes so I could enjoy that happy moment to the fullest degree.

I can't tell you, my darling, how very much your letter meant to me. It was the most wonderful letter I've ever gotten in my life. I've read it about three times, now – four – I just read it again. Each time I find something new to make me realize how much I love my little wife and how much she means to me. That dull ache of longing for you, Honey, is so strong I can hardly stand it. I'd give everything I own – except, of course, my lovely wife and little son – to be home with my family and live a normal life. I want to start doing things for you and taking care of you like I should.

Boy, oh boy! I've certainly been "shouting from the house-tops," except we don't have any housetops. That crow's nest can cover an awful lot of territory, though.

I wanted to go to the beach this evening and have a party for the fellas and celebrate, but last-minute stuff kept me from it. It'll have to wait I guess till next time.

Oh, by the way, tell that son of mine that he better take good care of his mom till I get back, or I'll spank him proper. (Bully that I am.)

Honey Beebee doll, I'm the happiest guy that ever lived. I can't wait till I get back and help teach little Mike the finer points of life. Inwardly I hoped Mike would be a little boy – although, as I said before, I would love a daughter just as much.

I'll have lots to keep me occupied during this run. I can dream about seeing my lovely little girl again, and seeing Mike for the first time. I can picture our little family at home, so deeply in love with each other. I can think of you holding little Mike as being the most beautiful picture in the world – sort of a "Madonna et filius" effect. Then I can imagine Mike in a couple of years toddling around our home, getting into everything, and climbing on his Dad's lap to read the funnies. Oh, what a lot of things I can dream!!

By the way, Darling, you can tell Mike his pop is one of the "glamour boys" of the service – the submarine boys. I was surprised to learn that myself, but it came straight from the zoomies that get picked up by submarines. They envy greatly the way we live and eat, and, as Lieut. Cary Alburn told me, they think we're in the most adventurous racket in the service. They think we have guts to go into shallow waters – guess they don't realize we think they're in a rough game themselves. The mutual admiration and cooperation between these two extreme branches makes you feel good.

Well, my darling, I'm afraid I'll have to stop now and finish my "ready for sea" work. I'd like to write on and on and tell you how awful much I love you and your courage and your tenderness. Until next letter, Honey, just keep praying and thinking of old Trace.

All my love,

H.A.

P.S. Hope you can get some snaps of you and Mike so I can get them when we come in (from next war patrol).

Michael Burgess Todd was born two months prematurely. Had he gone full term, his father would never have known of his birth. This was Hal Todd's last letter home.

Bill Mendenhall's Last Letters 1945

The following are excerpts from Bill Mendenhall's last letters:

9 April 1945

Do you remember my writing last night that today would be another day and maybe things would go better? Well it was and they did. So tonight I am not so discouraged although I am tired. It must be that in your own organization you don't see what is good because those things you expect, and the things that are bad take up the whole picture. Today the 'boss' went out with us and complimented the skipper very highly on the ship, and said that everything was just as he would want it. And he only has three or four Navy Crosses.

10 April 1945

The skipper told me that he expects to recommend me for qualification for command this next time in and that will be a big step toward my getting back and getting a boat also. I have certainly had the lucky breaks on this boat, haven't I. The old man is really a guy to work for. I do all of the ship handling, all of the personnel work, with the skipper only occasionally putting in a little advice. Every once in awhile he gets a little angry with me, I think and I do with him, but I think that is quite natural considering the strain we are under.

12 April 1945

This is another one of those hard letters to write. Yes, it will be the last one for awhile, and I'll try to make it just as short an 'awhile' as possible.

Tragic News
1945

On June 23, 1945, a telegram was received by Mrs. R.L. Hoppe of 103 Rhodera St., Peoria, Illinois. Mrs. Hoppe was a sister of MoMM1 Richard Fisher of Pekin, Illinois. The government wire related:

> I DEEPLY REGRET TO INFORM YOU THAT YOUR BROTHER RICHARD LOUIS FISHER MOTOR MACHINISTS MATE FIRST CLASS USN IS MISSING IN ACTION IN THE SERVICE OF HIS COUNTRY. YOUR GREAT ANXIETY IS APPRECIATED AND YOU WILL BE FURNISHED DETAILS WHEN RECEIVED. TO PREVENT POSSIBLE AID TO OUR ENEMIES AND TO SAFEGUARD THE LIVES OF OTHER PERSONNEL PLEASE DO NOT DIVULGE THE NAME OF THE SHIP OR STATION OR DISCUSSS PUBLICLY THE FACT THAT HE IS MISSING -
>
> VICE ADMIRAL RANDALL JACOBS CHIEF OF NAVAL PERSONNEL...

Telegrams identical to this, with only the name differing, went to all eighty-six next-of-kin of *Lagarto's* crew. The method of delivery varied somewhat. A little man on a bicycle came to Rae Todd Kinn's door to deliver the devastating telegram in Fort Wayne, Indiana. Sue Halstead Hill was working in the field on her grandparents' farm when she and her grandfather saw a dark official-looking car coming down their road to deliver the awful news. Vivid in the minds of many was the reaction of the mothers – more than one of whom fainted when given the news about her child. As the human spirit prevails in the most tragic of circumstances, hope sprung in the hearts of most family members. The telegram had said their loved one was "missing in action," and most in the country felt that the war was coming to a close. Hopefully, the missing crew would be found on one of the many Pacific islands – or even be languishing in a prison camp.

As horrible as the thoughts were, most family members clung to them – believing with all their hearts that their son, husband, brother, or friend would return to them. Rae Todd continued to write her husband and saved the letters for him to read when he returned home – praying fervently for that outcome every day. Other wives and mothers wrote each other to offer news and support.

In July, Eleanor Shackelford, the wife of SM2 Wes Shackelford, wrote to Margy Mabin. Eleanor and Margy were close friends and the Shackelfords and Mabins had spent much time together.

Mrs. Wesley Shackelford - 25 July 1945 – Great Bend, Kansas

Dear Marg –

I have the first definite news about the Lagarto and I feel encouraged to no end. Ruth, my best girlfriend in Gt. Bend, has a husband who's on a destroyer in the Pacific. They docked last week and as soon as he read the letter about Wes, he checked with their communications officer and found that Lagarto has not been taken off their call list. It seems that all the subs have a call letter with which they identify themselves when they approach our ships out there. That to me means the Navy isn't at all sure that our boat is lost. Isn't that encouraging? He said he would try his best to find out more for us while he is in and I'm sure that he will. He's that kind of guy.

I checked with the Red Cross director here and she said there isn't a thing that they can do. She did say that the Navy will give us an up-to-date report every three months. God let us hear from our "honeys" before the next letter from the Navy!

I drove to Wes' folks (60 miles) for the week end. Wes' Mother is so sure the boys are safe someplace, it's like a shot in the arm to talk to her. We sat up nearly all night talking. She is really swell in my estimation.

My sis is feeling pretty well up to now. I took your advice and tried to make her feel that she has to look after me. I think it works. Last night I was having company, a girl Wes and I knew in Larned. Jeanie went after cokes for me, had gasoline put in my car and did a lot of little things for me so I could be ready for her when she arrived. It gives Jeanie a feeling of importance I think. I've never before asked her to do a thing for me nor has any of the family. I think it makes a difference already.

There isn't much new, Marg, just wanted to tell you about the Lagarto still being on the call list. There is a very good chance for the boys. I really feel it inside. They are coming back, Marg, and what a wonderful day that is going to be!

Victory's Eve
1945

On the eve of victory in the Pacific hopes were high, and some newspapers began publishing the likely good news. The front page of *The Fresno Bee,* published on 10 August 1945, was typical. The bold headline at the top of the page read:

JAPAN MAKES OFFER TO SURRENDER

Smaller headlines all over the front page bespoke almost nothing but war news:

Truman Speech Warns Japan To Give Up Or Die

Carrier Pilots Destroy 259 Enemy Planes

Soviets Slash 100 Miles Into Manchuria

U.S. Gets In Touch With Allies On Peace Proposal

Tokyo Accepts Every Term But
Wants To Retain Hirohito Rule

Hirohito Removal Would Be Break in 'Eternal' Rule

Here Are Points Of Ultimatum
Hirohito Creates Peace Committee

Navy Ship Loss Costs 112 Men

Fresnans Greet Japanese Offer With Mixed Emotions

And finally – at the bottom right corner of the front page of *The Fresno Bee*:

Submarine *Lagarto* is Presumed Lost

Now that the war was almost over, local newspapers began reporting the losses of their own sons. One such headline in *The La Grange Citizen* read:

Bill Mabin, Signalman on Sub, Is Missing

It was not the only news of loss in the article. The item read as follows:

> Word reached La Grange Tuesday morning that Pfc. Ralph Leavitt, son of Mr. and Mrs. Edward Leavitt, 522 North Spring avenue, had died in Germany on April 17. He was taken prisoner along with Pfc. John Swett, Pvt. Clifford Armgard and Pvt. Don Candy on December 19 when the German armies made their last breakthrough.

> The Leavitts received four brief notes from him after he had been taken prisoner. For a time the La Grange boys were all together at Bad Orb, but about the first of February Ralph was moved to another camp and no further news had been heard from him. The telegram from the War department gave no additional information as to where he had been or the cause of death.
>
> Up to the time he left Bad Orb (a German prison camp), Ralph and John Swett had been together all through their army careers. They were students together at the University of Wisconsin in the A.S.T. program. They later went to Ft. Benning, Ga., and later to Camp Atterbury, Ind. They were sent to England in October and a few weeks later into France, where so many were taken prisoners.

The next part of the same article repeated part of the same headline – "'Bill' Mabin Missing." It then went on to say:

> William T. Mabin, signalman first class, is reported as missing in action. Bill was a veteran submarine officer and the sad message was received Saturday by his wife, the former Margaret Miles, and his parents, Mr. and Mrs. Gordon Mabin, 323 West Calendar avenue. They had not heard from him for about 10 weeks, but that was not

alarming, for sometimes the subs are away from base for quite a while.
Bill volunteered for submarine service when he entered the navy in '40, but he was assigned to duty in a signal tower at San Diego for a time before his application for submarine training was accepted. He attended the sub school at New London, Conn., and then was assigned to a sub that had its base in Australia for several months. He was on several "runs" into enemy waters and was in charge (signalman duties) of two of these. Later he was returned to the States and was here for a couple of weeks last August. He then went to Manitowoc, where a new sub was being built and to which he was assigned. His last visit at home was while the sub was making its slow journey down the drainage canal, the Illinois river and the Mississippi to New Orleans. There he picked it up and proceeded to the Pacific, where he has again been in action.

Mrs. Mabin and two-year-old daughter Nancy Jean, have been living with her mother, Mrs. Jean Miles, 124 South Sixth avenue.

Bill's many friends are joining with his relatives in the hope that the submarine will turn up safely in some port where it has taken refuge.

In the Friday, August 10, 1945 edition of *The Manitowoc Herald-Times,* the following article appeared:

Manitowoc-Built Lagarto Reported Lost

The U.S. submarine *Lagarto*, built for the United States Navy at the Manitowoc Ship Building company, and commissioned October 14, 1944, is overdue from patrol and presumed lost, the Navy announced today. The next of kin of casualties have been notified.

This is the fourth of Manitowoc's built undersea craft to be lost in the present war. The others were the Robalo, Golet and Kete.

On June 26 the Herald-Times carried a story that four members of the crew of a submarine which left here last year, were reported missing. It is presumed they were aboard the *Lagarto*, now officially listed as lost.

The *Lagarto's* commanding officer was Commander Frank DeVere Latta, a native of Indianapolis, who was graduated from the naval academy in 1932.

Latta wore the Navy crosses for successes in submarine actions against enemy shipping.

His wife, Holly W. Latta lives at St. Helena, Calif. His mother, Mrs. Peter Entringer, lives at Burlington, Iowa.

Four Listed. The four men who were reported missing in June off the *Lagarto* –

Machinist Mate First Class Thomas Hardegree, 27, husband of the former Joyce Mandel, Two Rivers.

Motor Machinist Mate First Class Oakley Frasch, 25, husband of the former Elizabeth O'Neil, 1110 South 14th street.

Quartermaster First Class William Graves, 23, husband of the former Eleanor Huske, 1018 S. 17th street.

Motor Machinist Mate First Class John Root, husband of the former Alice Cherney, Maribel Caves, Cooperstown.

Hardegree's home was in Vienna, Ga. Frasch came here from Lancaster, Ohio, and had been in service five years. Graves hailed from Portland, Oregon, and was a veteran of five years service. Root came here from Buffalo, N.Y., and had been in service nine years.

Submarines of the *Lagarto* class usually carry a crew of 90 officers and men.

<u>47th Sub Lost.</u> The *Lagarto* was the 21st submarine launched at the Manitowoc ship yards, on May 29, 1944. The ship's sponsor was Emily Taft Douglas of Chicago.

World War II Ends In The Pacific 1945

On August 14, 1945, headlines in every newspaper in the country told Americans the good news they had waited so long to hear – ***THE WAR IS OVER!*** Everyone was overjoyed at the news. Their boys were coming home!

Five days earlier, the War Department publicly released the news of *Lagarto's* loss. Many of the same papers announcing the good news also carried a smaller article on the same front page:

NAVY REPORTS SUB, CREW OF 90 LOST

> The Navy today announced loss of the 1525-ton submarine *Lagarto,* presumably lost in Far Eastern waters. The vessel is overdue from patrol and presumed lost, the Navy said, and its crew of approximately 90 is listed as missing in action. Next of kin have been notified. Loss of the *Lagarto* brings to 47 the number of submarines lost from all causes in this war and to 329 the number of naval vessels lost...

Margy's friends rallied round. One of them, Jane Borden, wrote the following in a note from Seattle, Washington dated Tuesday, August 14, 1945:

Margy dear,

I'm sitting listening to horns blowing and people shouting and everyone being slightly hysterical – and I'm thinking of you and Bill – others too, but mainly you, since I heard them announce the Lagarto missing the other day. Margy, I'm so sorry – I wish there were something more I could say – The price of V-J day is terribly dear. Of course there's nothing I can do way out here, but when I do come home again if there's anything I can do, I know you'll let me know. And no one who ever knew Bill will ever forget him.

A few days later, Marg received a letter from Bethesda, Maryland from her friend Francie Mehring:

Dear Margy,

I know, Margy, that now that things are over with that it's even harder for you, if that's possible. I pray for you that something will turn up shortly and that Bill & his crew will be found safely! It takes a lot of faith, Margy, but with the Blessed Virgin anything is possible. Please when you write, Margy, don't feel as though you have to control your emotions with me. I've heard you've been terribly brave with perfect self control – but Margy, I know you too well not to realize what a fight you have to put up to do that. Sometimes it makes one feel better to let all that emotion out and any time you have a desire to do it, I'll be there – and I certainly will still consider you a very wonderfully brave girl.

Marg was indeed brave and began an active correspondence with other *Lagarto* wives. One of the submarine wives to whom she felt close was Eleanor Shackelford. She wrote the following to Margy on V-J Day:

Mrs. Wesley Shackelford - 14 August 1945 – Bainbridge, Maryland
Dear Marg –

I wonder if you have the same mixed up feeling this day as I have. It looks as though the war will be ended within the next few hours. After waiting for three years for this I feel happy of course, but also scared, scared stiff.

Marg, I feel that we will get our news of the boys soon now. If only they can be well and safe in a prison camp.

Perhaps I shouldn't tell you this 'cause it made me hit a new all time low, but I agreed to tell you all I found out, good or bad so here it is. Frank, Wes' cousin here, has a very good officer friend with whom he served on the Lexington. He's now in the Navy personnel office in Washington. Frank made a trip to Washington to see what he could find out about the Lagarto from this Mr. McManus. He happens to be in charge of the office that handles all the casualty reports. He said the boat is definitely lost and the fate of the crew is unknown as far as the Navy is concerned. That along with the Lagarto being announced in the papers just makes the news about the end of the war almost unimportant as far as our little worlds are concerned, doesn't it? Oh Marg, why did we have to live in this horrible age?

I'm starting home today. The kids have been swell to me and the trip was beautiful, but it's no fun without Wes. I'm sure I'm a "wet blanket" to the kids' fun. Besides I called Mom once and have wired and had the folks wire me every other day to see if there has been any news. So I think I'll be easier in my mind if I get back home where my mail is.

This surely isn't a "pepper upper" of a letter but I don't have to put up a front with you. You're the one person who really understands because you live for Bill just as I do for Wes.

We've just got to hear from them Marg! I wouldn't know how to live with nothing to look forward to. It would be just my luck to be one who lives to be an old, old lady.

A week later, Margy received another anxious letter from Sylvia Davis, the wife of TM2 John E. Davis, Jr.:

Mrs. John Davis – 21 August 1945 – Little Rock, Arkansas
Dear Margy,

I've been meaning to write to you for some time. But not knowing what to say I keep putting it off.

I received a letter from the Navy Department yesterday and I am sure you did too. I don't know why but that letter made me feel better. I thought the Navy Dept. had forgotten all about us. I feel like they will let us know, as soon as they know.

I feel the same way about Ed that you do about Bill, but as you said, that doesn't help.

Now that the war's over, it won't be long until we find out about the prisoners. I've prayed that the boys will be found among these war prisoners.

I think it would be swell if we could all get together. I would like very much to be with you girls again.

Rae Todd, wife of LTjg Harold Todd, kept up her hopes by continuing to write her husband. She kept the letters for his return:

Mrs. Harold Todd – 1 September 1945 – Fort Wayne, Indiana

My Darling –

You're probably wondering why the long delay between letters – last week my other letters to you started coming back marked 'Undeliverable – Return to Sender' and your birthday boxes come back. It was a very cruel blow to my morale – I went clear under for a few days – thinking that now even the pleasure of writing to you was being taken away. Then I had a little talk with myself and decided there was no reason why I couldn't go on writing to you – and have the letters all ready to mail whenever you turn up someplace. What a huge big fat bunch you're going to have to read when that day comes – already 5 months worth of mail – and it will probably be longer. And all the pictures of Mike I have to send you –

just think – you have no idea what your son looks like and he's 5 mos. old. The news will all be terribly, terribly stale – but not the parts where I told you how much I love you.

Oh darling Buddy – if I only knew something. At first I thought maybe you'd had to go in hiding or something – or had run aground – but that theory sort of went by the board. Then I thought maybe you'd been taken prisoner – and gruesome as that thought was – at least it would mean you were alive. Every day I kept looking for a telegram – or some word that you'd been liberated from a prison camp. Then yesterday, I heard from two different – and fairly reliable sources, that the LAGARTO had been in trouble and supposedly gone down – and that any of those top-side might have had a chance to get off, but that's about all. As you can see that isn't too encouraging – it was a blow right square on the chin that really had me staggering for awhile. But if anybody could get off why couldn't it be my Trace – so I tightened my belt another notch and threw out my chin and started looking again for some word that you're all right. But there's something sort of incongruous in the whole. Wally wrote that he'd been several times over the spot the LAGARTO is supposed to have gone down – he didn't sound too encouraging. Then Ruth Auchard (wife of LTjg Frederick Auchard) *wrote that she'd talked to a sub officer who had heard from the skipper of the QUEENFISH quote 'We think she's (the LAGARTO) gone down. She was in trouble when we left her – and we're going back to see.' And that's what I don't understand – if they knew you were in trouble – and knew where you were, why couldn't they help you – or send help anyway? And if they had done that, why isn't there some news? And if they didn't, why oh why didn't they? I wrote Wally again to ask him just what happened. I mean, if it was operational trouble or if you were depth charged, or what? Whatever it was, I can't see why you couldn't get out – and yet if you did and the QUEENFISH went back, why didn't she find you? Oh darling, it's driving me crazy. Every day I ask myself how much longer I can go on not knowing, wondering, mulling over a million questions and trying to think up new answers. Although it's just as bad for you – you know we've been notified and that we're worrying ourselves silly – and there isn't anything you can do about it. Now that the war's over, there certainly should be some news soon. This is all the punishment I ever hope to have for all the sins I've committed – this is as bad a hell as I ever hope to go thru.*

If it weren't for Mike, I don't think I could take it at all. He's such a big boy now – has teeth, darling – and 2 more nearly thru. And he turns over now. Takes him about a half hour to do it, and he gets so mad when he can't make it. He has a terrific temper. Wonder who he gets that from??? Don't look at me! Can hold his bottle by himself now for a few minutes. I hate to think of you missing all this cute part of him. We'll have to have Becky right away so you can go thru it all.

Well, sweetheart, I have to get to bed. I have a date to meet my favorite H.A. in my very favorite dream.

Good nite, my darling. I'll never give you up no matter how impossible the odds seem. I love you, Buddy.

A Tenuous Homecoming 1945

Autumn of 1945 brought thrilling homecomings to the majority of the American population. From many different parts of the world, their boys were returning.

While all Americans celebrated the end of the war, there were plenty of families whose lives were still broken. In these families, sons, husbands, fathers, brothers and friends were gone from their lives forever. These sad outcomes were known by most, but others were yet waiting and hoping for positive news of their loved one of whom an accounting was still awaited.

Lagarto family members wrote to the person they believed most apt to give them news of her fate – Holly Latta, wife of CDR Frank Latta. While dealing with her own anxiety and the well-being of her own two little boys, Mrs. Latta responded to the other submarine wives and mothers. In a letter to Margy Mabin, she wrote:

Mrs. Frank Latta – 12 September 1945 – St. Helena, CA

My Dear Mrs. Mabin –

Thank you for your good letter – you are right in that I have gotten many letters from wives and mothers of men of the Lagarto, not one of which has shown anything but the same courage and hope you show. The only difficulty in my getting them is my dread in writing each of you that I know nothing about the boat. I still hope greatly and especially now that Singapore and the area all about the Gulf of Siam are being surrendered.

But dependable friends of Frank's and mine have gone to the operations offices both in Pearl Harbor and in Washington. There is simply nothing known whatever about the Lagarto. I suppose that can be construed in two ways – I find myself concentrating on the more optimistic one that at least there is no evidence that the boat and its crew are definitely lost.

I don't know how much you know about the schedule of the boat – the last war patrol was in the Gulf of Siam and I have fairly definite information that the last communication with her was that the patrol was completed and they were heading for base. That was May 4th and they were to go to Perth, Australia. One of my hopes is in the fact that the waters thru which they were operating were mainly shallow. That would give the crew so very much more opportunity to escape if the ship was sunk – and a submarine does not usually give up easily. As a friend of ours said lately who had just brought his submarine to Mare Island, it takes from two hours to perhaps several days for the boat to sink usually.

This same friend, while admitting that things look bad for us, did feel a definite bit of hope for at least some of the men on the Lagarto. He doesn't know anything at all of what may have happened. He is basing his hope on the area in which the boat must have been and the fact that the boat disappeared so late in the war action. If there is any chance at all, it must be in the Lagarto crew being in prison camps in the area of Malay, Siam or Indo-China.

I have heard many and varied rumors, and I've tracked down a few. As with these inevitable rumors, the whole thing goes off into nothing. Maybe some of them are actually true. But I'm not depending on any of them. They seem to crop up with the report of every missing submarine. The only thing that I know to do about them is to try to track down any I can and to ignore the rest.

If and when I get any definite news of the boat I will let you know at once. If your husband is a prisoner of war, you will be so notified by the Navy immediately. There is also a slim chance that word of men who are prisoners in such areas as Singapore, etc. might be broadcast on the air or in newspapers due to being let out by correspondents connected with the British forces who are in charge of that area. I admit that I'm watching news broadcasts and the papers myself, tho I don't really have much hope of getting anything from them.

So, you see, I can't give you much except my own refusal to give up hope. At least the Navy hasn't given up and until they do, I shan't.

Please write me whenever you wish and whenever I can be of any help to you.

While most of the young *Lagarto* wives understandably felt anxious for their futures, those with children were able to take comfort in them. One young mother, Nell Andrews, wife of TCM Harold D. Andrews, wrote to another, Margy Mabin:

Mrs. Harold Andrews – 15 September 1945 – Malden, MO
Dear Margy and baby –

I've been intending to write a line for so long – but writing letters these days are a job for me. I'm wondering how you & baby are getting along? Karen & I live through the days, weeks, & months but nothing means very much anymore. Yes, we're lucky to have our babies & I don't know what I'd do without mine. She's so much company, yet I can hardly stand to think of the future without her Daddy to help me teach her & bring her up. How awful it is for a child to lose a parent – especially this way. How unfair. But what can be done – Nothing. All we say, think or do may make no difference now. This thing has made me terribly bitter – I hope I'll be able to overcome this terrible feeling. I wonder if down in your heart you don't feel the same way. I pray every night that God will see fit to bring our boys back to us – but I'm so afraid. And why did this all have to happen, I just can't understand. About the only hope we have left is that they may be prisoners.

Eleanor sent me the letter you wrote her & I sent it on to Sylvia. Had letters from Sylvia and Dottie this week – they are both planning on coming to see me sometime before long. Sure hope they do come. Sylvia spent her vacation with me – we had a nice visit together.

Well, Dear, I can't think of much more this afternoon & my baby is up from her nap. So I must close & finish some other work.

Write us again, soon & Karen sends her love to your daughter. Always, Karen & Nell

Portraits in Courage
1945

Throughout autumn of 1945, the *Lagarto* families continued to write each other. They offered information and encouragement to each other.

One of the active correspondents was the mother of S1 Dick M. Paper. Photographs of Dick Paper show him to be a handsome young man – probably 19 or 20 years old. His mother adored him and was very active in urging other family members, particularly those who lived in the Midwest, to keep hoping and working toward finding a way to get their boys home. Her letters were often sent to multiple families, full of her own research into *Lagarto's* disappearance. The first part of the following letter names some of the family members who lived in the Midwest. The names in the parentheses designate the relationship of those addressed:

20 September 1945 – Davenport, Iowa

Margaret Mabin, 124 6th Ave., La Grange, Ill. (Wife of William Mabin)
Dorothy Peterson, 7524 Constance Ave., Chicago, Ill. (Wife of Robert Peterson)
Theodora Manhusen, 1523 Center St., Pekin, Ill. (Sister of Richard Fisher)

Allan Jobe, Tunnel Hill, Ill. (Father of Jesse Jobe)
Mr. & Mrs. Louis Halstead, Lynn, Ind. (Parents of Glen Halstead)
Mr. & Mrs. Wm. McKinley Moss, 129 S. 2nd St., Richmond, Ind. (Parents of Wm. Moss)
Marcella Wade, 211 1st St. SW, Mason City, Ia. (Wife of Arthur Wade)
Eliz. Frasch, 1110 S. 14th St., Manitowoc, Wis. (Wife of Oakley Frasch)
Joyce Hardegree, 1957 Roosevelt Ave., Two Rivers, Wis. (Wife of Thos. Hardegree)
Alice Root, Maribel Caves, Maribel, Wis. (Wife of John Root)
Mr. & Mrs. James Harrison, Hazel Park, Royal Oak, Mich. (Parents of James Harrison)
Gloria Spalding, White Plains, New York (Wife of Robert Spalding)
Mr. & Mrs. Jacob Hinken, Grand Rapids, Mich. (Parents of Walter Hinken)
Mr. & Mrs. Anthony Plushnik, R.R. 1, Ceresco, Mich. (Parents of Harry Plushnik)
Yolanda Moore, 515 Ash St., Lansing, Mich. (Mother of Willis Moore)
Mrs. Rae Todd, 1210 W. Washington Blvd., Fort Wayne, Ind. (Wife of Harold Todd)

Dear Friends –

I know you will all be surprised to hear from me, but I am writing to all whose addresses I found in the papers, and whom I know have sons or husbands on the

Lagarto. So I am taking this way of writing to you all and giving others the addresses at the same time. Maybe some of you would like to write to the others.

My husband and I were at Manitowoc last fall to the commissioning of the Lagarto, so that is how I had the names of the boys from my son's ship. I have been corresponding with the wife of the Skipper, and I would like to pass on to you all that she has found out. Their sub was refitted in Subic Bay in the Philippines around the 1st of April or last of March. At least that is when we had our last letter, although I know of some who wrote a little later than that. Anyway, their last patrol was in the Gulf of Siam, and they had completed their patrol successfully, and were headed for base, which was to be Perth, Australia. They were with another sub, and when they tried to contact the Lagarto, they couldn't. (May 15th). So they were between those dates. We believe they could have been taken prisoners, and if so, may be in Malay, Siam, or Indo-China. Those places are just now being opened up by the British. So we just can't give up until every prisoner is out, and maybe not even then. Only the other day I met a lady whose friend was lost on a submarine for four months, and was found on some little island.

There are so many rumors a person hears, but when you track them down they invariably vanish in thin air. I have talked to so many men home from the Pacific and from subs, and almost every one of them have a different story to tell. But I believe Mrs. Latta is in a position to know more than anyone else. However, if any of you people who receive this letter hear or know anything different, please let me know. Please write anyway, and let's all pray for our loved one's safety. I will surely let you know if I hear anything more. Please write.

Sincerely, Mrs. Herbert Paper

2910 Telegraph Road, Davenport, Ia.

One of Margy Mabin's best friends was Dorothy (Dot) Peterson, the wife of QM3 Robert F. Peterson – or "Pete," as he was often called. Since Dot lived in Chicago, and Margy lived in La Grange – a suburb of Chicago – they got together frequently. A few days after receiving Mrs. Paper's letter, Margy received the following:

Mrs. Robert Peterson - 24 September 1945 – Chicago, IL

Dearest Marg –

I don't know what I'd do without you, Margie – golly you boosted my morale tonight way up high again.

It's pretty late so I'd better concentrate on copying Bill's (Reno) *letter for you.*

Quote –

Dearest Dot -

I've been putting off writing you in hopes I could find out something definite about *Lagarto* from one of the thirty some subs that have been going through here from the Pacific. After being the first one over the gangplank on about twenty of the things, today I found out what I wanted to know, from an old friend of mine of the U.S.S. Sennet (sub). The *Lagarto* and the Sennet made the first part of their patrol together. The day after the two separated, the *Lagarto* sank a Japanese Submarine. That was all for the first one. On the Second patrol the *Lagarto* went out with the *U.S.S. Baya*. The *Lagarto* was the senior boat so she went into a Japanese Harbor while the *Baya* patrolled outside. The *Baya* heard gunfire and the *Lagarto* never came out. This is all official, Dot – no punches pulled. God, if any of them did get off – why haven't we heard? As far as I know, the chances were good, but Dot, I just don't know. If the *Baya* comes through here, well maybe I'll be able to find out something more. That's my letter for now, *Dot.*

Love, Bill

P.S. Dot, from what I could find out, Bill Graves was definitely still on *Lagarto*. I'm still in Panama and don't think I'll ever be discontented again...

Ask Mrs. Latta what she thinks about the above news. She might have known before, but like you said hated to write you about it.

I wrote to Bill tonight telling him about Mrs. Latta's letter. Maybe he'll write again soon and have more news for us. Let's hope it's good news – I still think they've got a darn good chance. I'm determined not to take "no" for an answer.

Keep your chin up, honey. Be seeing you soon.

Love, Dot

Mrs. Shackelford – 27 September 1945 – Great Bend, KS

Dearest Marge –

Today I received a letter from Dot. It was a copy of the letter from Bill Reno. What do you make of it all, Marge? I've thought about it all afternoon and I've come to the conclusion that, if what he said is correct, it is encouraging. If they were in a harbor, chances are the water is shallow and two, they would be fairly close to land. In both cases, their chances of survival are much greater than if they had been out to sea, it seems to me. Surely some of them at least are prisoners. Being prisoner used to seem a dreadful thing to me but now I find myself praying that they are. I'm sure if they got off the boat, they will be alright. And, certainly after they are home, we can make up to them for all the hardships they have had to endure. I've often thought, if we could only find out the name of the Sub that they were operating with, there would be something we could do, but now that we know, what's to be done? I never heard of the U.S.S. Baya but I have the Sennet.

I have an idea, probably not a good one. Mrs. Latta said she was trying to track down some of the rumors. If we wrote her about what Bill R. said, do you suppose she could contact the skipper of the Baya and find out any more detailed news? After all, she is in the dark about as much as we are and is just as anxious for any news. What do you think? Marge, would you please send me Mrs. Latta's address? I just feel that I would like to write her, not to ask what she knows 'cause she already told you that, but just to tell her that we had a lot of confi-

dence in Mr. L and assure her that we know whatever happened couldn't be caused by any lack of efficiency on his part. She must feel a little responsible to us all, don't you think?...

Margy and Mrs. Paper 1945

While active correspondence continued that fall, and all the wives, parents, and other family members still hoped and prayed for the safe return of their loved one, many realized that their lives would probably continue without the inclusion of their beloved missing sailor. The information they individually received from a variety of unofficial sources within the Navy was passed along, and at best, a confusing picture emerged. The roller coaster of emotions ran deep and fast with each good news/bad news letter they received. No one knew quite what to believe.

Such is obvious in the exchanges between Margy Mabin – a *Lagarto* wife – and Fern Paper – a *Lagarto* mother.

Mrs. Paper – 10 October 1945 – Davenport, Iowa

Dear Friends,

I have some more news to relay to you all, and I believe it is very definite and official. Dick's friend in Washington has written me, and he said he has found out from the secret files that the Lagarto was last heard from in the South China Sea. He said that he asked the official there what the odds were that they would be found alive, and the man said that, although they were pretty slim, it was a definite possibility. They were headed for Java and then to Australia. I believe they could have had an accident near Borneo, and if that is the case, it would probably be a long time before they would be found. Those places haven't been occupied as yet. I simply am not giving up hope. Every day there are reports of released prisoners, and I know it takes a long time for news like that to be reported. I know the subs have a way of shooting oil to the surface when they are in trouble and if nothing of that sort was found, wouldn't you think they have had some kind of trouble, or been taken prisoners? All the prisoners have not been liberated yet in those places.

I am trying to get the date that the Lagarto was in the China Sea, and when they were supposed to be in Java. There are so many little islands in that part of the ocean, they could be on one of them. The man in Washington said that nothing had been heard from the Lagarto or any of her crew. It simply did not report when it was supposed to. That would seem to indicate they are all together, and when one is found, they all will be found.

I enjoy getting all your letters so much, and find pleasure in the knowledge that we are all hoping and praying together. If there is anything new that comes up, I shall let you know at once. Please write again.

<u>Mrs. Paper – 26 October 1945 – Davenport, Iowa</u>

Dear Mrs. Mabin –

I have been intending to write again, but thought I might have something more to tell you about something I heard about the harbor story too. A boy home on leave told me that he was on the Guitarro and they were traveling with the Lagarto. He said they were in Singapore Harbor, and Lagarto never came out. I told Mrs. Latta about it, but she seemed to think there was nothing to it, as she believed they were never in Singapore harbor. I could not much stalk (sic) *of what this boy said, because I found out that he could not be relied upon for truthfulness.*

A Mrs. Hinken to whom I write, wrote me last week, or this week rather, and said that the minister from her church went through the Mero when it was in Chicago. He said that he talked to one of the boys on board, and he said that the crew from the Mero was made up of survivors from other subs, and that the sub he was on at the time was traveling with the Lagarto. They were in radio contact with them, he said, and suddenly the radio contact was broken. They never heard from them since. Of course that is just another rumor, and does not correspond with our most authentic story from Washington, because that report was that they broke silence, saying they would be in Java on April 30. I am hoping I will soon hear from my friend in Washington again. I know he will let me know if he hears anything else.

I knew of that boy who was taken off the Lagarto in Panama. Dick wrote me about him. His name was Dick Byrer. His story corresponds with the one Mrs. Shackleford (sic) *wrote about the Sennet. I suppose she told you about talking to the boy from the Sennet. Mrs. Latta said she found out that Lagarto's last patrol was in the Gulf of*

Siam, so that could have been the harbor they meant. I figure that they must not have been so very far from Java and Sumatra, and could very well be down there some place right now. They are having such a time down there now, that it might be a long time before they could be "processed." I watch the Tribune very closely for accounts of what is going on down there. In yesterday's paper it told about the natives seizing the only air field at a certain place, and not letting even the mail get through. Most of that country is not even occupied yet, by any allied forces.

Did you happen to go through the Mero? I wish the minister had gotten the name of the boy to whom he talked. There was a picture of a man in the Tribune last week whose wife was suing him for divorce. It said that he had been in a Japanese prison camp in Sumatra for three years. Something in the article made me think he might have been on a submarine. I save all clippings like that thinking that sometime they might come in handy, and if I came to Chicago very soon, I would go see him.

Do write to me whenever you can. As you say, it helps so much to correspond with people that are in the same boat that you are.

<u>*Mrs. Mabin – 21 November 1945 – La Grange, Illinois*</u>

Dear Mrs. Paper –

I'm going to try to work in this letter, but because I am at work, chances are that I might well be interrupted. I have put off writing you for a long time, for one thing, because I too had heard quite bad news, and that is always unpleasant to write about, and for another, because I have so much to say when I write you that I like to take my time about it, time which I never seem to find.

I am so very sorry that you could not find my telephone number when you were so close. However, I can well understand it, since I live with my mother, and her name is Jean Miles. At any rate, my home number is La Grange 74, but had you phoned any of the other Mabins in La Grange you would have gotten in touch with me as the only other Mabins are Bill's folks and his brother. Still, I probably would have been working. I work in Chicago, and will give you my office number too, as I think that would really be more convenient for you. It is Central 3995. I will be here any day except Saturday or Sunday, on which days I expect to be home. Would certainly love seeing you or talking to you.

Your letter, as usual, was wonderful, and very inspiring. When you mentioned the "bad rumor" you had heard, I wondered if it was the one I had heard (or one of the ones, by now) about Bill Graves. Someone sent me a clipping from an Oregon newspaper saying he had "perished at sea," and giving very definite details of what was supposed to have happened to the Lagarto, including the date, the name of the ship which sunk it, and the name of the submarine which supposedly sunk the ship. That being the "Hawkbill." If this isn't the one you were referring to let me know and I will tell you exactly what is said. It struck me as being quite odd.

On the same day on which I received your letter, Monday of this week, I received a letter from Eleanor Shackelford enclosing a letter she had received from a naval officer with an entirely different and contrasting story of what had happened, but just as definite sounding. He felt sure there was no hope. He was from the submarine "Kingfish" I think. He said that it had been sunk by a Jap Destroyer which had later been sunk by a British submarine......Eleanor will probably give you the details, it just simply proved to me what a Navy chaplain said to me in August that you shouldn't believe anything unless it came from the government. Bill has always been very emphatic about that too. He had heard so many rumors in the years he has been in the submarine service that proved not to be true.

Continued (Nov. 26)

As you can see, I was interrupted – in fact I have no business writing this now, as we have been and still are extremely busy, but I am so anxious to get it off to you, particularly as it is late now.

You asked about my hearing from Mrs. Latta. That is a long story. I will explain it to you, but would appreciate it if you did not mention my telling you about it.

Several weeks ago, I think it was in the last week of October – a friend of mine was making a business trip to San Francisco. As I had written Mrs. L about that Baya story and had received no reply I asked him if he would phone her when he got there, and so he did.

She told him to tell me that there was absolutely no hope for any of the boys. She said that she knew all the details of what had happened but was sworn to secrecy and could not relate any of them, but to tell me that she had given up, and that she wouldn't if she didn't <u>*know*</u> *there was no hope. She also told him that she planned to write all the girls and mothers to that effect when she was up to it – and also to tell them what had happened, but that she couldn't do that until the details were released from the Navy Department.*

He asked her if there could have been a "chance in a million that there were any survivors" and she replied "No, not a chance in a million."

Well there it is. And don't think it didn't get me down – but now, I'm afraid with the many conflicting stories I have heard, I don't even know whether or not I feel certain she was correct. For one thing she told him she would write me, and she hasn't and it has been almost a month. I have since written her telling her of a rumor I heard and asking if that were anywhere near the truth, and still have had no reply. I figure that could mean one of two things – either she thinks the best way not to say something she shouldn't is by not writing at all, or she is beginning to wonder if she has the straight dope and hates to say anything in case it is possibly wrong again. Of course she has never retracted her statement that it was "hopeless" – and maybe I'm completely insane or something, but I can't feel that it is. I was under the impression that whatever dope she got came from the officers from the U.S.S. Baya, but I'm not sure as she didn't say. But I do know the Baya was docked in San Francisco at that time.

Your letter was one of the most encouraging things I have received for a long time.

I hope your anniversary was a pleasant one. It is so hard to really enjoy anything now. I would like to talk to you. I feel like I know you. It is so hard to believe that that boat, new as it was, and so well commanded, and so near to the end of the war, could possibly have been destroyed. I wonder if we'll ever believe it, even if the government gives them up……

Much love, Margaret Mabin

Christmas Without War 1945

The Christmas that everyone had been looking forward to had arrived – except the crew of *Lagarto* was not home to enjoy it.

The letters between the families continued – the news not good. Hope was beginning to fade, and reality was taking hold.

Mrs. Latta – 3 December 1945 – St. Helena, California

My dear Mrs. Mabin –

Forgive me for not having written you sooner but, since the many talks I've had with friends still in or returned from the Pacific, I've not had the will power to write or talk of the Lagarto. The consensus of opinion from those who should know is that there simply is no basis for further hope for any survivors from the boat. I can't say that I've given up all hope for I've not, but I am deliberately setting my mind and heart to living without Frank.

The Lagarto is evidently one of the only boats (subs) about which the Navy knows nothing of eyewitness account as to its actual loss. Even the Japs didn't know that they'd actually sunk it. That must be the reason why it has not by now been moved to the lost rather than the missing list.

I do so admire you for going back to a job and plan to do so myself within the next months. It should serve a dual purpose, economically and psychologically. I want to buy a home eventually here and stay in this valley at least until the boys are thru high school.

I was glad to be able to talk with Mr. Wallace but sorry to have to relay such word as I did to you. As to Worth Scanland's having told Mrs. Graves that there is no hope for her son – Worth has been a friend of Frank's and mine and his wife, Karina, is a very dear friend of mine. Worth did sink the Jap minelayer that had reported to its headquarters that it had attacked the Lagarto. However, the Japs did not know that they had sunk the Lagarto, and as to Worth saying that he sank the Hotsuka (sp. – should be *Hotsutaka*), *he did so several weeks after the Lagarto failed to answer to radio calls by the Baya. Personally, I've been angry at him for his smug attitude of coming up to see me and expecting me to leer with delight at his self-styled 'revenge' for Frank's loss. I had been asked not to tell what I knew about the Lagarto – then come the reports that he has tried to gain hero credit at the expense of those who have lost so much. But, whatever my fury at his manner and tactics, I do agree with him that there is little or no hope.*

I know what you feel in loneliness. Sometimes I think I can't endure another visit from friends back from the war, bringing their families with them. They do so in the kindliest spirit but not realizing how completely the sight of them together again breaks the morale I've so carefully pieced together these months. But, in self-

defense, I seem to have concocted a shutter valve in my mind, which cuts off feelings and thoughts when they become too unendurable. Perhaps if one puts on a gay show for long enough it will eventually become habit.

I've dreaded the thought of finding and holding a job but your letter has done so much to help me know that that is the happiest solution. Right now I'm working on the prelude to work – a strict regimen of weight and strength gaining. And succeeding at it at long last. The lean and haunted look may be fascinating in Vogue but it must soon pall on friends and offspring.

Do write me whenever you need or want to. By the way, as to your wondering why the Navy still lists the boat as 'missing,' I have asked about that and the only answers seem to be these two – that there were no eyewitnesses of any sort, either by our men or the Japs, and secondly, the Navy wants to give us the financial benefit of as long continuance of the men's pay as possible. Unless the miracle of some good word should come to some or all of us, I rather expect the final settlement of all doubts to come in February or thereabouts, as that would be six months after the end of the war.

Affectionately, Holly Latta

Mrs. Paper continued to write letters filled with hope – even though the odds were against finding the *Lagarto* crew safe. The following letter was to Margy Mabin:

Mrs. Paper – 11 December 1945 – Davenport, Iowa

Dear Friend –

I have been trying to get a chance to write you, but I have been so very busy. I wanted to thank you for being so lovely to me when I was in Chicago. I don't believe I even thanked your mother-in-law for the swell supper. Please thank her for me, and if any of you folks ever come to Davenport, I hope I can repay your hospitality. I surely enjoyed my visit at both of your homes.

June Barstein in Manitowoc sent me a picture of the boys, taken at the party, like the one you have. I wonder if it would be asking too much of you to copy down the names as you have them so I can tell whom they are. There is no hurry – just sometime when you have "nothing to do." Also if you would make sort of a notation behind the names of those that you told me about, such as the one who was killed, the one taken off at Panama, the rich boy, and any other little thing you think might interest me....

I just checked on something. On the day our boys' names were published as "missing" in the Tribune, I copied all those names that were listed. That would probably mean they were missing at about the same time. Out of a long list, every one of those boys but one (outside of ours) have since been listed as dead. It seems to me that if they knew positively as Mrs. Latta said that there was no hope, they would release that information in their case, just as they have in the others. I think I'll take a run down to Burlington again some of these days to see Mr. Latta's mother. I'll be very careful not to let her know that I know about Mrs. Latta's information, & see what she says to me. I think I can tell whether she knows anything or not, even if she doesn't tell me.

Did you hear my husband & me on the radio that Monday morning? We went to Don McNeil's breakfast club & he called us up to the mike. It was quite a thrill. I think everyone in Davenport heard us except my mother. She didn't have the radio on, and she is still so mad at herself, she can't get over it. I had to laugh at her. Well, of course he asked us how many children we had & I said one boy who was missing aboard a sub. After the broadcast a lady came up & was talking to us about it. She said that her son just missed going out on the Amberjack when it was lost. Since then he has been on the Balao. He is in New York right now. I asked her if he had ever mentioned Bill Mabin, & she said she didn't remember but they probably knew each other, because her son had been on the Balao ever since he left the Amberjack. His name is Lt.(jg.) S.D. Saska. Ever hear of him? She said her son told her that when the war was over, he would tell her just what happened to the Amberjack. This friend of mine in Davenport who lost her son on that sub, was so pleased that I got his name & address. They never have been able to find out a thing, in all this time. She wrote to the Navy & asked them, now that the war is over, couldn't they tell them something at least. But they didn't hear a word from them. I haven't heard from my friend in Washington yet, & he always has been so prompt in answering. I can't help but feel there must be something in the wind, or he would have answered, and I know he wouldn't have hesitated to tell me even bad news because I told him to, that I could take it.

I was just reading over the letter I got from the mother of the boy who was a sub prisoner from the Tang. She said that her boy had said there were still prisoner of war camps yet to be located. Her letter was dated Nov. 21. I have also written to the boy who was a prisoner in Java, but I haven't heard from him as yet. He lives in Ft. Dodge. I am anxious to hear from the man in Perth, Aus., too.

Well, I guess I have rambled on enough, but I want to say so many things, I never know when to quit. Again, let me thank you for being so nice to me. I feel I have known you all for a long time. When I come to Chicago again, I'll give you a ring. And if you have time to do the favor I ask, I'll appreciate it very much.

Love to you all, Mrs. Paper.

Just before the Christmas that Bill Mabin had anticipated spending with his wife and almost three-year-old daughter, (it would have been his first Christmas home in five years) Marg wrote this response to Mrs. Paper:

Mrs. Mabin – 20 December 1945 – La Grange, Illinois

Dear Mrs. Paper –

It did me no end of good to receive your encouraging letter last Friday – I had been meaning to write you even before I got it – then even moreso after I received a letter from Mrs. Latta on Saturday. But I have been extremely busy, both at home and at work.

First I will give you a brief resume of what Mrs. Latta had to say to me. She told me things that apparently she is not telling generally, probably because I quoted that article I had seen in the Oregon paper, and that more or less let the "cat out of the bag."

Since I am not sure she still feels bound by her promise not to tell anything, and since I am not sure that what she told me wasn't at least part of what she is bound not to tell, I would appreciate your not repeating it to anyone or mentioning it to her unless she should happen to mention it first.

According to her, Comdr. Scanland did sink the ship that had reported "attacking" the Lagarto (although she did say, as to you that the Jap ship was not sure, at the time it happened, they had sunk the Lagarto). However, he did not sink this ship until about three weeks after the Baya had tried to contact the Lagarto. So you see the newspaper story was not actually true, but part of it was. She expressed great annoyance at Comdr. Scanland for telling this story around as she thought it was more or less bragging on his part and was being done at the expense of those who had lost so much.

Other than that, and the fact that she said she thought they were still on the missing list for two reasons – one that there had been no eyewitnesses, two that the Navy was trying to give us the benefit of as long continuance of the men's pay as possible – she said absolutely nothing which she didn't tell you. The rest of the letter was just telling me she knew what I was going thru – and also thanking me for telling her that it was better for me to work – as it had given her some encouragement about that, and that she planned to go to work herself soon. So, in that respect, you are correct, we married girls do have more adjustments we must make with our lives and so we must face the truth, if the truth it be ....

To tell you the honest truth I'm definitely in the middle on what I think about it. I'm afraid I'm not as hopeful as you are, but I still feel there is a great deal of logic in your encouraging ideas on the matter. However, as I have felt for a long time, the odds are probably 99% against their returning. Bill was never particularly optimistic about chances of survival when a sub was sunk.

And I can certainly see, in the face of all the people she has talked with, none of whom have encouraged her at all, it would be almost impossible to feel hopeful any more. Heaven knows I am sure she would like to, but she probably feels she simply cannot stand to build up her hopes again only to get the final blow.

I am sure it must be hard for her to have to insist to you that all is hopeless, but I am also sure that she must think it is for your own good. I too worry just a little about how hard it might be for you if you can't accept it at all, and have to go on, maybe years hoping against hope with no real reason for it. The one thing I'd like not to do is accept it, and I'll admit, I haven't quite, but I am going ahead on the assumption that I too will have to make plans for a life without Bill, and that should he return, I will have lost nothing, and be forever the luckiest person in the whole wide world!!!

It is certainly the hardest thing in the world to make yourself really try to imagine what happened, and so far I try to simply avoid that thought – it is one that I cannot take.

I shan't wish you a "Merry Christmas," for I know it can't be that, but I do wish you the best possible. I think we'll all have to avoid as much sentiment as possible on that day. Of course I must make it a happy one for Nancy, but I'll be very glad to have it over.

Much love, Margy

Supreme Self-Sacrifice
1945

Somehow everyone got through Christmas.

Then this letter from the Navy arrived at the homes of the *Lagarto* families – finishing off the year with the most somber of news. One of the families to receive this letter was that of 20-year-old F2 Richard F. Grace:

SUBMARINE DIVISION ONE HUNDRED ONE
29 December, 1945
Care of Fleet Post Office
New York, New York

My dear Mrs. Grace,

Now that the active war has been successfully terminated by the efforts and supreme self-sacrifice of men such as served in the U.S.S. LAGARTO, I am able to give you a few more details of her last patrol than would have been possible while hostilities were in progress.

The LAGARTO sailed from Subic Bay, in the Philippines, patrolling an area in the South China Sea which was very vital to the last efforts of the Japanese for survival and continuance of the war. She was operating in company with another of our submarines off the coast of French Indo China on May 2, 1945. Both submarines had contact with a Japanese convoy consisting of two large merchant ships and two modern, radar equipped escort type vessels. On the night of May second, the LAGARTO engaged in aggressive surface attacks on this convoy and the Japanese countered with strong but not too well directed gunfire.

Early in the morning of May third, the LAGARTO rendezvoused with the U.S.S. BAYA, the other submarine in company, and they planned to conduct further attacks the next day. The BAYA made the first of a number of attempts to contact the LAGARTO at three in the afternoon on May third but was never able to establish communication. During the day of May third, the BAYA sighted a Japanese float plane which had been added to the previous protection the convoy had the night before.

From this chain of events, I assume that the LAGARTO was probably severely attacked by surface and air escort while driving home her attack against the Japanese. The odds the LAGARTO were up against in having one escort for each merchant ship sailing, plus air coverage made her attack one of the most difficult that I know of.

However, it was only the splendid fighting spirit and grim determination of our men who would resolutely attack against such odds that drove the Japanese to their knees.

May I be allowed to offer as a small measure of condolence my whole hearted sympathy to you at this time of your sorrow. Those of us who are still here will do our utmost in the future to safeguard the ideals and heritage of our country for which those who are missing gave so much.

Most Sincerely,
C.O. TRIEBEL,
Captain, U.S. Navy,
Commander Submarine Division 101

ALONE

Alone I talk to a ghost –
Missing you still;
Your smile, when I speak wisely
Your wonderful eyes so deep
And lovely looking at me
Amused, but chiding me
For reading your mind.

I tell you my deepest thoughts,
You understand; you comfort me
Are you perhaps still here?
Agreeing, disagreeing, speaking
Of love.
I yearn simply to hold your hand
As before.

Margaret Mabin

A New Year
1946

The letter from Captain Triebel, coming at the turn of the year from 1945 to 1946, didn't leave much room for hope for the *Lagarto* families. It wasn't the final blow – that would come later – but it didn't offer much for the *Lagarto* families to hold on to.

Many of the young widows forged ahead looking for work. Some had babies to care for and were thrust into the roles of both mother and father. They assumed the responsibilities of both parents, as well as the breadwinner in the family.

Margy continued to commute to Chicago daily to her job as assistant to the manager of *This Week* magazine. Both sides of her family pitched in to take care of me. At the age of 3, I began nursery school at Mrs. Jensen's house in La Grange Park. Every morning, my Grandmother Miles dropped me off before she went to work in her real estate office in La Grange. At noon, someone (I don't remember who) dropped me off at my grandfather Mabin's real estate office in La Grange (my Grandmother Miles and Grandfather Mabin both had their real estate businesses on the same block), and I hung around there until Grandpa took me to his home for lunch. I spent the afternoons with my Grandmother Mabin until my mother returned from work. That was the general routine. I was very close to my Mabin grandparents and held a special place in their lives. While I could never replace their beloved son Bill, as his only child I knew I was very special to them. In spite of the loss of my father (with whom I had spent less than 6 months of my life), I always felt safe and loved.

The year following the end of the war continued on this way for the Mabin family, as it did for many – grieving their sons – and carrying on.

Spring of 1946 was a tough one for the Miles and Mabin families as the losses kept coming. Margy's sister Mary – long plagued with type 1 diabetes – lost a baby and her own life from complications during childbirth. Mary Miles Stewart left her husband Tod with two little girls – Jeannie, aged 7 and Mary Ellen, aged 3. Again, family came to the rescue. Stewart and the girls moved in with Mary and Margy's mother, who took on the task of rearing the two youngsters, in addition to working full time to support herself. While the Miles' house was spacious, it was getting a little crowded so Margy began to look for another place to live.

Then Margy and the other *Lagarto* families received the following letter from the Secretary of the Navy, written on 27 May 1946:

My dear Mrs. Mabin –

Your husband, William Tucker Mabin, Signalman first class, U.S.N.R., has been carried on the official records of the Navy Department in the status of missing in action as of 24 May 1945. He was serving aboard the

USS LAGARTO when that submarine failed to return from patrol operations and was presumed lost.

On 12 April 1945, the LAGARTO departed from Subic Bay, Philippine Islands, to conduct a war patrol in the South China Sea. At 1045 p.m. on 2 May 1945, the LAGARTO and the USS BAYA were both in contact with an escorted enemy convoy in the Gulf of Siam. Following this action, the BAYA and the LAGARTO rendezvoused at 240 a.m. on 3 May 1945 and made plans for again closing with this convoy. The BAYA proceeded on ahead of the LAGARTO about fifteen miles and was driven off by alert radar-equipped escorts. The BAYA had no further contacts with the LAGARTO. The LAGARTO had been directed to proceed to the Java Sea and depart from there for Fremantle, Australia, on 4 May 1945. She failed to arrive at Fremantle on or about 24 May 1945, in accordance with her schedule and, to date, no further information has been received by the Navy Department concerning the fate of the submarine or her crew.

In view of the strong probability that the submarine sank during action in enemy-controlled waters, and that your husband lost his life as a result thereof, because no official or unconfirmed reports have been received that he survived, because his name has not appeared on any lists or reports of personnel liberated from Japanese prisoner of war camps, and in view of the length of time that has elapsed since he was determined to have been missing in action, I am reluctantly forced to the conclusion that he is deceased. In compliance with Section 5 of Public Law 490, 77th Congress, as amended, the death of your husband is, for the purposes of termination of pay and allowances, settlement of accounts, and payment of death gratuities, presumed to have occurred as of 25 May 1946 which is the day following the expiration of twelve months in the missing status.

I know what little solace the formal and written word can be to help meet the burden of your loss, but in spite of that knowledge, I cannot refrain from saying very simply, that I am sorry. It is hoped that you may find comfort in the thought that your husband gave his life for his country, upholding the highest traditions of the Navy.

Sincerely yours,
James Forrestal

There it was. The awful pronouncement that no one wanted to hear. Barring some dramatic and implausible miracle, eighty-six young American sailors were gone forever. *Lagarto* parents never recovered from the loss of their sons. *Lagarto* widows lost their husbands to whom they had given vows to cherish forever. *Lagarto* children would always wonder what life would have been like if their fathers hadn't died. These were universal feelings of those closest to someone lost in war.

All of the *Lagarto* parents, many of the *Lagarto* widows, and some of the *Lagarto* children died not knowing what had happened to that submarine or even where it was.

With the official declaration of death received from the Navy department, individual memorial services were held for the *Lagarto* crew at churches, American Legion Posts, and VFW Posts across the country. Coping with the death of her sister and the memorial service for her husband, Marg suffered another blow the same month.

On her way to work one morning into Chicago, as her train approached Union Station, another train backed into it. The seat Margy was sitting in collapsed, and the car began to fill with smoke. Margy was convinced that if she didn't get out of the train, her three-year-old daughter would become an orphan. She managed to open the window next to her seat and hailed a passenger who had just alighted from the train. He stood below the window and shouted for her to let herself down; he would catch her. With strength hard to imagine, given her injuries, Margy pulled herself out of the seat and crawled through the window. The man carried her into Union Station and placing her on a baggage cart, signaled for help. Margaret Miles Mabin was admitted to Northwestern Hospital with numerous fractured pelvic bones (from the seat collapse) and spent the next four months at the hospital with both legs in traction.

Christmas Together - At Last 2005

Just prior to *Lagarto's* arrival in Pearl Harbor on Christmas Day of 1944, Bill Mabin had written to Marg:

I want you to send me an itemized list of everything Nance gets for Christmas, with her reaction to each. This was the Christmas I really wanted to be home. I pray to God I can be with you both the next one. This is the fifth Christmas in a row I've said that. The next one will be the one she'll talk of Santa Claus tho, so let's mark Dec. 25, 1945 as our big day.

It turned out that our "first" Christmas together was a little later than that. It was Christmas 2005, sixty years late.

In the months since *Lagarto's* discovery, I had become closer to my long-gone father than ever before in my life. The challenge of getting the Navy to acknowledge *Lagarto's* discovery, the plans for the submarine's memorial service, and the search for the submarine's other families had driven me day and night for the past seven months. My mother had urged me for years to read my father's letters, but I had resisted. I felt that reading them would make me sad.

Lagarto's discovery had opened a whole new world to me – one of getting acquainted with my dear father and doing something for him. Two weeks after the sub's discovery, I borrowed my dad's letters from my mother and began reading them. Even though many of his relatives and friends had told me what a wonderful and exceptional guy he was, I didn't know my father until I read his letters. After that, he seemed real to me, and I was obsessed with making sure that he and all the other *Lagarto* crew would receive the respect to which they were entitled. So Christmas 2005 was OUR Christmas.

That Christmas our family gathered at our farm in Lake Leelanau, Michigan and had a very special and blessed time together. Someone who had been missing all my life was to be part of a Christmas he had longed for sixty years earlier. His special blessing was that he now had grandchildren!

2006

As the new year began, things started to fall into place. More families were found, but the pressure to pick up the pace increased. Karen Duvalle and I estimated we had found almost half of the *Lagarto* crew's families, but we weren't satisfied.

Local newspaper stories about *Lagarto* had run their course, and we were stymied about what to do next. We decided to give the newspapers another try, and this time, instead of asking the publications to run a full-blown article about *Lagarto,* we sent letters to the Editor. Again we contacted the unresponsive papers from our first try, and waited for a hit. As a result of this new approach, the *Rocky Mountain News* in Denver, CO; the *Trinity Standard* in Trinity, TX; the local newspapers in Rockford, IL and Sayre, PA; and the *Hartford Courant* in Hartford, CT all printed an article or prominent item about *Lagarto* in their publications. Through their efforts, we found the families of Lt. Robert T. Ruble, EM2 Dennis J. Gray, S1 John L. Williams, and Ltjg. Walter B. Phelps. Unfortunately, we didn't find any family members of TM2 Justin M. McGee of Rockford, IL.

Our criteria for families changed somewhat. After reaching a number of dead ends in our searches for *Lagarto* families, Duvalle and I made the decision that friends who remembered and/or cared for a *Lagarto* crew member would be considered family. It was daunting to try, in a few short months, to find family members of submariners who had been gone for over 60 years. We had taken on the task ourselves with no help in tracking down relatives from the military.

We were thrilled, however, to receive help from unexpected sources. Patricia Pleska, Manager of the West Virginia Veterans Memorial Archives, looked for *Lagartos* from that state. David Dwiggins, who was living in the Philippines, began an active search for *Lagartos* from Indiana. Michael Mohl, who was the webmaster for the excellent *Navsource.org* stayed in constant contact with us and others who might have information.

Charles Hinman, Director of Education and Outreach for the Bowfin Museum in Pearl Harbor, coordinated the website *OnEternalPatrol.com.* He was an enormous help. Many who had read about *Lagarto* contacted me with their best wishes and support. The response to the discovery of this one lost submarine from World War II was touching and overwhelming.

The *Lagarto* families came together. I sent out an S-O-S to all of the family members we had found so far, and got a terrific response. It seemed that everyone who could, wanted to be helpful.

Carol Lawson, niece of MoMM1 Richard L. Fisher; Larry Halstead, nephew of RM3 Glen E. Halstead; Nancy Mendenhall Ford, daughter of Lt. William H. Mendenhall (XO of *Lagarto*); Ben Byrer and his wife Violet, brother of F1 Clark R. Byrer; Kelan Spalding, brother of PhMC

Robert B. Spalding; Laura Keeney Zavala, granddaughter of Lt. A.H. "Bud" Keeney; Heather Reichert, niece-in-law of F1 Raymond E. Reichert; and Sandra Summers, niece of EM2 Dennis J. Gray all took names of missing family members and were a great help. Just prior to finding Sandy Summers, I was contacted by Bill Epperson, who had been a good friend of Dennis Gray.

The primary mission of the *Lagarto* families and friends was that of finding as many other *Lagartos* as possible in the next two months. Time was flying, and it was important to notify those families of the new status of the submarine and apprise them of the memorial service that was scheduled for the first week end in May. We were racing the clock, and although the work ahead would take time, no one was bothered by it. We had the grand goal of finding as many families as possible, and everyone was enthusiastic about helping.

Dave Walker
2006

I had let myself go. My hair was shaggy, and my nails were chipped. So in the last week of February, I made an appointment with the Pavlova Spa in Traverse City for a haircut and manicure. One never knows what kind of weather you are going to be facing in northern Michigan in late February. That part of the country, always beautiful, gets a lot of snow in the winter, often leading to icy roads in the hills one must traverse from Leelanau County to the biggest town in the area – Traverse City, which is twenty-five miles away from my home. So I gave myself plenty of time to get there.

It turned out to be a beautiful day, and I arrived too early for my appointments, so I stopped in a coffee shop to kill some time. While I waited for my coffee, I spotted a familiar face sitting at a counter, sipping his coffee and reading the paper. The face belonged to a man who had visited our living room, through the wonders of television, many times. It was Dave Walker – a news anchor and manager of the Traverse City affiliate of NBC News.

I considered my approach for about 10 seconds and introduced myself.

"I hate to bother you, but I have a story that you might be interested in," I said. Walker was pleasantly receptive, so I continued. He listened while I told him the *Lagarto* story and expressed interest in doing something on it. Walker had also served in the Navy and found what I told him inspiring. We parted, saying that we would stay in touch.

A few days later, I sent Dave an e-mail:

> <u>24 February 2006</u>
> Dear Mr. Walker,
>
> I so enjoyed talking with you the other day. You were very gracious and kind. Thank you.
>
> ...My experiences in finding and contacting *Lagarto* families have been so profound, that I am determined to find as many other families as we can before the May service. As I told you, we've had wonderful responses from local newspapers (which include The Chicago Tribune and The Cleveland Plain Dealer). Our latest response has come through a recent article in The Hartford Courant. Hopefully we will find someone from the family of Lt. Walter Phelps. Everyone on that crew deserves to have someone remember them (sometimes, it's only friends).
>
> After going this route, we feel that we have done all we can. The only route open to us is through the medium of television. We believe that a story, with na-

> tionwide applications, would reach other families who still do not know the fate of their lost loved one on that submarine. It would help us enormously. Plus, it's a very good story!

Walker responded and said that he was talking with his boss at the station and contacting a national news friend in Washington D.C. to see if they had any interest.

I was encouraged by his speedy reply and wrote again:

> Dear Dave,
>
> Thanks so much for your response. In the past few days, a few interesting things have happened that I don't think I've told you about. We've found our 40th family – that of Lt. Walter Phelps from West Hartford, CT. It's the 10th we've found from a local newspaper. His niece (who always considered her uncle a war hero) was thrilled to read of the discovery and hopefully is planning to attend the ceremony. Other family members have now become involved in finding others...
>
> Some U.S. senators have become involved and are working to get American flags to give to the families. I believe that the navy band has been secured from

Great Lakes, and the governor of Wisconsin is scheduled to be there. The diver who found the *Lagarto* is flying in from Thailand earlier in the week, and I think I told you that the Commander of the Pacific Fleet (submarines) Admiral Jeffrey Cassias is coming from Pearl Harbor to be the keynote speaker...

...I believe this memorial service will honor more men (MIAs found from WWII or any other war) at one time than any that has ever been held. It's amazing to me that the TV media hasn't picked up on this. A couple of weeks ago, I saw a story on CNN about a man whose WALLET had been found after 40 years. This story should be at least as newsworthy as that!

Hope I don't sound too pushy to you. Whenever I think I might be, I remember a diary my father kept. It spoke of depth charges, the heat, the fear, and the courage that was part of the daily life on a submarine at war. Whenever I reflect on that, I know I'm not going too far. Those men (and all the other lost submariners) deserve to be remembered...

Dave replied the next day and said they needed to confirm the discovery of *Lagarto*. He asked who to call – "the U.S. Navy? Or the shipyard? Or – who do I call?"

That was the problem, and we'd encountered it before. The discovery of *Lagarto* was certain, but we had received no "official confirmation" from the Navy. Without that, some media sources were reluctant to broadcast or write about the story. Consequently, Walker was unable to take the story any further at the time. That would change.

Lost Families
2006

The request from Dave Walker – to confirm the discovery of *Lagarto* – was just the latest in a series of questions from journalists about the authenticity of the submarine find. We needed the Navy to acknowledge the discovery of the long-lost submarine in an official way.

The genuine and whole-hearted actions on the part of the Naval officers in Pearl Harbor had gone a long way in easing the angst many of us felt toward the Navy, but their well-meaning attentions didn't solve the basic problem. We also knew there were naval personnel working behind the scenes to help us, but we needed more.

We had found forty families of the eighty-six crew members. Karen Duvalle and I communicated with each and every family. I spoke on the phone with most of them and shared their initial shock and joy at the news. But that left more than half of the crew's families still in the dark about the fate of *Lagarto,* and the memorial service was coming up fast. There were forty-six men who hailed from all regions of the country, and we were determined to find as many of their families as we could before May.

The Mighty Lagartos
2006

The *Lagarto* families and friends of the project rolled up their sleeves and were reaping results. Their determination went beyond what Karen Duvalle and I expected. Most took the names of three missing crew members and contacted the newspapers, Chambers of Commerce, libraries, historical societies, genealogical newsletters, and local schools in the towns where a *Lagarto* sailor had once lived.

Through the aggressive efforts of the *Lagartos,* this diverse and strong group of volunteers got in on the act to find the missing families. They were touched by the long-ago sacrifices of the lost submariners and wanted to help find their families. Keith MacNeal, a grand-nephew of *Lagarto's* S1 John Leslie Williams, put a piece in the Rootsweb Newsletter. He also contacted Richard Bergen, a retired Lieutenant Commander of the Navy and military historian, whose wife was currently serving as a captain in the Navy. Their daughter was serving in the Navy Nurse Corps, and they had two nephews in the Submarine service. Solidly Navy! A resident of Upper Marlboro, Maryland, Bergen often taught at the Naval Station in Annapolis and was familiar with the Nimitz Library of the Naval Academy. He suggested other resources – the American Battle Monuments Commission and each state's Adjutant General's office.

On March 24, I was contacted by Sasha Stanley, a former research librarian and 40-year genealogist, who lived in Greene Co., Ohio. She took some names to search and told me her husband was career Navy, and her father was a Navy man. She was thrilled to be part of this project. Sasha's dedication to the project helped us find five families: Lois Friend, the sister of BM1 Eugene Robison of Boggstown, Indiana; Thayer, a relative of F1 Willis Moore of Lansing, Michigan; and Frank Marriott, a brother of S1 Joy M. Marriott of Columbus, Ohio. She also found Violet Heaton, a sister of TM3 Alvin Enns of Gray, Oklahoma, and Eleanor Anderson, the widow of QM1 William Graves of Portland, Oregon. Sasha was a godsend! The kind of research she was doing was typified in an e-mail:

> My husband, who was on and off ships for 34 years before he retired, says crews logged on for special missions, or were not on the lists because of sickness and someone took their place to round out the crew, etc. I found a small article in a newspaper about the *Lagarto* being overdue in port, and on the same page it told how the Navy was deactivating all its ships and the war was over. The *Lagarto* must

> have been on a special mission of some kind...

The 'special mission' possibility was always a question in my mind. U.S. submarines engaged in stealth, supplying ammunition and goods to troops on Pacific Islands. They also landed spies and evacuated troops and individuals. Before he became *Lagarto's* commanding officer, CDR Frank D. Latta, while captain of *U.S.S. Narwhal,* directed that submarine in numerous special missions. According to *United States SUBMARINE Operations in World War II,* CDR Frank Latta directed the following missions:

<u>May 4-11, 1943</u> Reconnoitered Attu landing beaches and disembarked 105 Army Scouts on Scarlet Beach, Attu.

<u>July 15, 1943</u> Bombarded Matsuwa Airfield on Matsuwa To in Kuriles with 31 rounds of six-inch shells. Also reconnoitered several Kurile islands.

<u>November 13, 1943</u> Delivered 46 tons of stores and landed 2 parties, Lt. Cdr. C. Parsons in command, at Paluam Bay, Mindoro, P.I.

<u>November 15, 1943</u> Delivered 46 tons of supplies and evacuated 32 people including 8 women and 2 children at Nasipit, Mindananao, P.I.

<u>December 2, 1943</u> Delivered 90 tons of ammunition and stores and evacuated 8 people including Lt. Cdr. C. Parsons and 2 women from Mindanao, P.I.

December 5, 1943 Evacuated 3 women, 4 children and 2 men including DeVries family from Majacalar Bay, Mindanao, P.I.

February 5, 1944 Delivered 45 tons of ammunition and stores and evacuated 5 servicemen and one British subject near Livertad, Panay, P.I.

February 7, 1944 Delivered 45 tons of cargo and evacuated 28 men, women, and children in vicinity of Balatong Point, Negros.

March 5, 1944 Delivered some cargo and received 10 passengers from Tawi-Tawi, P.I. Unloading interrupted by patrol boats.

June 13, 1944 Bombarded oil tanks at Bula Ceram I., N.E.I.

June 20-21,1944 Landed supplies and evacuated personnel in vicinity of Lipata Pt., Panay, P.I.

September 1, 1944 Landed 20 men and 10 tons of supplies on east coast of Luzon, P.I.

October 17, 1944 Landed 11 tons of cargo on north west coast of Tawi-Tawi, P.I.

October 19, 1944 Landed 37 men and 60 tons of cargo and evacuated 20 women and children plus 6 prospective mess boys and one steward's mate on southwest coast of Negros I., P.I.

This was CDR Latta's last special mission on *Narwhal.* However, from February 11-14, 1945, as commander of *Lagarto,* Latta directed an anti-picket sweep west of Bonin Islands.

Karen Christensen managed a department at Syracuse University and became very involved. She had seen our message in a genealogy newsletter, offered her services, and looked for men from New York. Christensen worked on finding the family of EM2 Donald George Stiegler of Rochester, New York and also took on the daunting task of finding family of *Lagarto* steward Robert Green of Titusville, PA. I was particularly anxious to find Green's family, as he was the only *Lagarto* crew member of whom Mike Latta had any memory. While *Lagarto* was engaged in sea trials in Lake Michigan, Mike was allowed to join the crew on a couple of occasions. He had warm memories of STM2 Robert Green. Christensen wrote me a short e-mail that rang with irony: "Nancy, I was just looking for Titusville, PA on the map. Do you believe it is down the road from a town named Torpedo?"

A combat veteran of the Korean War, Ed Maul served on the USS Wisconsin from 1951-1955. He offered to help and suggested several military and navy websites to search for information.

Donald Bishop, another retired Naval Lieutenant Commander who lived in Mississippi, joined the search and engaged numerous family members and retired naval associates to help him. He adopted crew members from Tupelo, MS; Amite, LA; Raymondville, TX; and two from Philadelphia, PA. It was amazing to see people from all over the country help us in a nationwide search for our missing families.

In the meantime, the *Lagarto* families themselves worked feverishly to find others. We knew our time was short if we wanted to find them before the memorial service. David Stanley, a nephew of MoMM1 Richard Fisher, found the brother of S1 John Franze of Ellwood City, Pennsylvania. Franze's brother couldn't talk about the loss of his brother, but a reporter from the local paper decided to write a story anyway.

Throughout this whole process, Karen Duvalle and I had learned to respect the various reactions of the *Lagarto* relatives. While the vast majority of the family members embraced the news, there were a few others who couldn't bear to open that door again. They had painful memories and weren't willing to dredge up the past.

Carol Lawson, David Stanley's cousin and Richard Fisher's niece, became involved in the search. She contacted Alva, Oklahoma Chamber of Commerce Director Alex Drenning for help in locating the family of RM2 Leslie M. Doud. According to a March 13 story in the *Alva Review-Courier* written by Helen Barrett:

> Drenning asked longtime Alva pharmacist Jim Holder if he knew the family. Holder steered Drenning to the local mortuaries. Drenning's first call to Marshall Funeral Home put her in contact with Doud's aunt, Moye Long and her son Lonnie. Doud's mother Mabel died in December 2000 without knowing of the discovery of her son's final

resting place. His father, Wesley, who formerly worked for the Alva Post Office, died earlier.

Lonnie Long, Doud's nephew said that his mother was "very, very relieved that there is finally closure."

All the *Lagarto* detectives had different reasons for adopting particular families. Carol Lawson told me hers in an e-mail:

> I would love to help to try and find some of the missing. One name stood out, RM2 Leslie M. Doud of Alva, OK. My father's name was Alva. When I was 12 years old, he was taking stunting lessons in a Piper Cub plane, and he and the instructor were killed. So that's just the guy I will try and help you with. If you would send me the sample letter, I'll get busy on this. I'll start on this in the A.M.

The following day, after Carol gave Karen Duvalle and me the news of a blessedly quick success, I wrote to her:

> Hey Carol, Nice going! Doesn't it feel great?

She replied:

> It was sooo exciting. I have had a busy week and it really topped it off. I spent about an hour on the phone telling friends about it. I am going to try more. I chose that family because my father's name was Alva and that was the town they lived in. WORKED!!!......Well, better try another family.

Larry Halstead, nephew of RM3 Glen Halstead was also enjoying success. In an e-mail note, Larry said:

> Just a quick update as to where I stand on my three families. I have not hit any pay dirt yet, but I am enjoying the task and I think I am making progress. I have now sent out three letters to the local newspapers......I also have a librarian at the Dayton Daily News doing some research on Mr. Kneidl. I also spent a half hour on the phone with a Mr. Brock near Busy, KY who is into genealogy stuff who is doing some research on the ground in the back woods of Kentucky for us.

Halstead's persistence was rewarded with two finds – Dayton resident John M. Kneidl, nephew and namesake of MoMM2 John W. Kneidl, also of Dayton and S2 Aaron Brock's brother Walter, a resident of Amelia, Ohio. Halstead was greatly moved by these finds as were Mr. Kneidl and Mr. Brock. Both gentlemen learned of the news in time to attend the *Lagarto* ceremony.

Lagarto's PhMC Robert Spalding's brother Kelan was doing well, also. In a series of e-mails, Spalding told me he had the newspapers in Little Rock Arkansas and Malden, Missouri looking for relatives of TM2 John Davis and TMC Harold Andrews, respectively. I suspect Spalding may have chosen those names because he knew they were good friends of his brother. They were good friends of my father, Bill Mabin, as well. The clues developed, and Spalding found a half-brother of Andrews living in Cape Girardeau, Missouri and learned that Andrews had a daughter. Andrews' daughter Karen was the baby her mother Nell spoke of when she wrote a letter to my mother. So I knew Karen and I were very close in age. On March 24, Spalding wrote:

Nancy, I received a call from an 88-year-old lady that had been a neighbor of Harold's. It was in response to a newspaper article I asked them to put in the Delta-News Citizen.....Also, they should be running articles in the Little Rock, ARK and Portland, Oregon papers today.

Two days later, Spalding wrote:

Nancy, received another call today. From a cousin of Harold Andrews. Cecil King, Vero Beach, Florida..... He said Harold's daughter is Karen Atkinson.....St. Petersburg, FL......Cecil is from MO and still receives the paper. How great is this??? Thought you would want to call Karen. You two must be about the same age...

I did call Karen Andrews Atkinson immediately. We shared feelings only another submarine daughter could understand. She said that her mother never remarried and moved to Florida, where her parents had talked about settling after the war. There were several photographs of Karen's father, *Lagarto's* CTM Harold D. Andrews, around the house, and she had always felt connected to him. I was thrilled that she was determined to attend the memorial service with her whole family.

March Madness 2006

The month of March was passing. Our search for additional *Lagarto* families was going well, and the Wisconsin Maritime Museum was receiving a flood of reservations for the *Lagarto Remembrance Week End.* Officers of high rank were expected in Manitowoc for the ceremony. RADM Jeffrey Cassias and LCDR Jeff Davis had been gracious and responsive. Other Naval officers – both active and retired – were working behind the scenes on *Lagarto's* behalf, and I couldn't have been more grateful. Things were falling into place, and we had accomplished as much as we could. Except for one thing.

The February issue of *Naval History* arrived, and I read an article that was interesting, informative and historical. Normally this article would have been appreciated, instead I found it infuriating.

It was about a group of historians, researchers and two government agencies – National Oceanic and Atmospheric Administration (NOAA) and Hawaii Undersea Research Laboratory (HURL) – that had taken part in surveying two Japanese vessels built for the purpose of attacking U.S. Naval vessels in WWII. The two agencies had teamed up with the Naval Historical Center and the National Park Service the previous August in an expedition to a Japanese midget submarine that had participated in the 1941 attack on Pearl Harbor. The prior March, HURL discovered the wreck of the Japanese World War II submarine I-401, one of three aircraft carriers built in 1944 to carry their submarines. These were fascinating and historical Japanese ships, and I understood the interest in learning more about them.

However, by the time the NOAA expedition took place, the discovery of *Lagarto* had been known for three months. The families of *Lagarto* had worked hard in trying to garner the interest of the U.S. government/USN to acknowledge her discovery. In return, the *Lagarto* constituents of many U.S. senators, contacting the Secretary of the Navy on their behalf, received the same tired form letter stating that the Navy was not going to do anything in regard to the newly discovered submarine. Even though our country was awash in patriotic fervor, that patriotism seemed to stop at *Lagarto's* hatch. Although the *Lagarto* families contained their frustration and forged on with little encouragement (except for the wonderful Navy staff in Hawaii), it was disheartening to think that the Naval Historical Center and the Navy were apparently oblivious to the families' feelings. Encouraged by the positive response of both RADM Cassias and LCDR Davis, our feelings toward the Navy's reaction were assuaged.

But after reading this article, the hurt feelings from the Navy's seeming disinterest in *Lagarto* resurfaced. I was shocked to learn that, at the very time the families had been rebuffed by the NHC, that same agency was involved in a project to learn more about our former enemy's midget sub - whose mission was to kill American sailors.

In a letter to NOAA in March 2006, I wrote:

According to an article in the February 2006 issue of Naval History, published by the US Naval Institute, NOAA worked with HURL on researching and surveying two Japanese vessels that were involved in the attack on Pearl Harbor. As an historian, I appreciate the value of the research.

However, it is curious to learn that these two agencies teamed up with the Naval Historical Center and the National Park Service last August in an expedition to the Japanese midget submarine, while the families of the American submarine, the USS Lagarto, were patiently awaiting US confirmation on the discovery of this missing WWII submarine. As a matter of fact, the Lagarto families are STILL awaiting confirmation on the discovery that was made almost a year ago.

Is there some reason why the same resources used in the Japanese projects cannot be used to positively confirm this American submarine? 86 sailors lost their lives on that boat. My father, William T. Mabin, SM1 was one of them. We have found 46 families of the 86-member crew, who will be gathering for a joint memorial service on May 6th in Manitowoc, WI. It is rather important for those families to know that the resources of our government would be used for the purpose of collecting data on the Lagarto rather than, historic though they may be, Japanese vessels.

Please see if you can clear this up for me. It will be difficult to explain to the Lagarto families if you don't.

I received the NOAA Public Affairs response on March 28, 2006:

Dear Ms. Kenney – Thank you for your message. I will check with the office that conducted this effort.

I never heard another thing from them.

Letters to the Admiral 2006

Reading the article about NOAA's expedition to survey the WWII Japanese midget sub in *Naval History* raised my hackles. While we were thrilled with the participation of the Navy through the attendance of the Pearl Harbor officers, we were still baffled by the reticence of the Navy to officially acknowledge *Lagarto's* discovery. We absolutely could not understand what was holding this up, and I got tired of waiting. After going through all the proper channels with no satisfactory result, I decided to go straight to the top.

The top man in the Navy was Admiral Mike Mullen, who was Chief of Naval Operations (CNO). I decided that sending him an e-mail expressing my concerns wouldn't hurt at this point since nothing else was working. Perhaps he was unaware of the situation (being a very busy man), or he didn't know how important it was to the anxious *Lagarto* families to have the Navy's confirmation of *Lagarto's* find.

On 13 March 2006, I wrote:

> Dear Admiral Mullen,
>
> I am writing you this letter as a daughter and a wife of the Navy. My father, SM1 William T. Mabin, was one of the 86

crew members who died on the WWII submarine, the USS LAGARTO. My husband, Lt. John M. Kenney (retired), was on the destroyer Gearing, which was the first ship to intercept a Russian vessel bound for Cuba during the blockade. I love the Navy! I frequently read articles in the *U.S. Naval Institute's Naval History* and have learned how interested you are in the Navy's future.

Of course, the Navy would have no future if it hadn't had a rich past. That past includes the countless sacrifices of those who gave their lives on submarines in WWII. The 50th of the 52 submarines lost in that war was the USS LAGARTO which, after 60 years, was found in the Gulf of Thailand, very close to its last known position.

Imagine how thrilled the LAGARTO families are to learn this news. We also learned that the boat went down fighting and no longer have to wonder how our loved ones met their deaths. So far, 42 families have been found, and I have spoken to most of them. The stories I hear are touching beyond belief. Many were lost, and each one was special.

To business. In the past few months since the discovery of the *Lagarto*, its family members have asked little of the Navy. The expectation was that the Navy would embrace this discovery. However, the reality has been quite different. We have only asked that the Navy officially acknowledge the discovery publicly (with a statement to the media), help find the families, and participate in a joint memorial service. We believe that the members of the *Lagarto's* crew should receive the same military honors that any other MIA receives when his/her remains are found. Imagine the Army not acknowledging a mass grave in a foreign country with the remains of 86 soldiers! Simply because the gravesite of the *Lagarto* is in the Pacific is no reason to not acknowledge it! The families have received an out-pouring of support from others – literally nationwide and worldwide. Some members of the Navy have been very kind and have gone out of their way to be supportive. It would mean so much to have that same support from you – speaking officially for the USN. A memorial service will be held at the Wisconsin Maritime Museum in Manitowoc, WI in May. We believe that's a most appropriate location, as the USS LAGARTO was built in Manitowoc. Things have come full circle.

One more thing – the "elephant in the living room." Apparently, the NHC is responsible for the determination of whether the USS LAGARTO has truly been found. After numerous requests from family and friends to acknowledge this important discovery – mostly through their members of Congress – the replies have been less than satisfactory. There is no doubt, based on historic data and physical evidence, that the submarine is the missing *Lagarto.* Yet the families have been informed that there is insufficient evidence that the boat is the *Lagarto.* The most recent communication stated that it may not be possible to make a positive identification. That is nonsense and totally insensitive to the families. For that attitude to come from the Navy is shocking and hurtful. Please move on, acknowledge the discovery, and join the families in their joy! It would be better for everyone involved.

This is not a trivial matter. There were 32 states represented on that boat. Newspapers across the globe have written of this story, and I know there are more articles to come. As yet, there has not been television coverage. But there will be. Just recently on CNN, there were two stories covered that were of much less import.

One was the recent identification of the WWII Army cadet whose frozen body was found in a California glacier. Yesterday, there was a story on a wallet found that had been lost in 1963. How do you think these stories compare to the discovery of a WWII submarine, on which 86 men gave their lives for their country? The families have been waiting patiently for the Navy to make the announcement. It would look better for you to make the announcement than us.

My father kept a diary that spoke of the depth charges, heat, fear, and courage that were part of life on a submarine at war. My mother kept all his letters that spoke of his love for his family and desire to finish the war so that he could be with them again. She also kept letters exchanged between herself and other wives and mothers of the *Lagarto* crew the year it was missing. They were heart-breaking as they spoke of their hopes that the crew would be found on an island somewhere – or even in a prison camp. Imagine what they went through. In recent months, I have spoken with widows, siblings, nieces and nephews on the phone, so overwhelmed with emotion that they cried – or could barely speak. The most emotional of all have been the conversations I've had with other children – mind you; most of us are in our 60s. We shared our feelings of loss as we grew up without our fathers. We often cried as we realized that we had all felt the same pain. Really, the Navy cannot ignore this. We are YOUR families, too.

Finding *Lagarto* families plus a million other things kept me busy while I awaited word from ADM Mullen. I knew that the top man in the Navy would be busy, so I didn't expect an answer immediately. However, after two weeks, I wrote him another e-mail on 29 March 2006:

Dear Admiral Mullen,

It has been over 2 weeks since I sent you my letter about the USS LAGARTO. I have heard nothing in response from you or your staff.

It has become increasingly apparent that the problem with *Lagarto* confirmation lies with the NHC. The *Lagarto* families and friends do not see it as a historical matter. We see it as personal. The USS LAGARTO did not have a long and dazzling record. It was built toward the end of the war and had a short life. The crew was led by a brilliant commander, Frank D. Latta, but many of them were young and inexperienced. However, they were deeply loved by their families, who never saw them again. IT IS TO THESE FAMILIES THAT THE NAVY OWES CONFIRMATION!

The USN and NHC have known about this for a long time. They had many opportunities to do something, but stated quite clearly that they wouldn't. In addition to other data, the NHC has the Steve Burton sketch of the wreck. Burton is one of the top divers in SE Asia. He also received degrees in engineering and really knows his stuff – both from the standpoint of a master diver and an engineer. I will quote from an article written by him recently. It is an excellent description of what the divers found, and I would be happy to forward it to you or anyone who hasn't already seen it. Just ask.

In the section of the article titled 'Final Moments,' it says, 'After each dive, it was possible to add more details to the dive sketch that would formally identify the USS LAGARTO. Unlike many other Balao class submarines, the LAGARTO had two 5-inch guns mounted in front of, and behind the conning tower. These were clearly visible mounted in a stowed position, which together with the wreck's location confirmed the identification.' It goes on, 'A forward starboard torpedo door is open, and it's possible to peer inside and confirm that it is empty. This suggests that the LAGARTO went down fighting and that a torpedo had been fired during her last moments. The rubber seals of the torpedo tube muzzle door are still in excellent condition even after 60 years under water.' And, 'Sadly, also visible was the massive damage caused to the port quarter forward of the conning tower. The LAGARTO had plainly sustained a direct hit from a depth charge or other large explosive ordnance. The destruction caused by this device had been sufficient to entirely destroy the external steel plating that contained several large buoyancy compartments and then penetrate much further into the sub to punch a large hole through the 1-inch thick high tensile steel inner pressure bulkhead that contained the crew's living spaces.'

...Admiral Mullen, I do not wish to be confrontational with the USN. The lack of interest from the Navy breaks my heart. But the question remains. What is the Navy going to do about this?

Four days later, I was encouraged by the following message from ADM Mullen:

> "hi nancy. just got your letter in this email. I will look into this and get back to you. i appreciate your concern. all the best, mike"

I was thrilled! With 27 words, Admiral Mullen signaled that he was paying attention and the *Lagartos* were finally being taken seriously.

Members of Congress 2006

There were others from whom we sought help. On day one, I had called the offices of both Illinois senators – Senator Barack Obama and Senator Richard Durbin. Senator Obama's office was responsive (I burst into tears during the call), and while Senator Durbin's office was not helpful at first, they later pitched in. Congressman Dan Lipinski's office went above and beyond (Lenore Goodfriend and Christopher Ganschow) in taking up our cause.

That was about it. I learned from the SubVets in Wisconsin that their U.S. senators – Senator Russ Feingold and Senator Herb Kohl – were also interested in the *Lagarto* situation and lent their support. As we approached the time of the memorial service, Congressman Mark Green, in response to my cousin Mike Walker, was helpful.

And prior to the time of *Lagarto's* discovery, Wisconsin governor Jim Doyle officially declared May 3rd of each year as *Lagarto* Remembrance Day.

In Missouri, Kelan Spalding, the brother of *Lagarto's* pharmacist mate Robert, had become very proactive in the *Lagarto* cause. Through his efforts, Missouri congressman Roy Blunt took steps to honor *Lagarto*.

As we began to find more and more families, other members of Congress were made aware of *Lagarto's* discovery and her connection to their constituencies. Senator Lindsey Graham of South Carolina contacted the Navy on behalf of Bess Torgerson of Columbia, SC – the sister-in-law of *Lagarto's* MoMM1 Caldwell T. Cook, who had also lived in Columbia.

One of our biggest breakthroughs came with getting the attention of Michigan's Senator Carl Levin. At the time, Senator Levin was the minority spokesperson on the senate's Armed Services Committee. His staff stayed in close touch with me.

However, even with the interest of many powerful members of Congress, others fell short. The *Lagarto* crew hailed from 32 different states, and their families lived in virtually every state of the union. Even though the family members contacted the senators from their states, most of them were either slow to respond or were disinterested. I faxed and/or e-mailed the senators of every home state of the *Lagarto* crew. That project turned out to be a dud except for the response of Senator Thomas Carper of Delaware. There were a few exceptions. Illinois Congressman Dennis Hastert, then Speaker of the House, responded to an inquiry from his constituent Brad Stahl, whose uncle EMC Jesse Jobe went down with *Lagarto*.

Then something wonderful happened. Art Keeney, the son of *Lagarto's* Lt. A.H. Keeney, Jr. (Bud), and I had become good friends and were e-mailing and speaking to each other on the phone at this time. He was well acquainted with North Carolina's Senator Elizabeth Dole, who also served on the Armed Services Committee. Art offered to help with the project of obtaining American flags for the *Lagarto* family members, many of whom had told me they never received a flag at the time of *Lagarto's* loss.

"Let me take the lead on this," he said.

Art discussed the flag project with Senator Dole, and she agreed to help. I told Art that Senator Levin was also interested in the *Lagarto,* and we hoped they would work together on this. They did.

It was disappointing that so few United States senators took an interest in this remarkable discovery, but those who did were wonderful.

Flags!!!
2006

Progress came fast and furious. In addition to finding more families, we confronted the issue of the *Lagarto* families receiving flags.

As busy as he was with his professional responsibilities as the President/CEO of the venerable East Carolina Bank group in North Carolina, Art Keeney was anxious to take on this project which meant so much to the families. We both knew that time was going to catch up with us soon. The *Lagarto* memorial events were going to take place in less than a month. When Art offered to take over the project of obtaining flags for the families, I was delighted.

We had both just learned that the Navy could not present flags to the *Lagarto* families without the submarine's discovery being officially verified, which the Navy was still reluctant to do. Art had been informed, through Senator Dole's office, that while we could get 50 flags that had flown over the U.S. Capitol, they couldn't be presented by Navy personnel. Art and I found this information confusing, but we were left with finding a solution which involved the family members somehow presenting the flags to each other.

It was hard to understand. I had attended funeral services of retired military whose families had received flags. Mourners stood proudly with them and recognized their service to their country. I couldn't understand why eighty-six submariners, who had made the ultimate sacrifice, were denied the same respect. This painful denial made no sense and made it more important than ever to have the Navy's official recognition.

The same day Art had his conversation with Senator Dole's office, I heard the same from an aide of Senator Levin. This was one of those times I found the struggle with the Navy fascinating, if not frustrating. Each setback forged a new determination to keep going, although sometimes I questioned my sanity in confronting the United States Navy! While it made me sad for our efforts to be met with obstacles, I became determined to continue fighting for *Lagarto's* lost crew. I had a commitment to them and hoped to give some measure of peace to their families. The men of *Lagarto's* crew died for their country, their young lives cut short in a violent way. Even sixty years after the fact, they deserved to have their country honor them. After getting to know their families, whose collective grief was as great as my own, I believed they deserved a simple acknowledgement of their sacrifice, too. An American flag was a powerful and appropriate symbol of this.

Senator Levin's aide told me *Lagarto* was quite the hot topic with the USN and that everyone knew about it. However, there was a process they had to go through before they could verify the submarine's discovery, and the NHC still didn't feel they had enough information.

I repeated this to Art in an e-mail and said, "Senator Levin's aide thinks we should keep up our efforts with the Navy. He thinks it HAS made an impact and kept it on their radar. I guess it's up to the *Lagarto* kids to speak up for our dads. If we don't, who will?" Art agreed, and we kept going.

Another wrinkle in the quest for flags came from a different angle. Owen Williams, the commander of the Wisconsin SubVets, told me that Senator Kohl had offered to obtain flags for us, but the *Lagarto* families would have to pay for them. While I appreciated Senator Kohl's interest, I told Williams that the families should "absolutely not" be required to pay for a memorial American flag. They had already paid the ultimate cost of that flag with the death of their loved one. Under those circumstances, it wasn't clear that we would receive flags from Senator Kohl after all.

In the end, all the flag glitches were happily resolved.

Behind the Scenes 2006

Entirely unknown to the *Lagarto* families, the Navy and the Naval Historical Center (NHC) had begun to work together to fashion a plan to verify the submarine's discovery. Initiated by CDR Tony San Jose, the complicated plan incorporated the many elements needed to accomplish the identification of the ship wreckage found in the Gulf of Thailand. This was a tricky project and was kept mum because of the possibility that identification of the submarine might show a different outcome – that the submarine was not, in fact, what everyone hoped: the substantially intact *Lagarto,* entombing the remains of 86 American sailors.

While official word was slow for the *Lagarto* families, it moved very fast for the Navy. Luckily for all involved, the person leading this task was CDR Tony San Jose, experienced in diving and salvage operations, connected to almost all of the parties to be involved and committed to the project itself.

Antonio P. San Jose grew up in Washington D.C. and was a self-described "Navy brat." His father, MSCS Antonio A. San Jose (ret.), joined the U.S. Navy in the Philippines, hoping to provide a path to a better future for his family. In 1955, racism was still alive in both society and in the Navy, and Tony's father's enlistment in the Navy was limited to the position of Steward. This meant cooking, cleaning, barbering, doing laundry and running errands for the senior officers. In the mid-seventies, this rate was changed to Mess Specialist and his hard work ethic earned him a recommendation to serve on the White House staff. Senior Chief San Jose worked on the President's Staff during the Nixon and Ford administrations and at Camp David during the Carter administration. After serving the Navy (and three Presidents) for 23 years, Navy Senior Chief Petty Officer San Jose retired and moved his family back to D.C. to run a barber business.

After finishing high school in Fort Washington, MD, Tony enrolled in the Naval Academy Preparatory School in Newport, RI in 1985. After graduation from a year of academic preparation, Tony went to the Naval Academy and graduated in May 1990.

He started his Navy career as a Surface Warfare Officer earning both his qualification on ships and his leadership as a division officer aboard ships. Tony served on *U.S.S. Rathburne* (FF1057) and *U.S.S. Worden* (CG18) in Pearl Harbor and *U.S.S. Princeton* (CG59) in Long Beach. Subsequent to this service, he went ashore to the Naval Postgraduate School in Monterey, CA, graduating in 1998 with a master's degree in Electrical Engineering.

It was while Tony was in Monterey that his interest in diving took root. After attending a luncheon featuring the senior Naval Diving Officer CAPT Chip McCord, who was promoting the diving/salvage specialty within the Navy, Tony decided that was "what I wanted to be when I grew up."

He didn't waste any time.

"In Spring of 1998, I finished my thesis early, skipped graduation ceremony and drove to Panama City, FL for the start of US Navy Dive training," San Jose told me in an e-mail.

He left in such a hurry that his wife Monica and their children caught up with him later. They all left Florida in late September 1998.

Tony's next tour was at Pearl Harbor Naval Shipyards with his duties requiring less emphasis on diving and more attention to managing ship and submarine docking overhauls.

San Jose was ordered to serve as the Combat Systems Officer on *U.S.S. Blue Ridge* (LCC 19) where he was in charge of the communications and computer systems on board the important Fleet Commander's ship. While *Blue Ridge* was at sea, his role was to ensure the Fleet Admiral and his staff could communicate and command all of the Naval ships operating in the fleet. This part of San Jose's service helped him later when he took on *Lagarto* as a project.

After the *Blue Ridge* job, Tony San Jose served in the salvage officer position in Singapore on the staff of the Commander Logistics Group Western Pacific. He served under Admiral Jeffrey Cassias, who later played a significant role in the *Lagarto* story. While working for Admiral Cassias, Tony coordinated annual diving and salvage exercises with foreign navies – Thailand, Philippines, Malaysia, India, Indonesia, Singapore, Korea, Australia, etc. This involved a fascinating array of activities which included combined diving operations, recovering crashed aircraft and getting ships off reefs when they ran aground. This experience and his close association with Admiral Cassias, laid the groundwork for his future *Lagarto* mission.

In the first few months of 2006, Tony worked behind the scenes to develop a plan and gather support for a Navy mission to *Lagarto* to verify her discovery. With his initiative in planning that year's Cooperation Afloat Readiness and Training exercises (CARAT) in the South Pacific, things began to fall into place. CARAT is an annual series of bilateral military training exercises designed to enhance cooperative working partnerships with several Southeast Asian nations.

By April, things were in full swing and the Naval Historical Center (NHC) approved CDR San Jose's plan. The NHC began corresponding with Jamie Macleod, seeking his guidance on specific matters. Macleod was asked to mark with buoys the location of *Lagarto's* bow and stern prior to the arrival of the Navy so they could anchor over *Lagarto* without putting an anchor down on the vessel itself.

Macleod responded that he would be pleased to work with the Navy operation, indicating his coordinates were precise. He also informed San Jose of the anticipated cost of fuel for the operation and the locations of the nearest ports to the WWII wreck site. He continued to offer help in any way he could.

While Jamie Macleod's support for the project was unequivocal, his own finances were limited. The Navy and the NHC wanted his help but could not help pay for the cost of fuel. Macleod had to work this out on his own. In the meantime, San Jose flew back to Thailand to brief the JOINT US MILITARY ADVISORY GROUP THAILAND (JUSMAGTHAI). JUSMAGTHAI is the U.S. Security Assistance Organization (SAO) in Thailand, as well as the in-country OPR for all U.S. bilateral and multilateral military exercises and operations conducted in Thailand.

At this point, the Navy and NHC were engaged and supportive of the *Lagarto* verification operation. More questions flew between the operations' principal participants – San Jose, Macleod, and the NHC: What was the depth of the conning tower, keel, propellers, etc? What was the current visibility? There were questions about the thermocline, the submarine's features, and additional damage to the sub other than the hole in the port bow.

Tony San Jose's strategy was to incorporate the *Lagarto* identification into an already established annual exercise to facilitate the chain of command's approval process. A new and separate operation would require specific funding, operational justification and approval process. Tony capitalized on his experience with planning bi-lateral exercises to fast-track the *Lagarto* identification operation.

At the same time, Macleod was concerned about whether the *Lagarto* families had been informed.

The Phone Call That Changed Everything 2006

On April 11, the day after Art Keeney and I had our flag discussion, I was standing in my sunny kitchen in Lake Leelanau, Michigan, when the phone rang.

"Mrs. Kenney?" asked the voice, which belonged to RADM (Ret.) Paul E. Tobin, the Director of the Naval Historical Center. Wow, I thought, an admiral calling me in the middle of the afternoon.

Admiral Tobin said that Admiral Mullen (then still the Chief of Naval Operations and later Chairman of the Joint Chiefs of Staff) had personally asked him to call me to try to work out, as much as possible, any difficulties between the Navy, the NHC, and the *Lagarto* families. He assured me that the Navy was indeed interested in *Lagarto's* discovery and hoped we could find a way to work together. It was music to my ears.

Admiral Tobin was friendly and firm, and I sensed he was a man who could get things done. I brought him up-to-date on the *Lagarto* families, and he explained the necessary steps the NHC must take before confirming the submarine's discovery. We were both candid and listened to each other.

He asked how he could help. I told him about the trouble Art and I were having with the flags. While

Senators Dole and Levin were working with the Veterans' Administration to get us flags, with Senator Kohl possibly doing the same, we had been informed that the flags couldn't be officially presented to the families because the Navy hadn't confirmed *Lagarto's* discovery. Admiral Tobin said he would try to do something about the flags. I sent this e-mail to the *Lagarto* families:

> I feel like a huge weight just rolled off my back. This afternoon, Rear Admiral Paul Tobin, who is now the Director of the Naval Historical Center (NHC), called me. He was very, very nice and very sympathetic to our situation. Admiral Mullen asked him to call me. Admiral Tobin must be a very brave man!
>
> Here is the story on the *Lagarto* confirmation. Basically, Navy officials believe that the boat in the Gulf of Thailand is the USS LAGARTO. They would love to confirm its discovery. The problem lies (as I guessed) with the historians at the NHC. Their thinking (five of them all agree) is that it PROBABLY is the *Lagarto*, but they are not POSITIVE. They are afraid to confirm that the submarine is the *Lagarto* for fear that at some future point, if the boat is determined to be something else, the *Lagarto* families will be devastated.

> In June, the Navy will be doing training exercises in the area of the *Lagarto*. After that, the USN divers will go down to see "our" submarine. Hopefully, they will find what they need to confirm the identity to their satisfaction, and this will put everything to rest.
>
> The USN is VERY interested in the *Lagarto*. Admiral Tobin said that the *Lagarto* is the main topic of discussion of all the WWII work they are doing now. He said they understand the feelings and frustrations of all the family members...
>
> We had a long conversation. In it, he mentioned that the emails to Admiral Mullen were helpful in letting him (them) know how we were feeling...
>
> Since I have sent some "rather strong" letters to the Navy, I plan to send Admiral Tobin and Admiral Mullen a note thanking them for their attention to this. Enough said.

After my conversation with Paul Tobin (he asked me to call him Paul, and I asked him to call me Nancy) things happened fast. The same day, I sent the following e-mail to RADM Paul Tobin (Ret.), ADM Mike Mullen, RADM Jeffrey Cassias (who was coming to Manitowoc), LCDR Jeff Davis, Captain P.O. Wheeler, and RADM Hank McKinney (Ret.), as well as civilian historians at the NHC – Barbara Voulgaris, Jack Green, Wendy Coble, and Robert Cressman:

> To all of you in the USN, especially those I have cajoled and worse, I hope this reflects my personal gratitude to all of you. Particularly the courageous Rear Admiral Paul Tobin. His call went a long way in easing the unhappy feelings I (and others) have had about the USN handling of this difficult *Lagarto* situation. Admiral Tobin's call eased the pain we felt in thinking that the Navy didn't care about the sacrifice of our loved ones.
>
> Communication is a good thing. Now that the ice is broken, I hope that others will feel no fear in calling or e-mailing me. My great hope had always been to work with you. As I've said frequently, I love the Navy!

Admiral Cassias responded right away:

> Nancy – thanks. I look forward to meeting you at the May 6 event. All the best, Jeff Cassias

Paul Tobin also responded very quickly:

> Nancy, Thank you for the good words. We are thinking positively. Best, Paul

Less than a week later, I heard from Robert Cressman, who worked with the NHC and was considered an eminent historian of American naval ships. He told me that Bill McKinney (CDR McKinney, son of retired RADM Hank McKinney) pointed out something interesting. Only three boats had the two-5"/25 configuration, *Lagarto, Sennet,* and *Haddock*, and they all went out in a group on *Lagarto's* first patrol. Sure enough, the ordnance register for June 1945 (when *Lagarto* was still listed as missing), showed those three boats fitted with two 5"/25 mounts.

Cressman continued his research and obtained the e-mail address for his Australian contact who'd made a study of Japanese convoy operations. He wanted to match up the one that *Lagarto* and *Baya* attacked with the convoy composition. He said that if it was *Hatsutaka* that sank *Lagarto,* the minelayer had been a pain in the neck to American submariners in the region. She had given the *Cobia* a good working over before being sunk by the *Hawkbill,* which was also a Manitowoc-built fleet boat.

(Ironies abound. The *U.S.S. Cobia* is today anchored at the Wisconsin Maritime Museum, in Manitowoc.)

Through the efforts of Senators Levin and Dole and RADM (ret.) Tobin, the Veterans Administration sent fifty American flags to the submarine base at Pearl Harbor, where they were flown above the base, folded in the military manner, and delivered to Manitowoc. At the memorial service, RADM Cassias graciously presented one to each grateful *Lagarto* family.

Finding My Father and Losing My Mother 2006

Toward the end of April, things were moving along for the *Lagarto* Memorial Service. More than half of the families had been found and contacted. The volunteers, both family and not, worked to bring us this success. Newspapers all over the country had pitched in; the latest being the *Hartford Courant* (Connecticut) and the *Mattoon Journal Gazette* (Illinois), whose published articles had reaped results. The United States Navy was solidly behind us, and a few dedicated Members of Congress achieved their quest to get special flags for the families.

Plans were underway with the Wisconsin Maritime Museum which had already registered 136 *Lagarto* family attendees. The SubVets and many current and retired members of all branches of the U.S. military services were expected to attend the ceremony as well. The media, both print and electronic, were on the story.

However, the moment was bittersweet for me. The joy of the impossible discovery of *Lagarto* – and my father – was tempered by the distressing decline in my mother's health. My parents' letters showed how much they were in love, and Mom's loss of her Bill was devastating – especially since they had begun making plans for their future.

Many war widows and their paternally orphaned children develop a unique bond reflecting that loss, and so had the small Mabin family. After Margy remarried and rebuilt her life with another husband and more children, she didn't spend much time talking to me about my father. She felt lucky to be starting over with a new husband and three more children.

However, she did save everything she had with Bill Mabin which, due to the brevity of their marriage and the long periods her husband was at sea, wasn't much. The most precious physical remnants of that union were my father's letters and a beautiful bracelet of sterling silver coins that Bill had made for her in Australia.

I had grown up, thrived, and was lucky to have a long solid marriage and three wonderful children. While there was a life-long hole in my heart for my missing father, and always would be, I had no conscious memories of him. Occasionally, I reflected on how we had missed all those special father/daughter moments that most families take for granted, but there was nothing of him that I remembered. It was a loss, pure and simple, but that loss had always been present in my life. I knew nothing else.

When *Lagarto* was found, it was an out-of-the-blue gift from the sea. Now I wanted to know everything about my father, and the only person alive who could tell me was my mother.

But for her, that time had passed. Margaret Mabin Chambers was 88 years old at the time of *Lagarto's* discovery, and not a healthy octogenarian. When I broke the news to my mother in early June 2005, she was physically disabled. Severe arthritis required her to use a walker to get around, and her hearing was limited. Her fierce independence and formidable stubbornness kept her going, and she was able to cope in her own home with the help of JoAn Skipski, her friend and 4 day-a-week housekeeper. JoAn had been a lifeline to the outside world for Mom for years. She did her shopping and took her to her doctor/dentist appointments and her twice-a-month beauty parlor appointments. My sister Katie, brothers Dan and Tom, and I tried to see Mom as often as possible, but our visits were limited because of the distance between Leelanau County, Michigan and the Chicago area where we all lived. Katie and her daughters Sarah and Maggie Haskins gave Mom the most support at the time. They spent many happy summers with her at her cottage on Glen Lake. Their support, as Mom began to need more attention, was important in keeping her at home as long as possible.

In 2003, we all began to notice that Mom's memory was getting hazy. She had always been so sharp – interested in politics and current events with keen insights and marvelous humor. She began to repeat the same things over and over. Sometimes, she would tell us something was missing, and then we'd find it in a strange place. We also noticed mood swings and irrational anger toward us. While her wit remained intact, it was often cutting and aimed primarily at Katie or me. Our brothers usually escaped Mom's frequent barbs.

About the same time, I moved from Illinois to Michigan and began to spend more time with Mom. On the days that JoAn was off, I visited Mom to fix her lunch and keep her company. By 2005, Mom's decline had become alarming to all of us. She often fell, and the Glen Arbor Fire and Rescue Squad (of which my husband was a member), was called. She had become a frequent flyer in the Munson Medical Center ER in Traverse City, 25 miles from her home.

When *Lagarto* was discovered, I had no idea what Mom's reaction would be. The news was shocking to me, but almost incomprehensible to her. When I first told her the news, her reaction was hard to read. She fidgeted and sighed and seemed uncomfortable with the subject, remarking that the crew were all skeletons now. My brother Dan surfed the internet to find *Lagarto* news that might be more understandable to her. She seemed to grasp the concept for awhile, and then it was gone.

In later attempts to discuss this subject, she became agitated and said the conversation was making her queasy. So I stopped talking about it. *Lagarto* had become an obsession to me. I longed to discuss this with was my mother, but I couldn't. This, more than anything else connected to *Lagarto's* discovery, was the most painful to me.

The months following *Lagarto's* discovery were hard on my mother. The falls that tore the thin skin from her legs and arms were accompanied with deep gashes. Several infections landed her in the hospital. Her shifting moods often predisposed her to anger which extended to my brothers, Tom and Dan. Our attempts to get help for Mom were met with fury. On more than one occasion, I was banished from her house for even suggesting it. Everyone aware of Mom's situation – neighbors, friends and her family – became alarmed at the danger that her situation presented. Mom forgot every fall and hospital visit. She could spend most of the previous night in the ER, and the next day not understand why she was wearing bandages. Her memory loss was shocking, yet, she refused to acknowledge that anything was wrong and would become irate if we suggested otherwise. Several times, with her grudging okay, I hired more help for her. Soon after, she fired them saying she didn't need help. To her, I was interfering. Even suggesting an assisted-living arrangement meant an immediate dismissal from her home. My siblings and I were alarmed and concerned about our mother, but were stymied at every turn. We knew a disaster was just around the corner. Yet legally, Mom was deemed competent to make her own decisions, and there was nothing we could do.

Ten days before the *Lagarto* events in Manitowoc, Mom was diagnosed with pneumonia and landed in the hospital, oblivious to how sick she was. I was emotionally torn in half. How could I leave my 89-year-old, very ill mother, who was due to leave the hospital? And how could I miss the memorial service for my father, reacquainted with me after 60 years?

Ultimately, my sister and niece Sarah were able to stay with Mom for a few days, and JoAn and other helpers pitched in. They arranged their schedules to stay with Mom 24/7 while I was away as they knew how much this trip meant to me.

My planned trip to Manitowoc and later Chicago to visit my children was downsized, and my husband and I left for Wisconsin for the experience of a lifetime.

Lagarto Memorial Weekend May 4-8, 2006

It was the most poignant of time machines. After being lost at sea for 61 years, the *U.S.S. Lagarto's* families gathered in Manitowoc, Wisconsin to honor that World War II submarine and her crew.

Thursday

As my husband and I entered the spacious lobby of the Inn at Maritime Bay, a comfortable hotel on the shore of Lake Michigan, the first person I saw was Kelan Spalding. Kelan's brother, Chief Pharmacist Mate Robert B. Spalding, was a shipmate and friend of my father. I recognized Kelan, as we had exchanged many e-mails and letters in the past year. He had sent photos of his brother Bobby and their family, who lived in Eugene, Missouri. It was a big family, and Bobby was the oldest son and Kelan the youngest. The physical resemblance between them was striking.

Bobby Spalding and Bill Mabin had much in common. They were some of the old men on the submarine. Bobby was 23, and Bill was an ancient 26. Both were married and had extensive submarine experience, something that the majority of *Lagarto's* young crew lacked. They'd had their share of close calls with death. While serving on *U.S.S. Puffer* (SS-268), Spalding tended to the nerves of her crew during a 38-hour submerged depth charge attack. On his four patrols in *Balao,* Mabin had also become well acquainted with depth charge attacks. Sixty-one years later, almost to the day that their submarine went down, the two sailors and their shipmates would be honored by almost 200 family members and friends.

It was a beautiful evening in Manitowoc, a charming Midwestern city with a lot to offer. The weather was cool but pleasant, and after I was settled in my room, I decided to stroll over to the Wisconsin Maritime Museum, which was just across a parking lot from our hotel. There was a grassy parkway along the edge of Lake Michigan, which made for an easy stroll between the two. For the second time that evening, I encountered Spalding and his wife Betty, and we chatted like old friends. I noticed another couple strolling along the parkway and recognized Nancy Mendenhall Ford. I called to her, and she and her husband Bill joined us. Nancy had just sent me a package of photographs of her father, Lt. William H. Mendenhall, the executive officer of *Lagarto.* In the package she included photos of herself and her family.

Nancy was an infant when her father died and still had the baby blanket he sent her from Australia. Bill Mendenhall was a man destined to be a great naval officer. He had graduated from the United States Naval Academy in Annapolis and was part of a prestigious naval family. He was handsome, smart, and had married Jayne Nash, his match in intellect and drive. She was equally good-looking.

Nancy was a special baby with special parents and had done them proud. Married to Bill Ford since 1967, she was the mother of three beautiful and accomplished children and the proud grandmother of three.

The two of us hit it off right away. When I told her I had to finish putting together some folders for the families, she and Bill offered to help and made my life much easier that night. Fortunately I got a good night's sleep because the next few days were a whirlwind of activity.

Friday

The next morning, excitement propelled me out of bed. I headed for the hotel's dining room, but it took quite awhile to get there.

Entering the lobby, I ran into Owen Williams, the commander of the Southwest Wisconsin Chapter of the U.S. Submarine Veterans of World War II (SubVets). A generous and energetic man, he was dedicated to the submarine veterans. His chapter was hosting several events for the *Lagarto* families that weekend. For years, the SubVets planned *Lagarto Remembrance Day* and worked closely with the state of Wisconsin to officially designate May 3rd as its day to remember the submarine. They were determined to make this weekend special for the *Lagarto* families.

A beautiful bronze plaque inscribed with all the names of *Lagarto's* crew stood in the lobby. Fund-raising for this memorial was undertaken by the SubVets, and a dedication was planned for that afternoon. After a brief chat with Owen, I continued to breakfast.

Caught up in the spirit of the day, I often stopped total strangers on my way to the dining room with the question, "Are you *Lagartos*?" They always they were, and we delighted in meeting each other. When I reached the dining room (by that time it was getting late, and most had finished eating), I spotted a couple and approached their table with my usual question. Ben and Violet Byrer were indeed *Lagartos*. We too had written each other, and I had learned a lot about F1 Clark Richard "Dick" Byrer, who was the second youngest of seven children.

After talking with the Byrers, I sat down to eat. By then, almost no one was in the dining room, and I was hungry. A few minutes after ordering, I looked up to see some members of my family enter the room. My brother-in-law and sister-in-law, Peter and Louise Abbruzzese, along with my niece Anne Abbruzzese and her fiancé had come all the way from Alexandria, Virginia for the ceremony. Our family was meeting Anne's fiancé, Lyle Perkinson, for the first time, and I thought he was a good sport to use this crash-course method of meeting Anne's relatives. We hugged, laughed and talked, and I noticed a young man approaching our table. He introduced himself as Clark Acton, a nephew of the handsome George Clark Harrington, MoMM3 on the *Lagarto*. A few minutes later, Clark's uncle, Floyd Harrington, who had come from Lehi, Utah, joined our table. When I had last spoken with Harrington on the phone, he had become very emotional about his brother. During that phone conversation, he apologized, saying that his family never imagined the *Lagarto* would be found. They thought they would never know what had happened to their brother. I assured him everyone felt the same way.

Floyd Harrington told me about the odd way in which their family had learned of *Lagarto's* discovery. Clark Acton, long interested in items with WWII navy relevance, had purchased an item through e-bay. He told the seller his uncle had died on the *U.S.S. Lagarto.* The seller said, "Did you know that the *Lagarto* has been found?" Acton got on the internet to learn more and then contacted his family. All of George Harrington's siblings, two sisters and a brother, were able to get to Manitowoc to say good-bye.

Caught up in the interesting conversation with Acton and Harrington, I almost forgot the time. I rushed through breakfast to get over to the museum to register for the weekend. Little did I know this would be the last meal I'd have for almost three days.

On my way through the hotel's lobby, I saw a sight for sore eyes. Entering the hotel, with two of my children, was Jamie Macleod. I had seen many photos of Macleod, and we corresponded, but I wasn't expecting that he would be jaw-dropping handsome. He was also every bit as down to earth, considerate, and sharp as he was good-looking. After quick hellos to Macleod and my children, I proceeded to the Wisconsin Maritime Museum.

Upon entering this marvelous museum, the first person I met was Karen Duvalle. Duvalle was young, lovely and smart. Her role was key in organizing the *Lagarto* events for the museum, and I considered her my valuable partner for the past 11 months. Duvalle had been dedicated to finding the *Lagarto* families and was very good at research. Our modus operandi had been that Duvalle, through her research, would find names and phone numbers of possible *Lagarto* family members. She would e-mail me this information, and I'd make the calls. Other families were found in different ways, but this was our usual method. It was a good starting point for our project, and we worked well together.

The museum was filled with *Lagarto* families checking in and abuzz with conversation. Norma Bishop, executive director of the museum, joined the group, and we all got acquainted. One of the museum's attractions was the *U.S.S. Cobia,* a Gato-class WWII submarine moored in Lake Michigan dockside of the building. Many volunteers led *Cobia* tours and gave folks an inside look at a real submarine that saw a lot of action in World War II. It was a sobering glimpse of the spartan conditions that submariners had to endure while winning the war for us.

While registering, my cousin Michael Mabin Walker arrived. Walker's father, my uncle Jim Mabin, was my father's sole sibling. He was my only close relative from the Mabin side of my family. Walker and his wife Millirose had never met my children or husband, so this was a grand family reunion for us.

All of a sudden, I realized that it was time for the dedication of the *Lagarto* plaque at the hotel. We rushed back for a ceremony sponsored by the SubVets. The *U.S.S. Lagarto* was the state submarine of Wisconsin, so this was very special. The huge plaque was unveiled, as was another plaque honoring one of the SubVets' members, Roy Leonhardt, who had tragically died a few months earlier. I think of Leonhardt as the 87th member of *Lagarto's* crew, since were it not for him, we wouldn't be celebrating *Lagarto's* discovery. Both plaques were financed by the generous friends of Roy and the *Lagarto*, and the reception was led by SubVets Owen Williams and Stan Coates.

The rest of the afternoon was spent meeting with *Lagarto* families as they arrived. One of my favorites was the Clouse family. Beulah Clouse Clark was the mother of *Lagarto* children Judie Sue and Terry. Beulah was a beautiful woman, inside and out, and everything I expected her to be. When we learned in July 2005 that *Lagarto* had fired off a torpedo before sinking, Terry Clouse mused aloud that his father, TM2 George Edward Clouse, was most likely one of the men who loaded it.

As soon as I saw them, looking solemnly at the *Lagarto* plaque, I knew that Albretta Kirtley Wilson and Joe Bagshaw were also *Lagarto* children. There was an expression of sadness, but pride, as they took everything in. I had spoken to both of them over the phone, and we hugged, smiled and posed for pictures. Their fathers, both very good-looking, were StM1 Albert Kirtley and Ltjg. Joseph Stanley Pash, who were of course, still together.

MoMM1 Richard Kirk Fisher, who hailed from Pekin, Illinois was stationed on the *U.S.S. Nevada* December 7, 1941. He survived the Japanese attack on Pearl Harbor and was later assigned to the ill-fated ship that carried the A-bomb to its eventual destination. Before the *Indianapolis* carried out her dark duty, Fisher was assigned to the crew of the *U.S.S. Lagarto.* Fisher's family was in full force in Manitowoc to honor him. It was touch and go for one of the Fisher family, Carol Lawson and her husband. Dewayne Lawson had been diagnosed with cancer and was scheduled for surgery when they returned from Manitowoc, but first they wanted to say good-bye to Dick Fisher.

Finally I got a chance to meet Rae Todd Kinn, a dear lady who had become my confidante. In her eighties, Kinn was still a beauty with warmth to spare. At her side was her son, Mike Todd, who was only a month old when his father died on *Lagarto.*

Then there was the Armstrong family. Virginia Grace Armstrong, the matriarch of the family, was a total charmer. Her brother, F2 Richard Fox Grace, was only twenty when he perished on *Lagarto.* Ginny Armstrong's daughter-in-law Amy appeared to be the quiet presence in the energetic Armstrong circle; brown-eyed

Amy is a rock for her husband Dick. Richard Grace Armstrong, often wryly described as the "All-American Boy," was a force of nature. He was named after his uncle Dick Grace, who wrote in one of his last letters to his mother, "Don't worry about me, Mother. If anything happens to me, I'll be in a million-dollar coffin with plenty of company." Richard Grace's mother was devastated by his loss. Many Armstrong family members believe that the death of her precious son led to her own death soon thereafter.

Dick Armstrong, the All-American boy, was just that. He was a guy with fun in his voice. Armstrong and I talked often on the phone. He would cheer me up when I was upset, and I would unload my anxiety on him. More often than not, after our phone conversations, I felt better and he felt worse. I placed my angst on his back, and he carried it well. Armstrong and I had become close friends, as we were both obsessed with the *Lagarto* situation. We had to know everything about it.

The *Lagarto* week end became a family reunion of relatives I had never met. The afternoon rushed on with many families getting acquainted. Before I knew it, it was time to get ready for a reception at the museum. There were more *Lagartos* to meet.

By the time I arrived at the reception, it was in full swing. The spacious, welcoming lobby and gift shop of the museum were filled with *Lagarto* guests, and an elegant buffet had been prepared. The first guests I encountered were RADM Jeffrey Cassias and his wife Terry. With them was another naval officer I was dying to meet, LCDR Jeff Davis. They had journeyed to Manitowoc all the way from Pearl Harbor to honor the crew of *Lagarto* and be with their families. RADM Cassias was the Commander of the Pacific Fleet Submarine Force, and LCDR Davis was its Public Affairs Officer. I was very happy to see them.

A distinguished man came up behind me, and when I turned to see who tapped me on the shoulder, I knew instantly that it was Art Keeney. He gave me a great bear hug, and we introduced each other to our families. In spite of his busy schedule, we had worked together on the flag project. In addition, Keeney was an invaluable sounding board, encouraging and calming me throughout the entire project. One of the things I enjoyed most about him was his laid-back, tongue-in-cheek sense of humor. We were on the same wavelength.

At some point that evening, I remember eying the buffet table. The museum had laid out a feast. It seemed that whenever I approached the appetizers, another *Lagarto* family would appear, and it would be old home week again.

After the excitement of meeting so many *Lagarto* families, my husband and I rushed back to the hotel for another reception hosted again by the Wisconsin SubVets. The veterans had asked Jamie Macleod and two of our children, John Kenney and Beth Kenney Augustine, to speak to the *Lagarto* families about the trips to the submarine and answer questions. The only audience in the room were the families and submarine veterans. A few *Lagarto* widows and a substantial number of siblings were there, as well as about ten children of the lost boat crew. There were also many nieces, nephews and grandchildren in attendance. Everyone seemed comfortable asking questions about a very painful subject. All had reason to want answers, if possible, to the questions regarding the deaths of their loved ones. Macleod did the best he could to answer some very sensitive questions. It was quite an evening.

When my husband and I got back to our room that night, I realized that I had eaten almost nothing since breakfast. John had purchased a can of peanuts the night before, and I snacked on them before I fell exhausted into bed.

Saturday

My family and I were up and ready for a big day. It began at 10 AM with a video presentation that Macleod had prepared with the help of Beth Augustine and John Kenney. It was held in the museum's hospitality room, a large space with a wall of windows overlooking Lake Michigan. The presentation was open to the public, and anticipating a large crowd, I skipped breakfast to get there early. As the room filled with people, I was astonished to find there was standing-room only by the time the presentation started. In addition to the *Lagartos,* submarine veterans, and museum personnel, many members of the USN – both officers and enlisted men – attended the presentation. Members of the public poured in, and I spotted several good friends who had made the trip to Manitowoc for this historic memorial service. Our friends, the Opper family, traveled from Dubuque, Iowa for the occasion. Jack Kenney (no relation) and his son David had driven up from Chicago for the day. I was happy to see that Chris Ganschow, my old friend and an aide to Congressman Dan Lipinski, had made the trip from Chicago as well. I will always remember their kindness for going out of their way to show support for *Lagarto* sailors, as well as personal support for our family.

After a few technical glitches, a nervous-looking Jamie Macleod began his presentation. He seemed a little uncomfortable in an unaccustomed suit and bright red tie. Macleod's usual attire, worn on the island of Koh Samui in Thailand, was substantially more casual than the outfit he wore for this formal presentation. The fact that very high-ranking members of the Navy were sitting in the front row probably increased his nervousness. But he looked great and did a wonderful job. Again he answered many questions from the audience about his historic discovery of *Lagarto.*

After the presentation was finished, and all the questions were answered, the museum brought in a casual buffet lunch of sandwiches, chips, cookies and soft drinks. I was very hungry. However, it seemed that eating was not on my agenda. I'm a people person and was enjoying the conversations with *Lagartos* and others. I never quite squeezed in a sandwich before it was time to go outside for the most important event of the day, the *U.S.S. Lagarto* memorial service.

The crowd reassembled on the parkway that ran along the Manitowoc River where the WWII submarine, *U.S.S. Cobia* was moored. Chairs were arranged for the *Lagarto* family members to view the service, which was held on the deck of the *Cobia*. There were so many *Lagarto* families there, that the museum had requested that only two members of each family sit in this viewing area. The others had an equally good view, but stood behind and around the seated family members.

The weather was gorgeous – sunny and cool. It was perfect for an outdoor ceremony. However, anyone familiar with the climate in that part of the country knew that spring could be skittish and quite chilly. All of the naval personnel were clad in their dress whites, but they had to be freezing – especially RADM Cassias, who was accustomed to Hawaiian weather. All through the ceremony, I kept wishing I had a sweater to throw him. But we Americans expect our military to be stoic, and they were.

As the audience settled in their places, they enjoyed the music of the Maritime Chamber Ensemble, situated at the bow end of the *Cobia*. Most of the service's participants were already seated in their chairs on the boat's deck when Admiral Cassias and his *Lagarto* companion, Nancy Mendenhall Ford, were piped aboard.

The service began with the Maritime Chamber Ensemble performing *I Hear America Singing*. Then Joe Maehl, who was a member of the U.S. Navy Band during WWII and who bugled off submarines from Manitowoc as they left for war, performed the Call to Colors. The placement of Colors was performed by Manitowoc area United States Navy Reservists. That done, everyone sang the *Star Spangled Banner.* Captain William B. Acker of the Chaplain Corps gave the Invocation.

The crowd was welcomed by Wisconsin Maritime Museum Executive Director Norma Bishop. CDR Jack Gadzala, USNR (ret.), Chairman of the *U.S.S. Cobia* Committee, introduced the Keynote Speaker, RADM Jeffrey B. Cassias. The Commander of the Submarine Force, U.S. Pacific Fleet, gave an address that touched everyone and brought bittersweet tears to the eyes of many.

Gerald Pilger, a member of the museum's Board of Trustees, wore many hats that weekend. He was the President of the Manitowoc Chapter of the U.S. Submarine Veterans of World War II and recited its creed. After that, Captain Acker recited the 139th Psalm just before retired USN member Stephen Petreshock performed the traditional Tolling of the Bell. The Reading of the Names of each member of *Lagarto's* crew was done by two retired submarine veterans, Stanley Coates and Gerald Striegel, who was an associate member of the SubVets. I glanced around at other family members; most were in tears. I was not; I had used up most of my tears.

A moment of silence was followed by a 21-Gun Salute performed by the VFW Rifle Squad Post 659 and the American Legion. The Maritime Chamber Ensemble then performed *American Anthem,* and all stood for the symbolic Placing of the Wreath, which meant tossing the wreath in the water, by Nancy Mendenhall Ford, the daughter of *Lagarto's* Executive Officer, Lt. William Mendenhall.

With the formal ceremony almost over, Joe Maehl played *Taps* and the assembled crowd sang *God Bless America.* By then, Nancy Ford and Admiral Cassias had been piped off the submarine, and Ford took her place next to her husband in the audience.

One of the most solemn and poignant parts of the ceremony was the *Presentation of the Flags* to the *Lagarto* families. Admiral Cassias and an aide said a few words to each family and presented them with an American flag. With this important gesture from the Navy, the angst and anxiety of the past seemed to melt away for the families. They accepted this singular American symbol of *Lagarto's* loss from their country, a precious gift of good-bye from Admiral Cassias. At last, the *Lagarto* crew's sacrifice was officially acknowledged by their nation.

After all the flags were presented to the families, everyone sang the hauntingly beautiful navy hymn *Eternal Father Strong to Save.* A solemn benediction was given by Captain Acker, and Joe Maehl performed a robust and uplifting *Anchors Away.*

While the *Lagarto* families were savoring one of the most emotional moments of their lives, they were startled by the loud blast of *Cobia's* horn and the start-up of her engines – enveloping those nearby in a cloud of smoke.

The flurry of activity that occurred after the ceremony took almost everyone in different directions. Some families headed to pre-arranged interviews with personnel and interns from the University of Wisconsin who were doing an oral history project on *Lagarto.* Some headed back to the hotel for a rest after an emotional afternoon. RADM Cassias headed for a hot shower. I had time to chat with the Oppers, whom I had seen only once since their move from La Grange. Chris Ganschow and I chatted for awhile. He delivered Congressman Lipinski's greetings and handed me a resolution showing that *Lagarto* Day had been placed in the congressional record. Chris had been a loyal friend for many years. We first met when I was a member of the La Grange Village Board and he was a reporter for the local newspaper. We discovered that his mother, Maria, had been a classmate of mine in grade school and high school. Chris and I later worked together in politics when I ran for the Illinois State Senate (the same year as Barack Obama's first campaign for the Illinois Senate). He had been one of the first to call me when he learned of *Lagarto's* discovery and encouraged me to pursue the objective of having the submarine's identity confirmed. I was touched to see Chris at *Lagarto's* memorial service.

After the excitement had subsided and most of the crowd had returned to the hotel or museum, I was approached by one of the Chicago newsmen who had come to cover the story. Chuck Coppola, then a reporter with Chicago's superstation WGN, asked if I would consider an interview. Of course, I agreed. Little did I know at the time that Chuck and I would become good friends, as well as collaborators on another *Lagarto* project. After I finished my interview with Chuck, Harvey Moshman, a special projects producer for CBS also asked for an interview.

The interview took place in the living room of the suite my husband and I had taken at the hotel. Anticipating get-togethers over the week end with family and friends, my husband and I had made these special arrangements for our rooms. Harvey and his cameraman rearranged the furniture in the living room and set up their lights and equipment. After my interview, Harvey did another one with my children.

When this was done and the afternoon almost gone, I realized I had barely had a chance to visit with our friends and relatives who had come so far for the special *Lagarto* service. I knew where I would find them – in the hotel cocktail lounge. I dashed there to visit with these people I loved, and I again lost track of time.

Suddenly, everyone was scrambling to get to dinner in the banquet room across the hall. By the time we walked in, we found a room overflowing with people, more than had made reservations for dinner. Many decided at the last minute to stay for the banquet, and there was no place to sit. Most of my family ended up back in the bar, but I was able to find a single seat at a table with two of my favorite families, the Armstrongs and the Keeneys. I loved both these families, so if I couldn't be with my own, I was happy to be with them. The dinner was a buffet loaded with plenty of chicken, mashed potatoes and vegetables. I discovered that most of the food was already gone, and I was really hungry. I managed to scrounge up a roll and a brownie, but that was about all.

One of the highlights of the dinner was an interesting presentation by Admiral Cassias on the role of the navy today. After his speech, he answered questions, both in general about the Navy, as well as some specifically about *Lagarto.* His presence and insights were appreciated. He and LCDR Davis seemed to feel the long trip from Pearl Harbor was worthwhile. I later learned that RADM Cassias had chosen to attend the *Lagarto* memorial service rather than participate in another event in California.

On my way back to the bar to join my family, I encountered Terry Leonhardt and her children in the hallway. In spite of Roy's tragic recent death, they wanted to be there. I thanked her for everything her husband had done for us and to tell her how sorry I was that Roy couldn't have been with us this week end. Terry Leonhardt couldn't have been more gracious. She and her children represented Roy well that day, and I couldn't help thinking how proud he would be of them all. I noticed their daughter had tears streaming down her face. Impulsively, I put my arms around her and told her that her father helped me to find my father after all these years. He had given all the *Lagarto* children a precious gift. That was his legacy to us, and we would always be grateful. Her father had given me my father. Then I started to cry. Before we all ended up in tears, I bade the Leonhardts good-bye and went to find my family.

I found them right where I had left them. They were none the worse for wear after being squeezed out of the dining room, although one of my children was a little annoyed he didn't get any dinner.

At some point in the evening, we heard fireworks. They were in celebration of a brand new luxury yacht, built by Manitowoc's Burger Boat Company for a wealthy sheik. The yacht was being delivered to the sheik that week, and he had arrived to celebrate its completion and deliverance to him. The irony was striking. Two big Manitowoc events the same weekend - a solemn, yet joyous memorial service for the crew that lived and died amid the harsh and cramped conditions of a WWII submarine and a lavish celebration for a sheik receiving a luxury yacht. Even the local press did an article on the strange paradox of the two events.

The cocktail lounge became crowded with *Lagarto* people relaxing and conversing. Although I didn't get a chance to chat with him, I noticed Admiral Cassias talking with numerous *Lagarto* families. Photo albums appeared. Two beautiful photographs of Clouse family members struck me. One was of Beulah Clark in the bloom of youth, probably at the time she married George Clouse. She was a natural beauty, and any young sailor would be taken with her. Another photograph showed Beulah's smiling husband posing with his baby daughter Judie Sue. One can only imagine how tough it was for George Clouse to leave his family, especially knowing that another baby was on the way.

I did get a chance to talk to Commander Davis for a long time. He had been very responsive to *Lagarto* matters since the previous fall, and I loved working with him. Each time I spoke with him, I became more and more convinced he truly wanted to resolve the issues that concerned the *Lagarto* families. I will always be grateful to him for the time he spent working with the museum, the SubVets and me in honoring our long-lost submariners. Davis chatted with many of the *Lagarto* families and Jamie Macleod, who at that point in the day was tired and ready to wind down from the continual stream of events of the week end.

Then, in a voice loud enough for anyone within earshot to hear, I said, "I'm hungry. Is there anything to eat around here?!" While most smiled with tolerant amusement, my son Bill responded. He hustled off to the adjacent dining room to see if he could get me anything, but it was closed. So, my only source of food was the bar snacks. Since breakfast the previous day, I had eaten only peanuts; I was living on adrenaline.

<u>Sunday</u>

Sunday morning, I arose a little tired, but still exhilarated. The weekend had flown by, and I knew it would be hard to see all the *Lagarto* families, who had such a dreadful thing in common, depart. At breakfast, the families spent a lot of time hugging each other, as they would relatives they wouldn't see again for a long time. LCDR Jeff Davis stopped at each table for a final good-bye and asked many families how they felt about the memorial service and other events of the weekend. He told me many said they had gained some peace in at last knowing their beloved submariner's resting place and having the opportunity to say good-bye. I agreed with those sentiments.

I joined my family and the Armstrongs and ordered a full breakfast. Within minutes of ordering, someone noticed it was time for the second flag ceremony. The SubVets had planned to present the American flags that Wisconsin's Senator Kohl had donated to the families. These flags had flown over the nation's capitol in honor of *Lagarto's* crew, and the SubVets and Senator Kohl had made a great effort to get them for us. Although ravenous at that point, I knew it was important to be at that presentation. Dick Armstrong and I left our families at the table and rushed to the hotel's ballroom where the presentation was held. It was very nice, and we were happy to be there. Some of the other families had already left, so the room wasn't as crowded as expected. Many of Wisconsin's submarine veterans were part of the solemn ceremony.

After the event was over, Armstrong and I returned to the dining room and were assured that our cold breakfast could be warmed. By this time, however, he had to leave for Milwaukee to catch a plane home to Delaware, and I had to rush to another activity.

Owen Williams had made arrangements for those of us who could stay a little longer to take a yacht ride on the river, courtesy of Craig Yort, a gentleman who was very interested in *Lagarto*. They thought it would be a nice way to unwind after a busy week end.

Only a few of us were able to accept Yort's generous offer. The passengers were members of the Kenney family, Rae Todd Kinn, Jamie Macleod, Karen Duvalle and a handful of SubVets. It was another sunny day, and the cruise was indeed relaxing.

When we returned to the hotel, it seemed deserted after the frenetic activity of the past few days. Most of the *Lagarto* families were gone. My husband had left for Michigan, and our children, with Macleod, drove back to Chicago. My plans were to drive to Chicago the next day to spend more time with my family and see some friends. I had an afternoon to unwind before leaving. Karen Duvalle and I were at loose ends. Together we had spent so much time finding families and working toward this weekend, that we couldn't let go of the day. Exhausted, we walked into town for a sandwich as we had missed lunch, and the hotel dining room was closed until dinner. On Sundays, many of the shops in town were closed, but we found a place to have some ice cream. We compared notes on the weekend's events and felt a happy kind of tired, knowing we had experienced something truly extraordinary. We were at peace.

After a nap, I remembered that my Abbruzzese in-laws were still here and not leaving until the next morning. The fast pace of the weekend afforded little time to spend with my relatives, who had come from the east coast to be with us. We had a quiet dinner and caught up on each others' lives, particularly the wonderful news of Anne and Lyles' engagement. It was a good way to end the weekend.

Norma Bishop, Karen Duvalle and I often discussed the ramifications of the astounding discovery of *Lagarto.* Many submarines and other U.S. naval vessels were lost in World War II. Of these, the *U.S.S. Lagarto,* a boat no one was looking for, was the one to be found. We believed the discovery and honoring of *Lagarto* was emblematic of those other long-lost ships of that hard-fought war. If we could remind people of the sacrifices of the *Lagarto* crew, all the others would be remembered as well.

Even with all that in mind, there was more – much more – to come in the amazing story of *Lagarto.*

Nancy Kenney and Nancy Ford at 2006 USS LAGARTO Memorial Service. The daughters of crew members, SM1 Bill Mabin and Lt. Bill Mendenhall (XO) hold American flags presented to them from the United States Navy.

Rear Admiral Jeffrey Cassias 2006

RADM Jeffrey Cassias had an enormous depth of experience in the Navy, especially with submarines. After graduating from the University of Texas in El Paso in 1974 with a Bachelor of Science degree in Chemistry, he was commissioned through Officer Candidate School in October 1974. His sea tours included serving on four nuclear submarines – *USS Haddock, USS Parche, USS Hawkbill, and USS Puffer.* He also served as Anti-Submarine Officer on the staff of Commander, Carrier Group One. Cassias also served as Commanding Officer on the nuclear submarine *USS Birmingham* from April 1992 to November 1994. On this tour, for which his ship received the 1992 COMSUBPAC Golden Anchor Award and the 1993 Commander, Submarine Squadron Seven Battle Efficiency "E" award, the *Birmingham* completed a deployment to the Arabian Gulf, as well as deployment to the western Pacific.

Leading up to his assignment as Commander, Pacific Submarine Force in Pearl Harbor, he also had vast experience ashore in San Diego and Singapore. Rear Admiral Cassias was a distinguished graduate of the Industrial College of the Armed Forces, where he received a master's degree in National Resource Strategy in 1999.

Rear Admiral Cassias' awards included the Defense Superior Service Medal, the Meritorious Service Medal, and numerous times – the Legion of Merit, the Navy Commendation Medal, and the Navy Achievement Medal.

His remarks to the *Lagarto* families, as prepared by LCDR Jeff Davis, were warmly received. The following is a partial text of RADM Cassias' address:

> ...I was just in Washington DC this week where I met with our Chief of Naval Operations, Admiral Mike Mullen, and he made a point of telling me to pass his warmest regards to all of the LAGARTO families. To all of you, please know that your nation is grateful for the service of these men...and that their loss was not in vain.
>
> It may seem somewhat odd to be in Manitowoc, Wisconsin, for a ceremony honoring men lost in World War II. After all, this was a peaceful place, far away from the war, and 800 miles from any ocean. But it was a place of vital importance to our victory in that conflict.
>
> Indeed, Manitowoc played a pivotal role in the amassing and projection of American naval power during World War II. It was here, on the banks of Lake Michigan, that the Navy's Bureau of Ships in 1940 contracted with the Manitowoc Shipbuilding Company to build submarines, first of the GATO class, and later of the BALAO class.

Manitowoc boats quietly became known as "fresh water submarines." In all, 28 were built, 25 of which saw combat. These submarines did all the things for which submarines are so well known –

- Manitowoc boats quietly patrolled the enemy's supply lines to inflict a stranglehold on their military-industrial machine.
- Manitowoc boats rescued a total of 76 downed aviators who had ditched their planes. And they engaged in special missions including conducting reconnaissance, landing guerrillas, laying mine fields, landing and taking off Coast Watchers, and making searches for enemy mine fields.
- Manitowoc boats made a difference in the war, and their crews always served with pride and professionalism – and often with bravery and sacrifice. They won a total of four Presidential Unit Citations and seven Navy Unit Commendations. And in total they sank 132 enemy ships displacing approximately 500-thousand tons.

But their contributions to victory were not without cost. Of the 52 submarines our nation lost in World War II, four boats – with a total of 336 men lost – were boats built at Manitowoc – ROBALO, GOLET, KETE, and LAGARTO.

It's the latter of these distinguished ships that we are gathered here to honor today. USS LAGARTO, a BALAO-class boat, was the 21st of the 28 boats built here at Manitowoc. Her keel was laid on January 12, 1944...and just nine months later, on October 14, she was commissioned.

A testament to American engineering and industrial ingenuity, LAGARTO was one of the most modern and most capable boats in the fleet. She had four General Motors diesel engines, two propellers, two 126-cell batteries, and carried 116,000 gallons of fuel. She could make over 20 knots surfaced, 8.75 knots submerged, and had a cruising range of 11,000 miles.

LAGARTO also packed a lethal mix of armament, including ten 21-inch torpedo tubes – six forward and four aft – 24 torpedoes, a 5-inch deck gun, and 50-caliber machine guns. And she was given a top-notch skipper, Commander Frank D. Latta, who had previously made seven patrols as Commanding Officer of USS NARWHAL. Every patrol made by Commander Latta was designated successful and earned the award of combat insignia, a record surpassed by no commanding officer in the Submarine Force.

But aside from Commander Latta and a few others, the vast majority of LAGARTO's crew was new to the submarine service.

They included people like LTJG Joseph Pash, who had been a football and track star at Carnegie Tech in Pittsburgh, where he graduated with a degree in mechanical engineering before being commissioned.

Or Stewards Mate Albert Kirtley from Springfield, Ohio. At age 27, he came into the Navy and the submarine force relatively late in life, leaving his family – including his little girl Albretta and son Billy – back home while he went off to serve his country.

Or Torpedoman Third Class Alvin Enns, who wanted badly to serve on a submarine but was too tall. He used to practice slouching so he wouldn't appear so tall, which apparently worked – and he was assigned to USS LAGARTO.

Following commissioning in October, Commander Latta sailed LAGARTO to Lake Michigan for sea trials and training, then onto a floating dry-dock, where she was floated down the Mississippi River to New Orleans, and then through the Panama Canal to the Pacific.

LAGARTO arrived in Pearl Harbor, Hawaii, on Christmas Day, 1944. As the crew marked the holiday – probably with little time for celebration – I'm sure they must have been met with a bittersweet mix of emotions. Surely they missed their wives and their families. But they were undoubtedly hopeful, because news from the war front was increasingly upbeat. The tide was turning, Imperial Japan was weakening, and there was even talk that the war might be over by the following Christmas.

Bill Mabin wrote home to his wife Margaret just before Christmas apologizing that he was missing his fifth Christmas in a row. Bill was a Signalman and he called his daughter Nancy, "Flags." "Flags" would be turning two soon, and Bill promised he would be home the following Christmas.

LAGARTO spent the first few weeks of 1945 conducting training and having new equipment installed, including a second 5-inch gun, two 40-mm gun mounts, and new communications equipment. She sailed from Pearl Harbor on January 24, made a brief stop in Saipan, then got underway for her maiden war patrol in the waters east of Japan.

LAGARTO's first mission was to lead a diversionary sweep so that another group of submarines could sweep the actual path to be used by the aircraft carriers of Admiral Halsey's Task Force 38 for an air strike on Tokyo. STERLET, POMFRET, PIPER, TREPANG, and BOWFIN were to sweep the actual path to Tokyo, while LAGARTO, HADDOCK and SENNETT were to feint to the South.

The diversionary sweep subs were placed under the command of Commander Latta, and became known as "Latta's Lances." They were instructed to attack picket boats with gunfire, but not to sink them right away, so that the pickets would have time to dispatch a warning. This way,

Latta's Lances would decoy the enemy to the area it was sweeping rather than the area where the aircraft carriers were actually coming.

At 0632 on February 13, LAGARTO and her sister boats opened surface fire on four Japanese picket ships – sinking two of them after giving the enemy plenty of time to radio an alert to headquarters ashore. The diversion was a complete success...so successful in fact that the actual sweep farther north never saw a single picket. Admiral Halsey's carriers reached their launch points safely, and the carrier planes reached Tokyo undetected.

Following that successful operation, LAGARTO moved south. On February 24, while patrolling submerged off Okino Shima in an operating area known as "Hit Parade," LAGARTO detected a Japanese RO-class submarine. At 1113 LAGARTO fired four torpedoes. Four minutes later, one of the torpedoes exploded, and screws on the Japanese submarine stopped. Then, at 1128, LAGARTO, in its War Patrol Report, describes hearing a "Heavy underwater explosion like a collapsed hull."

LAGARTO arrived in the Philippines on March 20, its maiden war patrol an unqualified success. She moored alongside the submarine tender USS GILMORE – named in honor of Cdr. Howard Gilmore who earned the first submariner Medal of Honor of World War II aboard GROWLER

– so she could be refitted for a second patrol in just three weeks.

It was there, in Subic Bay, where the crew enjoyed their last time ashore. It was there as well that Dick Fisher, the fun-loving and boisterous Motor Machinists Mate from Illinois, probably took his last motorcycle ride.

...And it was there, in Subic Bay, that the crew got their last letters from home...letters written weeks or months earlier. These letters probably talked about news back home, things like a baby's first steps, or words of love and support. It was there that LAGARTO's crew would also write their last letters home...letters that talked about hopes and dreams for the future, and letters that said, "don't worry."

One such letter was written by Dick Byrer of LAGARTO. On March 31, he wrote to his siblings, wryly complaining of the military censorship of mail at the time, by writing, "But I can say I am still alive which you can plainly notice, so it isn't a secret. That's all the news I have except the water in the Pacific, like the Atlantic, is salty."

Torpedoman Second Class George Clouse wrote his last letter home to his wife Beulah on April 6. His daughter Judi Sue was now about 16 months old, and Beulah was expecting their second child in just two weeks. Sadly, George would never get word that his son, Terry George Clouse, was born April 23, 1945, just nine days before George perished on LAGARTO.

But some did express their fears. Seaman Dick Grace, in a letter home to his mother about his experience being depth charged during LAGARTO's first war patrol wrote, "I was so scared. I said prayers the Pope doesn't even know." He was just 20 years old.

LAGARTO sailed out of Subic Bay on April 12, and was directed to patrol the outer part of the Gulf of Siam, which is now known as the Gulf of Thailand. On May 2, she made contact with USS BAYA, which was tracking a tanker in a convoy of heavy escorts. BAYA reported that the enemy escorts, equipped with radar, had detected her approach and driven her off with gunfire.

At 0240 on the morning of May 3, BAYA and LAGARTO rendezvoused to discuss plans for the day. LAGARTO would dive on the convoy's track to make contact at 1400, and BAYA would lie in wait twelve miles farther along the track, prepared to strike in the evening. The two boats parted company, and the convoy chase continued.

At 1500, BAYA attempted to send a contact report to LAGARTO, but LAGARTO did not answer. BAYA continued trying to raise LAGARTO every half hour for the rest of the day, but there was no response.

Nothing was ever heard again from LAGARTO. She was supposed to dock in Australia at the end of May, but never arrived. Soon she was declared missing, and across America, there were knocks on 86 doors. Eighty-six different families received the devastating news that their son, their husband or their brother was missing. We can only imagine the pain that they must have felt, particularly since it was mixed with uncertainty.

It wasn't until three months later – after the atomic bombs had been dropped on Hiroshima and Nagasaki – that the Navy finally declared LAGARTO lost. The August 10, 1945 edition of the Oakland Tribune had the banner headline saying that Japan had offered to surrender. But even with that joyous news dominating the wire services, the announcement of LAGARTO's loss was also front page news. Indeed, as the rest of the nation was celebrating victory, the families of the LAGARTO crew were just coming to terms with the fact that their loved ones were never coming home.

On the day she learned that LAGARTO really was lost, Motor Machinists Mate First Class Caldwell Cook's wife recalled seeing a dove tapping at her kitchen window. Years later, after her death, their daughter Maureen built a rock garden in her yard. She says that two doves come to visit on occasion, and she feels that it is the spirit of her parents, together again.

After the war ended, Japanese records indicated that the minelayer HATSUTAKA reported sinking a submarine near the mouth of the Gulf of Siam at the time LAGARTO was there. In just 30 fathoms of water, LAGARTO had little chance for evasion. And so, LAGARTO joined the solemn list of those boats lost. For the families, their worry and uncertainty slowly turned to sorrow and grief...

...Jamie MacLeod has reported, when he and his team of divers found that awesome sight 200 feet below the surface in the Gulf of Thailand, they noticed something. On the port side, the middle torpedo tube was open. And the torpedo inside was missing. USS LAGARTO apparently went down fighting.

Just recently, a gentleman by the name of Pat O'Brien sent a letter to the LAGARTO families. Mr. O'Brien ... joined the Navy at age 17 and served six war patrols on USS NAUTILUS before reporting to LAGARTO's commissioning crew. He was on LAGARTO during its first war patrol but transferred off before its second.

Mr. O'Brien wrote –

'(LAGARTO) had the best torpedo crew any submarine ever had. I don't think I ever heard an angry word out of anyone. They looked up to me as if I was an old sailor and I was only twenty-one years old at that time. I don't think a day has ever gone by that I didn't think of that crew. I feel it was an honor just to have known them and to have served with them. I still pray for them more than I do for my mother and father. They were so young and innocent.'

The Pacific Submarine Force paid a steep price in the fight for freedom. In all, 52 submarines were destroyed during World War II, which is about the number of attack submarines we have in our Navy today. More importantly, 3500 submariners lost their lives aboard these ships. They are a reminder of the courage and sense of duty required to serve in submarines...duty that was more likely to result in death than in any other warfare specialty of our armed forces during the War.

But their legacy is proud. Even though American submariners made up less than 2-percent of the U.S. Navy, they accounted for 55 percent of all Japanese shipping sunk in the entire war.

...Ladies and gentlemen, that legacy, as exemplified by the crew of LAGARTO and our other World War II submariners, is what drives the Submarine Force of today to be ready to defend the cause of freedom. And rest assured that we will never fail you.

RADM (Rear Admiral) Jeffrey Cassias addressing *Lagarto* family and friends at Wisconsin Maritime Museum in Manitowoc, WI. *Lagarto* Memorial Service.

Aftermath 2006

The feeling of euphoria generated by the *Lagarto Memorial Week End* in Manitowoc continued for quite a while. We *Lagartos* enjoyed reading area newspapers and seeing the television pieces produced by the Chicago CBS affiliate and the network. E-mails between family members who attended the ceremony were exchanged. We knew we had experienced something extraordinary.

My visit to the Chicago area was cut short when I arrived at my daughter's home. Jamie Macleod, who was a guest of the Augustines' greeted me at the door, and we had a chance to visit until Beth and Chris came home from work. Then Macleod remembered a message he had taken from my husband, asking me to call him.

My mother was back in the hospital, and the news was not good. Mom had fallen six times the previous week; three of those times she lost consciousness and required the services of the Glen Arbor Fire and Rescue Squad. Her helpers tried as long as they could to avoid telling me, not wanting me to miss the *Lagarto* events. I left for the long drive back to Michigan at daybreak the next morning.

When I spoke with Mom's physician, Dr. John Zachman, the news was dismal. Mom could no longer get around with the aid of a walker and would be confined to a wheelchair. Undaunted, she insisted on going home. She had just celebrated her 89th birthday in the hospital and was anxious to get back to normal – whatever that was.

My siblings and I were convinced that normal for Mom would not cut it anymore. I asked Dr. Zachman to speak with her about going to a rehab facility in order to regain enough strength to use her walker again. Mom agreed.

We found a wonderful place called Orchard Creek in Traverse City where our mother received the care she needed. The month of May had been an emotional roller coaster ride for our whole family. And the ride wasn't over.

Euphoria
2006

After a challenging winter and an exciting spring, summer finally arrived. I began to relax a little and do some necessary gardening. I enjoyed the balmy weather and was inspired to take long walks and read long books. After the emotional highs and lows of the past year, I slipped into my laid-back summer routine.

LCDR Jeff Davis and I stayed in touch, and he called one afternoon to tell me the Navy was going ahead with its promise of visiting *Lagarto*. Admiral Tobin had told me, prior to the *Lagarto* Memorial Service, that the Navy, in June, would be sending one of its ships to *Lagarto's* site to verify her discovery. We knew before Memorial Day 2006 that would happen, but we didn't know exactly what to expect.

On June 14th, I received two messages from Macleod. In one he said:

> Everything went very well with the Navy although it was a strange feeling for both me and Stewart handing over 'our' very special submarine. They've promised to let me know their results when they are able. I suspect we may have to wait until they've finished and reported back.

With the second message, Macleod attached some fascinating photos he'd taken, which included one of the *Salvor* approaching his dive boat, with the American flag flying from the British MV Trident, in honor of her meeting with the American navy.

Macleod's message said:

> We flew the US flag from the Trident, a first time for everything! Your family flag (the U.S. flag Beth Augustine brought from Chicago) is still attached to the *Lagarto*. We gave it a clean and left it for the Navy. You should have seen the sailors' faces when the ROV picked it up – they patched the image all through the ship.

Another huge player in the process of verifying *Lagarto*'s discovery was the Wisconsin Maritime Museum. Their historical resources were impressive, and they worked with the NHC to find a way to make *Lagarto*'s identity indisputable. The museum, via Karen Duvalle and Norma Bishop, kept the *Lagarto* families informed every step of the way. Duvalle sent the following e-mail to the families:

> Good news, the dive is underway! We have been put in contact with a Lieutenant that has direct contact with the SALVOR. He will be copying us on any offi-

> cial press releases, and I will pass the information on. So keep an eye out in the next few days for some hopefully good news!

After a day and a half of nail-biting, I heard from Admiral Tobin. He told me COMSUBPAC (Commander of Submarine Force in the Pacific) was going to announce the sub was, in fact, the *U.S.S. Lagarto*. He said he was convinced that it was and would say so and didn't foresee any surprises.

Later that day, I received a call from LCDR Davis relating the same information. A press release had been prepared, and he wanted me to know before it hit the news. I was euphoric! Grinning ear-to-ear, I hung up the phone. Then, with tears filling my eyes, I raised them upward and said out loud, "We did it, Daddy. We did it!"

I almost went crazy waiting to tell my husband about this. He had been such a supportive partner to me throughout the past year of emotional upheavals. But he was at a meeting and couldn't be reached. I resisted the temptation of telling my children, who were first on my list of calls, because I wanted John to be the first to hear the news. Soon he arrived home, and when I looked out the window and saw him approaching, I flew out the front door! I rushed into his arms and received the big hug I was expecting. He was as happy as I was to hear the news.

After I calmed down, I went on the internet to find the story LCDR Davis had told me about.

Sunken Sub Appears to be *USS Lagarto*

From Commander, Submarine Force, U.S. Pacific Fleet

(PEARL HARBOR, HI) – Navy divers completed six days of diving operations June 16 on wreckage in the Gulf of Thailand believed to be that of the lost World War II submarine USS *Lagarto*.

Divers will send photographs and video of the submarine to the Naval Historical Center in Washington for further analysis.

The divers' observations appear to confirm the discovery made in May 2005 by British wreck diver Jamie MacLeod.

'Without a doubt it's a U.S. submarine, a Balao-class,' said Seventh Fleet Diving Officer Cmdr. Tony San Jose.

San Jose and his fellow divers reported identifying twin 5-inch gun mounts both forward and aft, a feature believed to be unique to *Lagarto*. They also reported finding serial numbers and the word "Manitowoc" engraved on the submarine's propeller. *USS Lagarto* was one of 28 submarines built in Manitowoc, Wisconsin.

The operations were conducted from the rescue and salvage ship USS Salvor (ARS-52) with embarked divers from Mobile Diving and Salvage Unit One, or MSDU-1, based in Pearl Harbor, Hawaii. The Japan-based mine countermeasures ship USS Patriot (MCM-7) assisted by first pin-pointing the location of the wreckage with its SQQ-32 sonar and remotely-operated Mine Neutralization Vehicle.

The mission to positively identify *USS Lagarto* was carried out as part of the Thailand phase of the exercise Cooperation Afloat Readiness and Training of CARAT. A Royal Thai Navy liaison officer was embarked onboard USS Salvor to assist during the mission.

San Jose said that the diving operations were very challenging because of short bottom times, strong currents and limited visibility. Due to the depths involved, the dives had to be conducted with mixed gas.

'We are deeply grateful to the divers of MDSU-1 and USS Salvor for their efforts to confirm this discovery and bring closure to the families of *Lagarto's* crew,' said Pacific Submarine Force commander Rear Adm. Jeffrey Cassias.

For 60 years, crewmembers' families did not know the exact circumstances surrounding the 86 submariners who perished. *Lagarto* was last heard from on May 3, 1945, as it was preparing to attack a Japanese convoy under heavy escorts. Japanese war records later revealed that the minelayer Hatsutaka reported sinking a U.S. submarine at roughly the same time and location.

Cassias met May 6 with *Lagarto* family members at the Wisconsin Maritime Museum in Manitowoc, where a memorial service was held to honor the lost crew. Last year, Wisconsin Gov. Jim Doyle signed a proclamation making May 3, the day the craft was presumed sunk, as USS *Lagarto* Remembrance Day in perpetuity.

'We owe a great debt to these men, and to all of the World War II submariners,' said Cassias. 'In the world's darkest hour, they faced the greatest risks, and demonstrated the most noble courage to preserve the freedom of our nation.'

Lagarto was one of 52 submarines lost on patrol during World War II.

-USN-

The Associated Press 2006

I had barely had time to digest all this, when I received another call from LCDR Davis. He told me that a reporter with the Associated Press had called him seeking information on the *Lagarto* discovery. He told the reporter he believed the real story was about the *Lagarto* families and sought my permission to give the AP reporter, Audrey McAvoy, my name and phone number. Of course, I agreed.

McAvoy called me and conducted an interview. Her article appeared in newspapers and the internet the same day.

LONG-LOST WORLD WAR II SUB LIKELY FOUND

> HONOLULU (AP) – For 60 years, Nancy Kenney wondered what happened to her father. The submarine that William T. Mabin was in disappeared while he and his crewmates were on a mission to attack a Japanese convoy in the last months of World War II.
>
> Now, the Navy says a wreck found at the bottom of the Gulf of Thailand appears to be the sub, the *USS Lagarto*.

'I have never in my life, unequivocally, felt such a high,' said Kenney, who was 2 years old when her father and the submarine did not return from their mission in May 1945.

'We can just feel a sense of relief and a sense of peace in knowing what happened and where they are,' said Kenney, of Lake Leelanau, Mich.

Navy divers on Friday completed a six-day survey of the wreckage site. They took photos and video of the 311-foot, 9 inch submarine for further analysis by naval archeologists.

The divers found twin 5-inch gun mounts on the forward and rear parts of the ship – a feature believed to be unique to the *Lagarto*.

They also saw the word “Manitowoc” displayed on the submarine's propeller, providing a connection to the Manitowoc, Wis. Shipyard that built the *Lagarto* in the 1940s.

Eighty-six sailors died when the *Lagarto* sank in May 1945. The Japanese minelayer Hatsutaka reported dropping depth charges and sinking a U.S. sub in the area, though it was never known what ship it destroyed.

The Navy sent its divers to examine the ship to provide the sailors' families with some answers after a British professional shipwreck diver last year found what looked like the *Lagarto*, said Lt. Comdr. Jeff Davis, a spokesman for the U.S. Pacific Fleet Submarine Force.

'It was important to bring a sense of closure to these families and it was important to do it in a way that would honor our fellow submariners,' Davis said.

The Navy wouldn't do anything with the ship even if it conclusively determined it was the *Lagarto*, considering the sea to be a proper final resting place for 'our people who are killed in action,' he said.

The wreckage site over 100 miles off the eastern coast of Thailand is also likely to go undisturbed.

U.S. laws and international agreements already protect sunken U.S. warships from looters or others who would disturb the site, Davis said.

Since Kenney was just a toddler when her father went to war, she has no conscious memories of their life in La Grange, Ill. But she said news of the Navy's dive 'was the most important piece' of a puzzle about her father that she's been trying to put together for six decades.

The children of the *Lagarto* sailors feel closer to their fathers now more than ever, she said.

'We feel like we've found our fathers,' Kenney said.

The Media
2006

No one could have prepared me for what would follow after a story like that hit the media. The news first came out with the press release issued by the Navy's Public Affairs Office in Pearl Harbor, but began snowballing on Saturday, June 17th with Audrey McAvoy's Associated Press article, which appeared in hundreds of newspapers and became a favorite story on the internet. I was watching the news on CNN and was startled to see news of *Lagarto*'s discovery on the crawl at the bottom of the screen.

My phone rang off the hook. A continual stream of e-mails popped up in my mailbox. It shouldn't have been a surprise, but it was – especially after a full year of trying to get the electronic media's attention and being rebuffed. Not so for the newspaper establishment. Those print reporters were a big help in finding *Lagarto* families.

Among some of the more poignant responses were those from family members who had just learned of *Lagarto*'s discovery. The name of one of them had a familiar ring – Robert Ruble:

Dear Mrs. Kenney,

I just sent an email to your local newspaper, hoping they'd forward it to you, but discovered an article from the Chicago Tribune with your e-mail address and am presuming to contact you direct, hoping it is not an intrusion.

I was born in late May, 1945. My father had been unable to enlist due to deafness, but found a way to aid the war effort by moving to Seattle and working for Boeing, doing shakedown flights on bombers before they were shipped to the armed forces. He had two brothers in the navy. One survived the war, on carriers, narrowly missing Pearl Harbor on the "Day of Infamy." The other did not. He and his family members got word in June of his loss on the *Lagarto*. He was Lt. Robert T. Ruble, USN. Soon after that, my name was changed to his, in his honor. I have his medals, and the approximate location of the *Lagarto*, but just tonight learned that she was found. I did some internet research, found the articles, and learned of the memorial service held last month.

I'd like you to add my name to the list of family members, and to learn any more that you care to relate to me.

> Thank you so much for your efforts, and the work you've obviously done to reach out to others.
>
> Sincerely, Robert T. Ruble, MD

Dr. Ruble lived in Billings, Montana and was one of the *Lagartos* we had sought, but not found before *Lagarto's* memorial service. I responded:

> Dear Bob,
>
> Welcome to the *Lagarto* family. We've been looking for you! Isn't this all amazing? I feel like I have so much to tell you that I don't know where to start. First of all, we were looking for the Ruble family in Denver and ran into a dead end. The Rocky Mountain News contacted me to do a story about your uncle, but that went nowhere. And now you've found us.
>
> I am forwarding your message to Karen Duvalle at the Wisconsin Maritime Museum. Karen and I have worked together all year in locating families. I'm not sure of the exact count at this point, but a year ago, we knew of 4, I think. Now we've found 55 or 56 of the 86 crew members.
>
> Since there is a lot to tell you, I would suggest this. There is a lot of info on the internet. Just google USS LAGARTO and you'll get tons. With this recent an-

nouncement from the navy, there may be quite a lot of media coverage. We sure hope so, because that should help us find others.

You will love this "family." They really are the nicest group of people I've ever met.

BTW. There is a photo of your uncle on the website "oneternalpatrol.org." It's run by Charles Hinman, the curator of the Bowfin Museum in Pearl Harbor. Great guy. He found your uncle's photo through the naval academy.

He wrote back the next day:

Thanks for your prompt reply. Denver would have been the logical place to look, but only one family member, an older brother of mine, still lives there. I just forwarded him your letter, and did the same to my other brother, in Florida. They may be contacting you.

There is only one other relative from our generation, another nephew – a cousin with whom I've lost contact. I believe he lives in southern France. I'll try to locate him. Isn't the internet a phenomenon, the way it spreads information and facilitates connections!!...

I couldn't have agreed more about the internet. If not for its existence, *Lagarto* would still be lost. It is easy to communicate these days. If our mothers, fathers, grandparents and other relatives had been able to communicate as we do today, it would have been much easier for them. But then, we might not have all these beautiful, hand-written love letters.

Sunday morning, June 18th, I went to Mass at the Roman Catholic Church of Blessed Kateri Tekawitha. This parish sprang from an Indian mission in Peshawbestown, Michigan. My family and I have enjoyed attending Mass in the tiny church building, embellished with beautiful Native American blankets and artwork. The music was perfect – sung from the heart – and included Native American flourishes, such as the beat-ing of the tom tom. The parish was ministered to by Father Andy, a Franciscan priest in his eighties, with a heart of gold and a down-to-earth manner. My heart was bursting with joy with the latest news of *Lagarto*, and I thanked God that morning for my gift from the sea.

When I returned home, John was full of news. He'd been handling the phones in my absence and had fielded some pretty interesting calls. One was from Lois Friend, a sister of BM1 Eugene Robison, who had gone down with *Lagarto*. I called her back, and we had a wonderful conversation.

Another phone call came from the president of American World War II Orphans Network (AWON), and we talked a long time. She said the members of AWON had been following the *Lagarto* story and were happy for all of us. I heard from other members of AWON, an organization whose members know how it hurts to lose a father to war and are very supportive of each other.

One of them lost her father in Palermo, Sicily in 1943. He is buried in the Sicily-Rome American Cemetery. In an e-mail, she said, in part:

> ...My father was also killed in World War II and I, too, had a difficult time all these years dealing with his death. ...I had these emotions and dealt with a wall of silence concerning his death. As children in the 40s, we weren't talked to about so many issues. As an adult, I knew I had to know all the details to fill in my broken heart...

In the days and weeks to come, her sentiments would be echoed over and over again as many other orphans from WWII found a way to contact me.

That night, I received a google alert for *USS Lagarto* which listed articles that had appeared in the *Kansas City Star* (Missouri), the *Winston-Salem Journal* (North Carolina), the *Myrtle Beach Sun News* (South Carolina), and *Scotland on Sunday* (Edinburgh, Scotland, UK). This was only a taste of what was to come. The public appeared to be very interested in the story. For awhile, the *Lagarto* story on the CNN website was third in the most e-mailed and first in both the most viewed and printed categories. The results were virtually the same on the MSNBC and AOL websites.

The results of these reports were immediate. In 24 hours, we found two more families and knew there would be more.

It was Father's Day! This time, my father gave me a gift – himself. I spent most of the afternoon re-reading the letters he wrote my mother. Before reading his letters, I had only known my father through photographs and occasional stories I had been told. Through his letters, I found him – his warm personality and his great love for my mother and me. These letters brought him back to me.

The media continued calling. A producer from the popular "Spike O'Dell" morning radio show, which is broadcast widely on WGN in the Midwest, called to set up an interview for early the next morning. Associated Press radio called on Saturday for an on-the-spot interview.

That was one of the things that surprised me about the electronic media. When someone called for an interview, they meant then. One day I received a call from Fox News in Honolulu with a request for an interview. When I agreed, the caller said, "Stay on the line." I was doing my laundry at the time. While waiting on the line, throwing clothes in my washing machine, I could hear voices, far away in Hawaii, referring to the fact that they had a family member of the *Lagarto* crew on the line, and then the interview began – live. It was a little surreal.

On Monday, I received more feedback from the week end news. One of the first came from a La Grange friend, Tom Morsch. His e-mail note said:

> The New York Times on Sunday, and WGN on Monday! Wow! I'm proud of you, Nancy...

On the same day, I received a note from another *Lagarto* relative who had just learned the news, Stacy Wright, whose uncle had gone down with the boat. She wanted to know if there would be another memorial service.

There were calls from the *Washington Times,* the *Minneapolis Star Tribune,* the *Herald Times Reporter* in Manitowoc, the *Traverse City Record Eagle,* the *Honolulu Star-Bulletin,* the *Austin American-Statesman* in Austin, Texas, and the *Bangkok Post* in Thailand, and *World War II* magazine. I heard from TV-radio networks *Fox News, WIS* in Columbia, SC, *ABC 4* in Salt Lake City, *CNN*, and *KXLY* in Spokane, WA.

At the same time, I heard from all kinds of wonderful people. A few were personal – old high school and college friends and the former village manager of La Grange, Scott Randall.

Others were strangers with whom I shared an awful bond. They too had lost someone dear in World War II, and they wrote and spoke about their feelings of loss. Many were 60 to 70 year-old sons of military men who died in WWII. Several of them broke down in tears while telling me they had never been able to tell anyone of their feelings of loss for their fathers.

Toward the end of the week, the calls from the media slowed down. Then came the most surprising phone call of all. Alyssa Litoff, a producer with ABC News, called to ask if I would do an interview for ABC's *World News Tonight*. There was a problem, however. At that time, ABC didn't have a local bureau in Traverse City, the closest big town to Lake Leelanau. The nearest news bureau was in Grand Rapids, about a three-hour drive away. Producers are made to overcome problems, and Alyssa found an independent camera crew to do the taping. The next morning, the crew joined me in my home and facilitated an interview with ABC's Ned Potter. It was shown a few days later.

This whole experience, coming on the heels of an intense year of working on *Lagarto* issues, began to have an adverse emotional impact on me. One day, while having my hair cut, my beautician asked me for recent news on my *Lagarto* activities. Without warning, I burst into uncontrollable sobs.

A few days later, the same thing happened at a routine visit to my dentist. The same question was asked, and I again burst into tears. Both outbursts were extremely embarrassing to me.

For a year, I had suppressed my emotions because I felt I had to in order to continue moving forward with *Lagarto* issues. I had been successful at doing this, focusing on the impact of the submarine's discovery on other family members, rather than myself. I didn't give in to my own feelings of grief because I had so much to do. I suppose it would be similar to a year-long preparation for a memorial service for 86 people. After more than a year of tamping down my own emotions, I seemed to be succumbing to them. I felt out of control.

When John came home that night, I told him about both incidents. Throughout the whole *Lagarto* experience, his primary concern was always my well-being. He urged me to let go of *Lagarto* for awhile and concentrate on something else.

Last Words
1944 - 1945

With all the media attention, we did find many more families. As the other families, they were thrilled with the news and wanted to share their stories. The following personal missives were written by *Lagarto* sailors and shared by their families:

HOWARD E. ORTEGA – Pastura, New Mexico
November 7, 1944
Dearest Loved Ones,

Never having written a similar document, I hardly know how to begin, but here goes anyway.

First of all, I want to say that you will read this after I am dead, and I request that this letter be fulfilled to the letter. I also want to say that I was not afraid to die – I am fully ready because I have never really done anything bad in my life, and I am squared away with my god. I even welcome it in some ways. I am sure mother will be waiting for me and I can be with her again, not for a short time but forever. She is the one who really loved me, and I realize that now after it is too late.

I request that my estate be disposed of as follows:

My cattle will be divided, equally among my brothers and sisters, including my brother and sister-in-law. If it is not convenient for any of them to keep the cattle, they shall receive the value thereof.

The Church of Santa Elena, Pastura, shall receive one of my fifty dollar war bonds.

Miss Helen Beckman, 655 Algoma Blvd, Oshkosh, Wisconsin shall receive one of my twenty five dollar war bonds, and a good large picture of me. Also my spurs.

Albert Clancey Ortega III will receive my saddle, my horses along with all of my money that is left after the aforementioned items have been fulfilled. (If I have any.)

My boots will be returned to John Maher – I am confident that HE will be alive.

Daddy is not included in this letter, but he will receive my insurance, so he will be well remembered.

You may wonder about Miss Beckman – I am sure she will tell you about it.

Before closing this letter I want to say that I am a very happy boy. I will have made the supreme sacrifice for my country, the thing I hold next to my god. I am not scared but I find a certain bliss in the thought. I know I am young to die, but I have lived a very full life and I have enjoyed every moment of it.

On closing I say – pray for me so that my stay in purgatory be a short one. Have faith in god that you may join me in time.

I love you all and am sorry to die for your sakes. I know Carolyn will take hardest of all for she has been sister and brother, father and mother and constant companion to me all of my life.

Good bye and god bless you all.
The late Howard E. Ortega
S 1/C U.S. Navy

S1 W.C. WARNICK – Raymondville, Texas
March 30, 1945
Dear Family:

Hi, Mom! I feel in one of those moods you know when you are at peace with your soul and all your fellow men and just want to talk to someone that really means something to you. I will tell you now don't worry about me because you know every person has some job they must complete in life before they are ready to die and I know that somewhere, sometime, there is a job to do, it may just be a small thing that will never receive any distinction, but I feel that somewhere sometime there is a big job that no one can do but me. Sometimes I wonder if I'm a normal person for the most of the fellows that I know just seem to live, not driven, but just for the fun of it, sometimes I try to throw off all cares and just live for today, but I never can quite seem to manage it, for I keep looking for this job that I must do. Maybe I've already done it, so if I have, there is no reason why I should go on, but I don't think it is yet finished.

I long for my family, my wife and my babies, with every fiber of my being and try to fill my waking hours with thoughts of what we will do when I can come home to be with them. My sole ambition is to help beat the people who were so blind as to think they could beat a nation where nearly everyone believes in God. I have seen people who suffered under the hand of the aggressor, most of them are very peaceful people, much the same as ourselves, who fight only when driven but when forced can be more barbaric than any other. It seems kind of queer in a way that a people so peaceful can start in to live only to kill, that their children may live in peace. Personally, I don't think I will ever make much of a killer. I can do it and have done it, but I will keep wondering if the ones we kill aren't also just little people who have been forced into emotions and ambitions or desires which without a driving force they could never have achieved. But we do our best and hope that someday soon there will be peace and our lives can again be lived in the manner in which man was intended to live. Mom, when I'm so scared that my tongue feels like cotton and my stomach tied in a knot, I can always say Psalm 23rd and get peace and relaxation. Just read it again:

The Lord is my shepherd. I shall not want. He leadeth me in places of plenty, He comforts me when all else fails, and yea though I sail where death is, I'm only a little afraid. Never beyond my endurance, for You are with me, my Lord. Surely when this is over goodness and kindness will make me a better man than I could hope to be of my own accord, and I will live in a peaceful way, which suits the nature you have given me, throughout the days, which are written in the Book for my life, and I shall live with you forever, never alone. Amen.

The more I read it the better I like it and it suits me. I will close now because if I write more it would only be words, but the things I have written, I really feel.

Your son,

W.C. WARNICK, S 1-c

U.S.S. Lagarto

Loose Ends

While I didn't exactly take the rest of the summer off, I did let go of *Lagarto* concerns for awhile.

My mother needed my attention, and after weighing all the possibilities and outcomes of our choices for her, my siblings and I decided she should remain at Orchard Creek Assisted Living. When she required more care than assisted living could supply, we moved her to another part of the Orchard Creek health facility system, their Supportive Care Unit. It was a brand new building with 20 separate suites for each of its residents. Since Mom was one of the building's first guests, we arranged for her to live in a unit with one of the best views.

Her suite had a small living room, separated from the bedroom by a set of bookshelves on the living room side and dresser drawers on the bedroom side. Off the bedroom was a spacious bathroom, designed to accommodate those with disabilities. The living room and bedroom windows looked out onto a heavily wooded area, through which a paved hiking trail ran. In the summer, Mom could see joggers and cyclers, and in the winter, cross-country skiers. We decorated her rooms with furniture from her own home, family photos, and lots of books. It was a cheerful and pleasant place to live. Mom maintained her precious privacy, and at the same time was cared for by kind and professional healthcare providers. She enjoyed her meals, and to our surprise, participated in many of the facility's activities. She became the queen of bingo.

With Mom settled, I began to think about some of the questions I still had about the *Lagarto* verification from the Navy. After the Navy had confirmed the submarine's identity, I inquired if the divers had come to any conclusions about what caused her sinking. We had found that the Japanese records matched up with the location of *Lagarto,* but differed in the description of their attack. Their report didn't groove with the damage found to the submarine.

When I inquired of the Navy if, on their identification dives they had determined the reason *Lagarto* went down, I was told it was not their mission to do that. They dove on *Lagarto* for the purpose of verifying her identity.

We had learned so much about the boat and were so lucky to know her definite location, after all these years, that it seemed too much to want any more explanations. However, that didn't stop the desire to know more.

In the meantime, my daughter Beth and I had begun corresponding with *Shadow Diver* Richie Kohler, who had become very interested in the *Lagarto* story and shared our belief that the submarine's story should be told. *Lagarto* had been found, her identity verified by the United States Navy, and her official memorial service had been held. I wondered what he could do at this point.

I hadn't been aware that, less than a month after *Lagarto's* original discovery in May 2005, British diver Steve Burton (SubVet Roy Leonhardt's original contact in Thailand) had fired off an e-mail to Richie Kohler with some questions on how to positively identify the sunken submarine. Kohler replied with suggestions and added that he was on the road, doing a book tour with John Chatterton. Ironically, Traverse City was on their tour, and we lived in that area. My husband and I had considered attending the *Shadow Divers* book signing, but I was still reeling with the news of *Lagarto's* discovery and wasn't up to hearing another submarine story. Little did I know that Kohler was interested in *Lagarto's* situation. A year later, after a series of e-mails between Kohler, Burton, and Macleod, Richie Kohler got in touch with my daughter, and the rest was history.

Another irony was connected with my mother's health care. The medical director of Mom's assisted-living facility at Orchard Creek was a wonderful woman named Denise MacMaster. Denise's husband Greg was the chief meteorologist of the NBC news affiliate in Traverse City and an avid diver. Through the same book-signing event that I declined to attend, MacMaster became acquainted with Richie Kohler and John Chatterton. Everything went full circle, and it turned out that all involved were interested in the fate of the long-lost submarine *Lagarto*. Months later, when MacMaster and

I discussed my wanting to learn the reason for *Lagarto*'s loss, he said, "Nancy, that's what they do. Richie and John can find out what happened to *Lagarto.* They are forensic divers." Why didn't I think of that?! Kohler's e-mail backed up MacMaster's analysis, and he seemed interested in helping. I was thrilled to death.

The Shadow Divers, The Producers and Walloon Lake

One of the most satisfying aspects of the year-long quest to find *Lagarto* families and honor her crew was meeting so many wonderful people.

Few come better than the noble foursome – *Shadow Divers* Richie Kohler and John Chatterton and television producers Harvey Moshman and Chuck Coppola. They all came from different backgrounds. Kohler and Chatterton were renowned technical divers, who lived on America's east coast and had worked everywhere in the world – as long as there was water. Moshman and Coppola were well-known TV producers whose careers had settled them in the Midwest. Both had won Emmys and loved a good story. Coppola's face was familiar to me, as he had covered many Chicago stories and was an on-air television journalist. He was professional and told news stories clearly.

I met Coppola and Moshman the weekend of the *Lagarto* memorial service in Manitowoc. They interviewed me after the service for their respective news organizations. While I didn't see much more of them after that, my daughter did. Beth stayed in touch, and they kept the idea of a *Lagarto* documentary moving along.

Other things moved along as well. The Navy's verification of *Lagarto's* discovery and the resultant publicity helped us find more families. By fall, we had identified 16 more *Lagarto* families through news articles, and they contacted Karen Duvalle or me.

Earlier that year, I decided to write about this experience, and signed up for the Walloon Lake writers' retreat held annually in the Petoskey, Michigan area. The site of the workshop was Michigania, a beautiful campground nestled on the shores of Walloon Lake (where Ernest Hemingway spent many childhood summers), and is owned by the University of Michigan alumni.

Staffing the seminars were ten successful professional writers – novelists, non-fiction authors, poets, and a screenwriter. Forty participants attended four workshops each day, socialized together, and dined together. In the evenings, we were entertained by the professionals reading from their works. Among the distinguished staff were Jane Hamilton who wrote the beautiful novel *A Map of the World* and Doug Stanton, author of the best selling non-fiction works, *In Harm's Way* and *The Horse Soldiers.*

My favorite faculty member was screenwriter/novelist/non-fiction author Chuck Pfarrer. I met him at a cocktail party the first night. After I told him the *Lagarto* story, we bonded. Pfarrer is a Navy SEAL and wrote a memoir on his experiences entitled *Warrior Soul.* He had just finished a new novel *Killing Che,* which came out in April 2007. Among his screenplays were *The Jackal* and *Red Planet*. Several of the writers were fascinated by the *Lagarto* story and were very encouraging. This gave me the confidence to write this book. Pfarrer, in particular, gave me a lot of guidance and became, in a way, my writing mentor.

In the meantime, the Wisconsin Maritime Museum continued to pursue the possibility of doing a documentary on *Lagarto*. They discussed this with Harvey Moshman and were hopeful that Chatterton and Kohler would be interested in working with them. Plans were underway to dive on *Lagarto* again in March 2007.

Other things were going on, as well. Bruce Abele, the eldest son of *U.S.S. Grunion* (SS 216) skipper, LCDR Mannert L. Abele, believed that his father's submarine had been found near Kiska in the Aleutian Islands. It had been missing in that area since July 1942. Abele and his brothers Brad and John were as determined as we were to confirm *Grunion*'s discovery and honor their father and his crew.

Karen Duvalle and I stayed in touch with Charles Hinman, our friend at the *Bowfin* museum in Hawaii. Hinman was involved with planning a memorial service for another discovered boat, the famous WWII sub *U.S.S. Wahoo* (SS 238). *Wahoo's* captain was the renowned CDR D.W. "Mush" Morton. *Wahoo* was reported missing in September 1943. Her discovery was confirmed by the Navy in 2007.

Also found in 2007, was the submarine *U.S.S. Perch* (SS 176) scuttled in March 1942, after the enemy had rendered her inoperable. Her crew spent the rest of the war in a Japanese prison camp. All but a few of the sub's crew survived the horrendous experience.

By early December, Moshman and Coppola were still working out the details of a documentary. They knew they had a great story, but needed to nail down the business end. They were in discussions with PBS to air the doc, but needed to find a way to fund it. By this time, the *Shadow Divers* were interested in the project, so paying for it was the only major problem.

Just before Christmas 2006, Moshman forwarded the following e-mail from Coppola. It read in part:

> Ben Jarvis, skipper of the USS Baya will talk with us on camera. His daughter will also, if we want. Both are in northern California. He is confident he is the last person outside the *Lagarto* to have spoken with Frank Latta, the *Lagarto's* skipper before the sub went down.
>
> Jarvis told me the story of the Japanese convoy he had been tracking for several days, talking across the water by megaphone to Latta while the subs floated on the surface about 25 yards apart. ...He's looking for letters he wrote his wife after the *Lagarto* went down. ...There may be mention of the *Lagarto* and Latta in the letters.
>
> He regarded Latta as more than another commander, to him. Frank Latta was

> a mentor and personal friend whom he first met while Latta was commander of another submarine connected to Gen. McArthur's efforts in the Philippines...

Moshman, in the meantime, continued tracking down information and photographs of *Lagarto's* crew at work. LTjg Harold Todd told his wife Rae that a photographer had lived on board the submarine in an attempt to film a "day-in-the-life aboard-a-submarine." Moshman contacted his photo researcher in Washington to see if she could find the photos. In his December 23 e-mail to me, he said in part:

> Since we spoke, I heard back from my photo researcher in Washington. Her response to my request of the whereabouts of the day-in-the-life-aboard-a-submarine film that was alluded to in a letter home from Lt. Hal Todd. ...was 'most of the ship-board life footage was not saved when lots of WWII footage from the NVY made its way to NARA (National Archives) about 25 years ago. NARA has no obligation to save everything it's given, so they chose to save change of command ceremonies over ship-board life. So I'd say unless the *Lagarto* and its captain were some sort of stars to the Navy, it's a long shot...

On the same day, I sent Jamie Macleod the following message. In part, it read:

> Yesterday, Harvey Moshman called. ...I was happy to hear so much progress has been made in getting a documentary started. ...I gather plans are being made to dive on *Lagarto* again in March with the documentary crew. That sounds very exciting. It also sounds as if Chatterton and Kohler are in. Great...

The day after Christmas, Mike Latta and I exchanged e-mails. I said:

> ...I got an interesting phone call, yesterday, from Harvey Moshman. I met him earlier this year in Manitowoc and like him. He is quite committed to telling *Lagarto's* story in a documentary for PBS, and I say, good for him. I was astounded when he told me that CDR Jarvis (Baya) was still alive and willing to talk to him. That's pretty amazing....
>
> At this stage, I think the Wisconsin Maritime Museum is going to write a grant to ask for funding for the project, but it sounds as if all parties are going ahead with plans to go to Thailand. In March, I believe. The two divers I told you about –

> John Chatterton and Richie Kohler (the subjects written about in 'Shadow Divers') are still enthusiastic about being a part of this and are going to Thailand, also. ...I am anxious to meet them. Everyone tells me they are terrific guys...

Back from Mike:

> Good to hear from you again. Ben Jarvis is a hell of a guy, and I am glad to hear that he's still kicking around. His memories of the last time anyone spoke to *Lagarto* and my dad are riveting...

Everyone got through the hectic holidays and began looking forward to the next trip to *Lagarto*. My son John decided, once again, to go along on the trip to the Gulf of Thailand and began preparing his professional and personal time to conform with the documentary's schedule.

Beth and I stayed in touch with Kohler and Chatterton for months. Even though we knew they were interested in diving on *Lagarto*, it was far from a given; they were very busy men. But everything came together, and the *Shadow Divers* and the producers, along with their crews and my son John were off to meet Macleod and Oehl in Thailand in March 2007. Correspondence had flown between all the major participants in this exciting expedition, and Mike Latta and I received a kind e-mail from Kohler just days before they left. He asked if there was anything special he could do for us while on the *Lagarto* expedition.

Latta was curious to know if they might locate any sign of his father's motorcycle, carried around with Frank Latta on his many submarine tours. However, the divers were barred from looking for this motorcycle for two reasons. First, the sub was intact and physically closed, preventing anyone from entering it. Second, it is against the law to enter a sunken American ship, which is considered a war grave.

I asked Kohler to take a minute to place his hand on the sub and say a silent prayer – telling my father that we loved him and were all okay and that I was taking care of Mom. He did this wonderful thing for me, knowing that I would never be able to visit my father's grave.

On 16 March 2007, Mike Latta and I received this message from Richie:

Dear Nancy and Mike,

I have just settled back into my home here in NJ and wanted to write to each of you my thoughts and detailed findings on this past trip to the resting place of the USS Lagarto. First and foremost, I want you each to know that I took a few moments as each of you requested and conveyed your personal thoughts and desires to your fathers. The site is very peaceful, quiet and secure...

In the same note, Kohler related that alongside his partner John Chatterton and cameraman Evan Kovacs, he made four dives to the boat - for a total of three hours on the bottom – searching and documenting the site with still and video cameras.

They found that the *Lagarto's* stern planes were in the dive position, as were the bow planes, indicating that no survivors had tried to raise the boat. The rudder was left full, indicating a hard port turn. The only apparent damage, which was on the port side, did not appear to breach the hull. The size and shape of the damage was what would be expected from the direct hit of a depth-charge.

Lagarto had fired a torpedo. The outer door of the Number 4 torpedo tube was open, showing it empty. The periscopes were still in place, in the retracted position with Beth's American flag still flying from them. All the hatches were closed and appeared secure.

Kohler and Chatterton drew the following conclusion: *Lagarto* went down fighting.

The submarine was on the surface and in very close proximity to the enemy. After firing a torpedo at her attacker, she turned hard to port and dove. Before the outer tube door could be closed (which takes between 30 and 45 seconds), she was struck by a depth charge on the port side and sank. It all happened very fast. Kohler said, "The diving planes, rudder, and torpedo tube are frozen in that moment in time."

That was it for us. After knowing little about *Lagarto* for sixty-two years, the families then learned the submarine's exact location and what caused her to go down. While we all believed the crew were war heroes, we then knew, in fact, that they went down fighting. What an incredible gift to *Lagarto's* children to know that the fathers they missed their entire lives died fighting for their country until they took their last breaths.

I, for one, found a certain peace in knowing that. My dad had been doing his job and fulfilling his duty to his country until the very end. We all hoped the crew died quickly and mercifully and didn't have time to anguish about those they were to leave behind. I couldn't bear to think otherwise.

The following May, the Wisconsin Maritime Museum held its annual *Lagarto Remembrance Day*, and a few more *Lagarto* families attended and said their good-byes. Chuck Coppola and Harvey Moshman were there again, and we were joined by a new visitor to the event. Richie Kohler. He was gracious and warm and mingled easily with the families and the museum staff. Our family spent a lot of time with him, and Kohler was so easy to be with, that he seemed like part of our family. We will always feel that way about him.

The other *Shadow Diver* was unable to make the event. John Chatterton had headed back to the Gulf of Thailand to see *Lagarto* again. Chatterton wanted to tie up a loose end, and at his own expense, returned to the submarine to try to determine whether or not the inner door of the # 4 torpedo tube was open or closed. After sending a remote operated vehicle (ROV) camera into the tube, Chatterton saw that the inner door was closed. Water had not entered the submarine through that torpedo tube. Although this information did nothing to solve the mystery of our sunken sub, it was a relief to know that the crew hadn't drowned as a result of its unclosed inner door.

Macleod continued to dive on *Lagarto* every year. On one dive, he discovered that Beth's American flag was gone. Determined to find another American flag (not an easy task in Thailand) to replace it on his next dive to *Lagarto,* Macleod found one hanging from the ceiling in a bar. He purchased it from the bar's owner, and the flag gained a more dignified position – above the lost submarine, waving in the ocean currents.

There were still questions about *Lagarto's* sinking, but it seemed little more could be learned in the future.

In 2009, on a subsequent dive to *Lagarto,* Jamie Macleod performed a dangerous maneuver. He felt his way past the depth-charge damage made to the outer pressure hull and found a breach in the inner hull. It was a place where water could have entered the sub.

He also found breaks in the main induction piping, which would have allowed water to gush into the submarine under great pressure. These breaks were most likely caused by the heavy depth charging.

All the forensic evidence showed that *Lagarto* was subjected to violent, sustained depth-charge attacks by the Japanese minelayer, *Hatsutaka,* and supporting enemy aircraft. The American submarine was pinned down by her aggressive, merciless enemy. That is the tragic nature of war.

Although it is likely the crew succumbed to drowning, other evidence showed the violent nature of the attack and the direct hits by multiple depth charges rendered the crew unconscious by the time water entered the boat.

Diver Richie Kohler going down line to dive on *Lagarto*. Notice American flag hanging from periscope shears. 2007.

Margy
2010

Mom was a fighter. In her last years, she had a range of life-threatening health problems that qualified her for hospice. While her severe arthritis limited her movements, she exercised by wheelchair walking around the halls of the Orchard Creek facility. I was told this was the equivalent of pacing.

Mom had lost the ability to transfer herself to and from her wheelchair, and before she joined hospice, I needed help getting her in and out of my car to get her to doctor appointments. Even though she weighed less than a hundred pounds, an aide had to assist me lifting her, as she was dead weight and had no strength to help. After getting Mom in the car, we then had to collapse her heavy wheelchair and wrestle it into the back of my car. No doubt this took a physical toll on me and the aides. Transportation became a little easier when we began using Orchard Creek's van which had a lift.

Mom was getting worse. There were times her face lit up when she saw me, and she seemed to know who I was. But when that glint of recognition faded, and she folded herself forward in her wheelchair, it broke my heart. And more often than not, she stayed that way until the end of my visit.

She did have some bright moments, and those were a precious gift to both of us. At those times, she might talk for a few minutes about something in her past or participate in a game being played in Orchard Creek's family room. I stayed with her as long as I could, not wanting to let go of the moment.

Orchard Creek's 2009 New Year's Eve party, held at noon, was the last time I saw Mom having fun. She smiled as she sipped champagne and listened to the singer crooning familiar old favorites of her time. Although I brought her a plate of appetizers she liked – cold shrimp and a variety of cheeses and fruit, she didn't eat much, but she enjoyed the festive atmosphere. Watching her socialize made me happy and sad at the same time.

In November, three months before Mom died, our phone rang around 10 PM. The nurse on duty at Orchard Creek called to say she couldn't get a pulse on Mom, and the hospice nurse had been called.

"Should I come right away?" I asked. Mom had had many close calls.

"Yes, I think you better."

John and I lived 25 miles from Orchard Creek, and an early Michigan blizzard had snowed in our driveway. My husband went out to plow, and I called my siblings. Twenty minutes later, just as John had finished clearing the drive, Mom's nurse called back saying that her vital signs had returned, and she was out of danger.

That was not unusual. For the prior seven years, I had dealt with numerous emergencies concerning my mother. She was losing ground fast, and we all knew it.

On January 31, 2010, when my husband and I visited Mom, we were both shocked at what we saw.

When we arrived, we found her in the hallway outside her room, sprawled backward in her wheelchair. When we talked to her nurse, she told us Mom was failing. I knew she had been eating little and, for the most part, was living on Boost shakes. Now she was refusing them.

"How long do you think Mom has?" I asked.

"Roughly two weeks."

My brothers, sister, and I had been through this before with our parents, and they had survived much longer than any of us expected. However, I knew Mom, and this was different. I decided to put everything else in my life aside and stay with Mom every day. I knew she would get excellent care in the evenings when I went home.

When I arrived the next morning, Mom was at Orchard Creek's in-house beauty salon for her weekly hair appointment. She looked better than I did. *She's done it again. She'll pull through,* I thought.

The nurse told me she had stayed up later than usual to watch a movie the night before and seemed to enjoy it very much. Since this was rare for her, I asked the name of the movie.

"It was 'South Pacific," she said.

My heart skipped a beat because I knew how much this show meant to Mom. When I was eleven, she and my stepfather had taken me to see the stage play in Chicago. Rogers and Hammerstein's wonderful musical featured the Navy in the Pacific in World War II, and I couldn't help thinking Mom, even in her confused state, had made the connection between the movie and her Bill.

I took her to her room, and we watched television and chatted. She commented on a scarf I was knitting and said she liked the colors. I enjoyed the morning and felt like I had my Mom back for a little while.

When she went to lunch, I felt it was okay to run some errands.

When I returned an hour later, she was a different person. She was agitated and called "Help" over and over again. She also called my name, and became panicky when she thought I was leaving her room. I assured her I would stay. Her terror was so great, she had to be sedated. At 6 PM, she succumbed to exhaustion and drifted off to sleep. I headed home with John, who had responded to my anxious call. I cried all the way home.

I anticipated a middle-of-the-night phone call, but it didn't come. When I arrived at Orchard Creek the next morning, Mom was feeling better and had even attended some activities that morning. *She's done it again,* I thought.

At lunchtime, she didn't feel like eating and wanted to lie down. I told her I would stay while she napped. As I sat next to her bed, she kept glancing around to make sure I was there.

Soon she became agitated again, and it was worse than it had been the previous day. She tossed and turned in her bed and when she tried to climb out, I summoned the nursing staff for help. They came running, and I moved out of the way.

They removed Mom's clothes and put her in a hospital gown. Then they put the sides up on her bed. Someone said, "She's active." What they were saying was that she was actively dying.

Mom's hospice aide, who had been so good to her and had become Mom's best friend, took me aside.

"If your siblings want to see your mother alive, you better tell them to come now," Penny said. "It's a matter of days."

At this point, Mom was administered morphine to ease her pain. This calmed her, but she was no longer able to speak. She was in the final stage of dying.

My siblings and nephew, Sean Chambers, drove up from Chicago the next day, and we all had a chance to say our individual good-byes to our mother. She was surrounded by her family when she died.

Shortly before they arrived, I had my last time alone with Mom. Her eyes were closed, and she was peaceful. I took her hand to let her know I was there and carefully considered what to say.

"Mom, you've been a wonderful mother, and I love you very much. It's okay for you to go now. Your mother and father are waiting for you. You'll see Dad (Hank

Chambers) and Mary and Bud (her sister and brother) and your family you've loved so. Your friends will throw a big party for you." (She mentioned, one time, that her friends would have a big party for her when she arrived in heaven.)

"And Mom, your Bill has been waiting for you so long. When he sees you, he will take you in his arms and hold you and kiss you and love you. He will be so happy to see you."

Tears streamed down my cheeks as I said this, but through them, I could see a little smile brighten Mom's face. After sixty-five years, she was young, pretty, healthy, and would be with her beloved Bill again.

Acknowledgments

When I began thinking about how many individuals were involved in helping me get this book done, it became almost as overwhelming as writing the book itself. There were so many kind and encouraging souls, I knew if I began naming names I would leave someone out.

Many of them are already mentioned in the book. But there were others who boosted my spirits, let me talk, and just kept me going. You know who you are, and you will always have my deepest gratitude.

A few critical mentions. Tricia L. McDonald was my editor, publisher, and friend. She was my first contact with the Peninsula Writers. When Tricia took me in hand, things began to come together. Several authors have been supportive and have given me critical insight into the world of writing. They are Chuck Pfarrer, Doug Stanton, Jim Harrison, McKenzie Magee, John Darnton, P.T. Deutermann, Gary Moore, George Weeks, and Mary O'Donohue. While U.S. Naval Institute Press sent me a glowing rejection letter declining to publish my book, they did publish my article about *Lagarto* in their prestigious journal, *Naval Institute Proceedings.* That gave me confidence to tell the *Lagarto* story, and I am grateful.

I can't imagine what I would have done without the unequivocal support of the Wisconsin Maritime Museum. Their staff, especially Karen Duvalle and Norma Bishop have been *Lagarto* partners from day one. We worked together in concert – finding the families, planning (and hosting) the beautiful memorial service for *Lagarto's* crew, and contributing to the information that led the Navy to verification of *Lagarto's* find. Beyond that, the museum took on the daunting project of financing and co-producing an Emmy Award winning documentary – *"Lost and Found: The Legacy of U.S.S. Lagarto."* They have given me permission to use the poignant Todd letters, which were generously donated to them by LTjg Harold Todd's widow, Rae Kinn, who also gave me her blessing to use the letters in this book. The museum also allowed me to include photographs of *Lagarto's* crew, donated to them by their families. Harvey Moshman and Chuck Coppola, also producers of the *Lagarto* documentary, have been great partners and friends.

Until *Lagarto* was found, I never dreamed I would have technical divers in my life. These are the most daring and courageous of men – and women. For the extraordinary underwater photos in the book, I want to thank Dr. Mike Gadd, Wilco Both, Ayeesha Cantrell, Jamie Macleod, Evan Kovac, John Chatterton and Richie Kohler. The iconic photos of the American flag waving from *Lagarto's* periscope shears were taken by Chris Clark and Mike Gadd.

I am grateful to my friends who listened to me with patience as I talked about *Lagarto* and my book – Jeannine McLaughlin, Ann Carr, Sandy Wischmeyer, and Patsy Beck. I am especially grateful to Dr. Dennis Trybus – my mentor, friend, and former boss, who even read the manuscript.

My family has been wonderful. *Lagarto's* discovery was thrilling, but traumatic. My husband, John, and children – John Jr., Beth, Bill, and daughter-in-law Linsey and son-in-law Chris - were conscious of the emotional impact the submarine's discovery had on me and always made sure I was all right. Now Bill Mabin and his Marg have four great-grandchildren, Allison, Clint, and Grant Kenney and Charlie Augustine. Their Grandma Nancy will tell them about their brave great-grandfather.

The Crew of the *USS Lagarto*

Charles Breithaupt, Y2 — William Carleton, RM1 — George Clouse, TM2

LT Bill Mendenhall — LT Robert Ruble — John Peterson, TM3

Ralph Simmerman, TM2 — LT JG Harold Todd — CDR Frank Latta

Bob Spalding, CPHMA

Clark Richard Byrer, F1

Aaron Brock, S2

Lloyd Cathey, MOMM3

Frank Turner, CGM

Gerald Price, CMOMMA

John Kniedl, MOMM3

William Graves, QM1

William Honaker, EM3

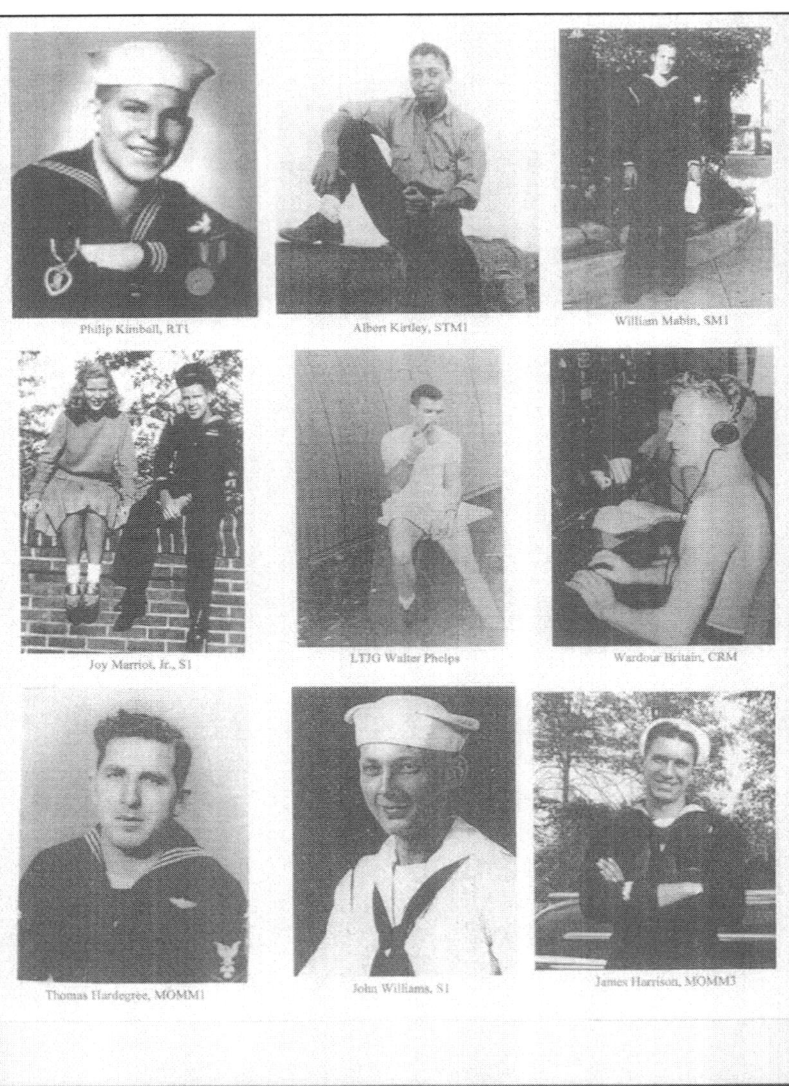

Philip Kimball, RT1

Albert Kirtley, STM1

William Mabin, SM1

Joy Marriot, Jr., S1

LTJG Walter Phelps

Wardour Britain, CRM

Thomas Hardegree, MOMM1

John Williams, S1

James Harrison, MOMM3

James Gregory, S2

John Johnson, CEMA

John Joseph Franze, S1

Wesley Shackelford, SM2

Howard Ortega, F1

James Harris, S1

Charles Bjornson, F1

Oakley Frasch, MOMM1

Richard Fisher, MOMM1

Raymond O'Hara, RT2 — Glen Halstead, RM3 — Leslie Doud, RM2

LTJG Joseph Pash — Jesse Jobe, CEMA — LT Arthur Keeney, Jr.

Raymond E. Reichert, F1 — George Clark Harrington, MOMM3 — Walter Hinken, TM3

The Lost Submarine

About the Author

The discovery of the *USS Lagarto* in 2005 was a "gift from the sea" for Nancy Kenney and the submarine crew's other relatives. This, her first book, is a loving memoir for all lost WWII submariners. Ms. Kenney lives with her husband, John, in Lake Leelanau, MI and La Grange, IL and enjoys life with her three children and four grandchildren.